HYDRANGEAS

for American Gardens

HYDRANGEAS

for American Gardens

MICHAEL A. DIRR

Illustrations by Bonnie L. Dirr

TIMBER PRESS

Portland • Cambridge

Frontispiece (colored pencil drawing of *Hydrangea serrata* 'Miranda')
and other illustrations by Bonnie L. Dirr.
All photographs are by Michael A. Dirr.

Published in 2004 by
Timber Press, Inc.
The Haseltine Building
133 S.W. Second Avenue, Suite 450
Portland, Oregon 97204, U.S.A.

Timber Press
2 Station Road
Swavesey
Cambridge CB4 5QJ, U.K.

www.timberpress.com

Printed through Colorcraft Ltd., Hong Kong

Interior design: Karen Schober

Library of Congress Cataloging-in-Publication Data

Dirr, Michael.
  Hydrangeas for American gardens / Michael A. Dirr ; illustrations by
Bonnie L. Dirr.
      p. cm.
Includes bibliographical references (p.).
  ISBN 0-88192-641-8 (hardcover)
  1. Hydrangeas--United States. I. Title.
SB413.H93D57 2004
635.9'3372--dc22
                                        2003019842

A Catalogue record for this book is also available from the British Library.

TO THE DIRR FAMILY . . .

Bonnie, Katie, Matt, and Susy . . .
all unique human beings,
whose love and
laughter are forever
cherished

Hydrangea macrophylla 'Taube'

CONTENTS

Hydrangea macrophylla 'Mousmée'

ACKNOWLEDGMENTS

Most of the time when I obtain a new book, I skip this section. Perhaps the reader will also, but it was a team effort with the pen in my hand.

Hillary Barber types, proofs, organizes, and cares as if her name were on the cover.

Timber Press is malleable and allows the author's voice and experiences to come to life with minimal editing.

Vickie Waters-Oldham, research technician and orchestrator of our hydrangea improvement program at the University of Georgia, provides attention to detail.

The above three and I function as a team, the whole greater than the parts. This has been an inspiring and easy book to write because we were collectively excited about the process and product.

Thanks too to the great gardens and the staffs who run them; the breeders—amateur and professional; every gardener who shared his or her views on hydrangeas; and especially Penny McHenry, Atlanta, Georgia, who via sheer will, persistence, and love founded the American Hydrangea Society, which has opened the floodgates to new friends and information.

Appreciation and respect to all.

INTRODUCTION

Known, grown, and loved worldwide, hydrangeas, or at least one, can be successfully cultured in American gardens in Zones 3 to 10(11). Most modern literature on hydrangeas is based on European or New Zealand experiences. Please refer to References for the work of Haworth-Booth (England), Lawson-Hall and Rothera (England), the Mallets (France), and Church (New Zealand). Their books are the major references on the subject but do not adequately detail the cultural idiosyncrasies associated with this vast garden, the United States of America. Also, their coverage of our native species, *Hydrangea arborescens*, subsp. *discolor* and *radiata*, and *H. quercifolia* is frail, i.e., lacking in specifics, depth, and cultivar currency.

This new book addresses the voids and presents a pragmatic overview of the cultivated species and their cultivars. Thorough literature, nursery catalog, and Internet searches framed portraits of the species and cultivars grown and offered in U.S. commerce. *Hydrangea anomala* subsp. *petiolaris*, *H. arborescens*, *H. macrophylla*, *H. paniculata*, *H. quercifolia*, and *H. serrata* are discussed in detail. I have conducted research and evaluation of various hydrangeas for most of my career. Since 1996, an active breeding and improvement program has been in force; the principal American landscape species, *H. arborescens*, *H. macrophylla*, *H. paniculata*, *H. quercifolia*, and *H. serrata*, have received significant attention. Over 15,000 seedlings from open-pollinated and controlled crosses have been grown to flowering, evaluated, selected, and introduced.

The major breakthrough for *Hydrangea macrophylla* improvement in the program occurred in September 1998 when a true remontant (reblooming) form that flowers on old growth and new growth was identified. This means that even if all preformed flower buds are killed by cold, new flowers will develop on the current season's growth. This unique plant was patented and trademarked as Endless Summer™ ('Bailmer') by Bailey Nurseries, Inc., St. Paul, Minnesota.

Since the initial discovery, I was given four other remontant types ('David Ramsey', 'Decatur Blue', 'Oak Hill', and 'Penny Mac'). They are now being utilized in controlled breeding programs with 'Ayesha', 'Lilacina', and 'Veitchii'. Early crosses with 'Veitchii' ♀ x Endless Summer™ ♂ produced seedlings with remontant flowering and mildew resistance.

I have been fortunate to work at a great university that supports and encourages the faculty to improve their subject-matter competency via sabbatical and travel. A respectable professor is an even better student. Plants are neither learned nor appreciated from Internet gleanings. They must be observed, stroked, studied, grown, and photographed at different times and places. With hydrangeas on the brain, I have traveled to many collections for such activities. At one garden in the southwest of England, approximately 360 cultivars of *Hydrangea macrophylla* unfolded before my purview. The mind became mush, the knees buckled, and the camera imploded.

For success in plant breeding and garden writing, one must understand the variation within a genus. With *Hydrangea*, the learning process is forever. I hope this *small* addition to the *Hydrangea* literature educates, excites, and inspires. I am always enthused about readers' observations and opinions and would appreciate feedback.

The size of this book limited the number of photographs, and so I produced a CD-ROM, now with more than 900 photographs, in concert. All photographs on the CD-ROM are labeled and are fully printable for enjoyable viewing, design projects, and creating signs and labels; it is available from Varsity Press, Inc., 337 S. Milledge Ave., Suite 125, Athens, GA 30605; tel: 706.613.0046; Web: www.nobleplants.com

Hydrangea macrophylla
Endless Summer™, pink

Hydrangea macrophylla 'Schwan'

CHAPTER ONE

Characteristics, Taxonomy, and Nomenclature

Hydrangea resides in the family Hydrangeaceae, which includes the vining relatives *Decumaria* and *Schizophragma*. In older literature the genus is included in the Saxifragaceae. *Hydrangea* was originally described by Thunberg in *Flora Japonica* (1784) as *Viburnum macrophyllum* and transferred by Seringe (1830) to the genus *Hydrangea*. The genus is difficult to compress under a small umbrella. There is no common vegetative characteristic that readily links all the species together. The fruit, a conical to top-shaped capsule, with a small opening (pore) at the apex, is the most universal reproductive feature.

Hydrangea usually has 8 to 10 stamens, 2 to 5 styles, the latter which persist as woody "antennae" on the ripened fruit. The fruit contains many seeds, estimates of 50 to 75 to 200. I have never counted them; the literature and a fellow hydrangea breeder supplied these numbers. Flowers vary from all fertile, to lacecap, to largely sterile in the mophead, or hortensia, types. Gradations between and among these inflorescence types are apparent in the species and cultivars.

The inflorescence is a corymb, by some authors, a cyme. A corymb is a compound inflorescence with many flowers, typically indeterminate, meaning it can continue to elongate, with the outer flowers opening first. *Hydrangea paniculata* and *H. quercifolia* flowers are borne in conical to broad-conical panicles; the central axis is a peduncle with flowers attached. Flowers open from base to apex (acropetally), with the inflorescences increasing in length as the flowers develop.

The showy portions of the flower are the sepals, which are grouped in clusters of 3 to 5. The individual sepal may be entire or serrated, elliptical, oval, to rounded. Sepal colors of *Hydrangea macrophylla* and many *H. serrata* change in response to aluminum in the soil or medium—typically pink in non-aluminum, blue/purple in aluminum-based. Sepals of several species also change from white and pink to rose, burgundy, and red, regardless of aluminum availability. This occurs in *H. serrata*, *H. heteromalla*, *H. paniculata*, and *H. aspera* taxa.

When sepals are arranged in a ring around the outside of the inflorescences, the term lacecap is applied. Typically, the center is made up of fertile flowers. These sepalous clusters on the periphery are often called the ray or sterile florets.

When the sepals are dominant in the inflorescence and form a more or less solid head, dome, or mass of color, the resultant structure is called the mophead or hortensia type.

The leaves of hydrangea are opposite, simple, evergreen, deciduous, serrate, entire, glabrous, or woolly pubescent and provide no consistent clues as to generic affinity.

Hydrangeas grow as vines, shrubs, and small trees with their flower buds either formed on the growth of the previous season or, in a few species, on current year's shoots. The best pruning strategies to optimize flowering are presented under the species' discussions.

Taxonomy and Nomenclature

Elizabeth McClintock (1957a) streamlined the classification and nomenclature of *Hydrangea*; in her monograph, she divided the genus into two sections, the first *Hydrangea*, comprising 11 species:

> *H. arborescens* Linnaeus [subsp. *discolor* (Seringe) E. M. McClintock, subsp. *radiata* (Walter) E. M. McClintock]
> *H. quercifolia* Bartram

H. aspera D. Don [subsp. *robusta* (Hooker f. and Thomson) E. M. McClintock, subsp. *sargentiana* (Rehder) E. M. McClintock, subsp. *strigosa* (Rehder) E. M. McClintock]

H. involucrata Siebold

H. sikokiana Maximowicz

H. anomala D. Don [subsp. *petiolaris* (Siebold and Zuccarini) E. M. McClintock]

H. hirta (Thunberg) Siebold

H. scandens [subsp. *chinensis* (Maximowicz) E. M. McClintock, subsp. *kwangtungensis* (Merrill) E. M. McClintock, subsp. *liukiuensis* (Nakai) E. M. McClintock]

H. heteromalla D. Don

H. paniculata Siebold

H. macrophylla (Thunberg) Seringe [subsp. *chungii* (Rehder) E. M. McClintock, subsp. *serrata* (Thunberg) Makino, subsp. *stylosa* (Hooker f. and Thomson) E. M. McClintock]

Within several species are subspecies, the most important being *Hydrangea macrophylla* subsp. *serrata*, which by many horticulturists is maintained as a true species, *H. serrata*. For ease of presentation, I have treated *H. serrata* as such. Subspecies differ from the species in several characteristics, such as flower, leaf, and distribution in the wild, and these morphological characters are inheritable from seed, generation to generation.

I read McClintock's monograph and have doubts about several of the subspecies designations. My thoughts are expressed in the text under the lead species. The *Hydrangea aspera* group is a mess, and I don't know anyone who could reliably identify the middle-ground variants between *H. aspera* and subsp. *sargentiana*. Judging by the labeling in many collections, I know the pros have qualms.

Also, all (most) of McClintock's work utilized herbarium specimens. These flattened, discolored, dried leaves, stems, flowers, and fruits do not tell the entire horticultural story. For example, her *Hydrangea macrophylla* subsp. *chungii* with hirsute hairs is known from only three collections (McClintock

1957a, page 225). Having assessed thousands of *H. arborescens*, subsp. *discolor*, and subsp. *radiata*, living and dried specimens, noting extreme variation in degree of pubescence (a fact that McClintock acknowledges with subsp. *discolor*), I ask: how with definitiveness can a subspecies be delineated from three herbarium specimens?

Most modern garden and horticultural literature simply recognizes McClintock's *Hydrangea macrophylla* subsp. *macrophylla* and *H. macrophylla* subsp. *serrata*, not subsp. *chungii* or subsp. *stylosa*. The latter was collected by Dan Hinkley and offered through Heronswood. His collection was from southern Japan, although the taxon grows in China, Bhutan, Sikkim, India, Burma, and Vietnam. The lone plant in my possession has narrow leaves and wispy, pubescent stems compared to typical *H. macrophylla*, serrated sepals in 4s, either pink to blue depending on aluminum, and a lacecap inflorescence. DNA analysis, coupled with old-fashioned field botany and horticultural common sense, will more clearly hone the edges of these fuzzy subspecies.

The second section is *Cornidia* with 12 evergreen vines, all self-supporting. They range from Mexico to Chile, with *Hydrangea integrifolia* Hayata found in the Philippines. *Hydrangea seemanii* Riley and *H. serratifolia* (Hooker and Arnott) Philippi f. are the only two species in "common" cultivation. All, to my knowledge, are Zone 9 and warmer adapted, although West Coast nurseries list Zone 7.

For anyone who wants a taxonomic education I recommend reviewing McClintock's great contribution. The real problem is sorting through the literature, Internet, and nursery catalogs and making botanical, horticultural, and garden sense of the potpourri of scientific names. In this book, *Hydrangea angustipetala*, *H. lobbii*, *H. indochinensis*, and *H. umbellata* are discussed. I have grown, studied, and/or photographed them; they appear unique. My best estimate, using McClintock's classification and talking to hydrangea experts, is their affiliation with the *H. scandens* complex, the exception being *H. indochinensis*, which McClintock places under *H. macrophylla* subsp. *stylosa*.

Also, the *Hydrangea serrata* complex with subsp. *acuminata*, subsp. *yezoensis*, and subsp. *angustata* as put forth by Mallet is presented under *H. serrata*. Perhaps McClintock did not see the essential characteristics of identification, inheritable from seed population to seed population, to warrant the various subspecies delineations. I can readily separate *H. macrophylla* from *H. serrata*; I have observed and studied subspecies and/or varieties *acuminata*, *angustata*, *chinensis*, *koreana*, *thunbergii*, and *yezoensis* in garden settings and via the literature, and they have the foliar traits associated with *H. serrata*. This is as far as I can travel without developing a case of "hydrangea-in-mouth" disease.

Hydrangea japonica, particularly 'Coerulea Lace' ('Coerulea', 'Caerulea'), is offered in commerce and was legitimized by Haworth-Booth. McClintock includes the species (cultivar) with *H. macrophylla* subsp. *serrata* (*H. serrata* of this book). It is a cold-hardy, remontant (reblooming) taxon with pink to blue, lacecap flowers. I suspect it might be a hybrid of *H. macrophylla* and *H. serrata*, and Haworth-Booth intimates this also.

Hydrangea maritima is the name Haworth-Booth gave to the true *H. macrophylla*, a lacecap type, representing the wild form growing around Tokyo Bay and the outlying islands. E. H. Wilson named this type *H. macrophylla* var. *normalis*. Occasionally, nurseries use *H. macrophylla* var. *normalis* and the cultivar name. This tells the buyer that the cultivar is a lacecap. However, the nomenclature is incorrect and should only list *H. macrophylla* and the cultivar name. In truth, this mixed bag of names equals the species that gave rise to the large showy mopheads, which equates with McClintock's *H. macrophylla* subsp. *macrophylla*. Hortensia is a term assigned to the mophead or largely sterile-flowered forms and has no botanical standing. It was used by the French botanist de Jussieu in the late 1800s and is inextricably linked, for better or worse, with the large-flowered forms.

With collectors such as Dan Hinkley, Heronswood Nursery, Washington, and Bleddyn and Sue Wynn-Jones, Crûg Farm Plants, Wales, probing Japan, China, Vietnam, Taiwan, and the Philippines and collecting hydrangeas in myriad forms, the potential for taxonomic restructuring is possible. Visit their Web sites (see Resources and Nursery Sources) to comprehend the scope of the collections.

Additional Nomenclatural Musings

Obviously, there are differences of opinion as to the composition of species and subspecies in *Hydrangea*. Kartez (1994) legitimizes . . .

1. *Hydrangea cinerea* Small, which equates with McClintock's *H. arborescens* subsp. *discolor* (Seringe ex de Candolle) E. M. McClintock
2. *Hydrangea radiata* Walter, which equates with McClintock's *H. arborescens* subsp. *radiata* (Walter) E. M. McClintock

. . . based on Pilatowski's 1982 master's research. See chapter 3's discussion of *Hydrangea arborescens* and chapter 16, on breeding and improvement.

Also, *Hydrangea serrata* (Thunberg) Seringe and *H. scandens* (Linnaeus f.) Seringe are difficult to pigeonhole taxonomically because of the great variation in the genetic soup. McClintock reduced *H. serrata* to a subspecies of *H. macrophylla* and lumped all the so-called varieties and subspecies, like *acuminata, angustata, koreana, thunbergii, yezoensis*, within. The reader can visualize this *H. serrata* complex as comprising smaller plants, more narrow, elongated leaves, thin stems, and smaller inflorescences. As mentioned in the *H. serrata* chapter, Mallet describes three subspecies and their characteristics. Lawson-Hall and Rothera (1995) and the new *Hillier Manual* (2002) list no subspecies under *H. serrata*.

The greatest shades of gray are evident in the *Hydrangea scandens* complex, which includes subsp. *scandens*, a small, wispy, almost scandent shrub with small leaves, typically to 2 inches, and the subsp. *chinensis* (Maximowicz) E. M. McClintock, a larger plant from the east Asian mainland and other areas outside of Japan. Herein presumably reside *H. lobbii, H. umbellata*, and *H. angustipetala* as presented in this book. The variants within subsp. *chinensis* comprise shrubs or small trees to 12 to 14 feet high, leaves 2 to 7 inches long, 1/2 to 3 inches wide.

Two difficult-to-reconcile subspecies of *Hydrangea scandens* are *liukiuensis* (which may equate with *H. luteovenosa*, see below) and *kwangtungensis*, the latter never observed by me. See chapter 11's discussion under *H. scandens*. Yamamoto (2000) believes and presents textual and photographic evidence for the uniqueness of *H. scandens* subsp. *liukiuensis* and *H. luteovenosa*.

Communications with Luc Balemans of Hydrangeum vzw, Belgium, about the state of *Hydrangea scandens* and *H. serrata* were helpful. I queried him about the above, and he responded: "If you are agonizing over inconsistent descriptions while writing your book, we're [fellow collaborator, Paul Goetghebeur, University of Ghent] agonizing for the same reason trying to determine what plants we have in the collection." His taxonomic thoughts:

- *Hydrangea aspera* is so variable it is difficult to fit the plants into McClintock's key, except for subsp. *sargentiana*, which is unique.

- *Hydrangea lobbii*, although best suited for inclusion with *H. scandens* subsp. *chinensis*, really doesn't match.

- *Hydrangea scandens* subsp. *liukiuensis* is recognizable on the basis of the yellow band along the leaf veins and small leaves (<2 inches). The name *H. luteovenosa* is synonymous with this subspecies.

- *Hydrangea scandens* subsp. *chinensis* has larger (greater than 2 inches) leaves without yellow bands, but there is considerable leaf variation thus creating difficulties distinguishing the plant from *H. scandens* subsp. *scandens*.

For *Hydrangea serrata* Balemans recommends maintaining McClintock's *H. macrophylla* subsp. *serrata* designation based on morphological (leaf, bud, stem, flower, fruits) characteristics. In a pragmatic sense this makes classification "easy" for it is not necessary to delineate the miscreants, i.e., subspecies. For the presentation herein, I utilized *H. serrata*, primarily because most plants are marketed as such in the United States.

Bertrand (2000) utilized 292 cultivars of *Hydrangea macrophylla* and *H. serrata*, and applied 28 qualitative and 5 quantitative criteria to their identification. She was able to separate the two species (subspecies) and identify several hybrids. Her conclusions? The serrata and macrophylla groups are characterized as follows:

SERRATA GROUP

- Red, pubescent, and short petiole
- Invisible or red lenticels
- Pubescence on both sides of the leaves
- Very acuminate leaves
- Early flowering
- Small diameter inflorescences
- Pale color sterile (sepalous) flowers

MACROPHYLLA GROUP

- Glabrous leaves or only axillary hairs beneath the leaves
- Large leaves with long green petioles
- Vigorous (strong) plants
- Mid to early flowering with large inflorescences

The Missouri Botanical Garden published the *Flora of China*, an English-language revision of the *Flora Republicae Popularis Sinicae*, with taxonomy reflecting the current understanding of each group. Based on the *Hydrangea* treatment in volume 8, it is obvious the revisionary experts failed to read McClintock. For example, the *Flora* mentions approximately 73 species worldwide, 33 of these in China. The authors, Wei Zhaofen and Bruce Bartholomew, apparently do not agree on the legitimacy of the 33 species as Bartholomew surmises there are 18 recognizable species. Many of the names did not appear in McClintock's 1957 revision. Also, the two authors assign the genus to the Saxifragaceae.

A key is presented that supposedly separates (?) the 33 species. I read through this *mess* on several occasions and believe it would prove *impossible* to correctly identify the species with the characteristics presented. A reasonable analogy might relate to 33 types of brown-skinned potatoes, which look similar. Now they are peeled, cooked, and mashed. Then the diners are given a key to the 33 varieties and requested to separate them by color and taste. Pure fantasy? You bet! So is the key!

Out of 33 species of mashed Chinese hydrangea, McClintock recognizes 5 species and 7 subspecies, and present-day experts question the validity of several subspecies within *Hydrangea aspera*.

All this taxonomic and nomenclatural information might prove daunting to the casual reader. When I was a young student, everything was taught and accepted in black and white terms. With time, I learned that the shades of gray in biology are more prevalent than the absolutes. In actual fact, there are exceptions to almost all taxonomic descriptions. Keys are based on the available literature, study of herbarium and living material in the wild and gardens, and the interpretation of same by the author(s).

The future, through field and DNA studies, the latter already in play, may witness a legitimate reshuffling of the *Hydrangea* taxonomic deck. Regardless, the plants will not change their characteristics and will remain as beautiful and vivacious by any name.

Hydrangea anomala subsp. *petiolaris*

CHAPTER TWO

Hydrangea anomala
D. Don subsp. *petiolaris* (Siebold and Zuccarini) E. M. McClintock

CLIMBING HYDRANGEA

If accolades were afforded vines, this species (formerly *Hydrangea petiolaris* Siebold and Zuccarini) would be crowned Queen of the Twining World. Somewhat shy and unassuming in youth, developing rather slowly, she then rockets skyward, never looking back as she climbs and clambers over, along, and next to the structure by which she was placed. This, in a nutshell, is the garden life of climbing hydrangea.

Great and noble specimens have interrupted my travels, particularly in the Midwest and New England, where venerable giants hug the bricks and mortar of arboreta and college campuses. Climbing hydrangea is a true climbing vine, attaching to structures with rootlike holdfasts. Initially the stems plaster themselves to the wall or tree in a flat-planar configuration. With time and continued growth, the secondary branches form a shrublike configuration. I liken this to the transition between the juvenile and adult stages that occurs on *Hedera helix*, English ivy, and *Euonymus fortunei*, wintercreeper euonymus. The multibranched adult stage also produces the most abundant flowers.

With age, the branches exfoliate in papery sheets and flakes of cinnamon-brown. The stems, if removed from buildings, leave a residue that is difficult (impossible?) to remove. I remember an old stucco mansion in Massachusetts, with the vines removed; it appeared as if someone had crayoned the walls.

Hydrangea anomala subsp. *petiolaris,* clinging to brick

Hydrangea anomala subsp. *petiolaris,* staring

Climbing hydrangea develops into a pretty shrub and at Kew Gardens, England, and the University of Guelph, Guelph, Ontario, was artistically fashioned as such. Plants also are appealing when stretched over rock walls, fences, and arbors. A climbing hydrangea was planted at the base of a sweetgum in our Urbana, Illinois, garden, and three years later, before moving to Georgia, it had not moved (much). Friends report that the vine is now in the sweetgum. This serves as a kind admonition that patience will, indeed, be rewarded.

Culturally, *Hydrangea anomala* subsp. *petiolaris* is a great candidate for shady environments, north and east sides of structures, and under canopies of deciduous trees. Remarkably, it is also served well by full sun situations. Almost indifferent to soil conditions, requiring well-drained, it thrives in the clays of the Midwest and acid sandy spodesols of the northeastern states. Maintain even moisture in youth, and keep fertilizer at a minimum initially (since little growth is occurring); once established the plant becomes self-sufficient. This may appear too casual, but the vine operates under the adage that less is more. Time is its biggest ally.

Why the love affair with this shy biological entity? To experience the large flattened inflorescences, dripping with honey fragrance, the showy white sepals in 3s to 5s extending from the margins, is to understand the appeal. I have observed flowering plants with few shiny sepals, in fact some inflorescences with none. Also, flowers in Zone 7 are fully expressed by early May. Flowers are at their best in June and July further north, the sepals aging to green, parchment, and finally brown by fall. The corymbs range from 6 to 10 inches across, attached to the stem via a 1- to 1½-inch stalk. The entire inflorescence stares at the passerby, establishing eye contact, actually slightly arching downward, making the effect more striking when viewing a large specimen that is 50 feet high and wide on a wall. Flowers originate from old wood (botanical floral characteristics are presented under "Identification Characteristics," which section appears toward the end of each species chapter).

The foliage is seldom praised, being overwrought by the flowers, but the lustrous dark green leaves, almost rounded in outline, provide great foil for the flowers. Leaves are fully developed by mid-April in Athens. Never acknowledged for fall color, on a late fall day (7 November) at Bernheim Arboretum, Clermont, Kentucky, a tree-hugging specimen, dressed in magnificent yellow, winked at me. I took notice!

Young stems start green, turn brown, and develop aerial roots along their length. All the aforementioned may be evident on one year's growth increase. These roots "cement" the stems to bark, wood, bricks, mortar, and vinyl. The exfoliating, rich cinnamon-brown bark develops on two- to three-year and older stems, becoming more prominent as trunk diameter increases. I liken the bark development to that of *Hydrangea quercifolia*, although the pieces are scaly and smaller sized.

Propagation, particularly stem cuttings, is somewhat difficult. Cuttings should be collected early in the growing season when shoots are green and soft. Although I have had miserable cutting success, the plant is widely available in the trade, and the nursery industry has solved the mystery. Seeds offer an easy reproduction method. Simply sow on the surface of the medium and keep moist. See discussion under "Seeds" in chapter 13.

Hydrangea anomala subsp. *petiolaris*, fall color

Hydrangea anomala subsp. *petiolaris*, bark

Cultivars and Varieties

Subspecies *anomala* has many of the fine qualities of subsp. *petiolaris* but differs in the longer, elliptic-ovate, 3- to 6-inch-long, 1- to 3-inch-wide leaves, fewer sterile sepals, and 9 to 15 stamens (versus the 15 to 22 of subsp. *petiolaris*). A venerable specimen on the north wall of the Arnold Arboretum's Visitor's Center grows next to subsp. *petiolaris*. The side-by-side comparison makes horticultural evaluation much easier. The inflorescence is more lax and floppy than subsp. *petiolaris* and not as ornamentally potent. Seldom available in commerce, it is probably only for the domain of the serious collector. Native to the Himalayas and China. Zones 5 to 7(8).

Subspecies *anomala* '**Winter Glow**' has evergreen, thin-textured, serrulate leaves that turn purple in winter; produces coral-green domed corymbs of lacy flowers in April and May. Grows 60 feet or more. Collected by Crûg Farm in Sikkim.

Subspecies *glabra* with elliptic-ovate leaves has terminal, 6-inch-wide, pink, lacecap flowers in summer; grows to 60 feet. Collected in Taiwan by Crûg Farm from an isolated colony. May be called 'Crûg Coral'. The veracity of subsp. *glabra* is dubious but presented herein for informational purposes.

Subspecies *petiolaris* '**Firefly**' (Miranda™) produces green leaves with wide-banded, irregular, yellow margins that do not revert. My single plant, maintained in shade, lost much of the yellow in the heat of summer. Leaves 3 inches

Hydrangea anomala subsp. *petiolaris,* shrub form

by 2 inches, slightly smaller than the species. This is a patented selection by Dan Benarcik and listed as adaptable in Zones 4 to 8. Based on limited experience, not suited to Zone 7 and higher of the Southeast and Southwest.

Subspecies *petiolaris* '**Furuaziai**' produces terminal and axillary inflorescences of small, white fertile flowers and large, white ray florets in late spring and summer; grows to 25 feet. Crûg Farm introduction grown from seed from the Shamrock Hydrangea Collection in France.

Hydrangea anomala subsp. *petiolaris*, foliage

Subspecies *petiolaris* '**Kasai**' produces predominantly white new leaves with small amount of green stippling. With maturity, leaves turn essentially green, with white mottling and white margins. A patented plant from Hines Nursery. Discovered by Seiichi Kasai, Japan.

Hydrangea anomala subsp. *anomala*, foliage

Subspecies *petiolaris* '**Kuga Variegated**' is an unusual small-leaf selection with young shoots yellowish orange, pink, maturing to cream and green, the leaves irregularly splashed, streaked, and speckled. Unfortunately, mature leaves turn green with nary a trace of the variegation. Mature leaves roundish, 2 inches high and wide, dark green, finely serrated, glabrous, except on the reddish petiole.

Hydrangea anomala subsp. *petiolaris* 'Kuga Variegated'

Young stems reddish with fine bristlelike hairs; with maturity becoming glabrous. Aerial roots are evident on the young stems. A patented plant from Hines Nursery. Discovered by Toshiro Shimizu, Japan.

Subspecies *yakushima* is from the island of Yakushima; possibly like the species. Validity of name unknown. From Crûg Farm.

Several dwarf or less vigorous, prominently serrated leaf forms—including the following—are available, but I do not know their true taxonomic pecking order. The literature is not clear about characteristics, so be leery when purchasing. I grew subsp. *quelpartensis* for a time. Largely nothing but a small, jagged, crinkled leaf, juvenile form that never wanted to mature.

'**Cordifolia**' has small heavily toothed, heart-shaped leaves; possibly the same as 'Brookside Littleleaf' ('Brookside Miniature'), which was originally linked to *Schizophragma hydrangeoides*. Plants I observed are without question attached to *Hydrangea anomala* subsp. *petiolaris*. Leaves (juvenile) are much like subsp. *quelpartensis* and eventually mature to smaller versions of subsp. *petiolaris*. I have not observed flowers.

'Brookside Littleleaf'

'Tillaefolia', mature flowers

Subspecies *quelpartensis* is less vigorous, again with smaller, strongly toothed leaves. It resembles a juvenile form, but I have only grown and seen small plants and am unsure whether it matures out of this stage. Have not observed

'Tillaefolia', foliage

flowers but they are reported in literature.

'Tillaefolia' ('Tiliifolia') has large leaves, to 4 inches long, and typical inflorescences. Leaves are lustrous dark green, sharply and uniformly toothed, with extended acuminate apices. Flowers on a plant at the JC Raulston Arboretum, 8 May 2003, look identical to subsp. *petiolaris*. Crûg Farm introduction via seed from Korean island of Ullüngdõ. Confused(?), Forest Farm sells 'Tillaefolia' as a 20- to 30-foot vine with dainty tiny-leaved foliage. A plant of this description with leaves about 2 to 2 ½ inches long, lustrous dark green, with an extended apex, grows on a post in the shade house at the JC Raulston Arboretum. Flowers with showy sepals were present on 25 May 2003. Both the large-leaf and small-leaf forms labeled as 'Tillaefolia' were distinctly different in leaf shape from the typical subsp. *petiolaris*.

Climbing hydrangea is considered adaptable in Zones 4 to 7(8) and in the severe heat of the Southeast requires more coddling, i.e., shade and consistent moisture. A respectable specimen in the University's Botanical Garden, now about eight years old, has reached the 10-foot mark of a large oak. It grows in deep shade and has yet to flower. Several beautiful 25-foot-high flowering specimens cover tree trunks in the garden of Penny McHenry, Atlanta, Georgia. Flowers outside in Minneapolis, Minnesota. Rose et al. (2001) list hardiness to -25°F. I experienced venerable, 100-year and older, specimens in the North—nothing with that vine-span in the South. The vine grows over a large area from Japan, Taiwan, Sakhalin, and South Korea (Dagelet and Quelpaert islands).

Identification Characteristics

Leaves: Opposite, simple, broad-ovate to ovate-oval, 2 to 4 inches long, nearly as wide, acute or acuminate, cordate or rounded at base, sharply and uniformly serrate, nearly glabrous, dark green and lustrous above, paler and often with tufts of down in the vein-axils beneath; petiole ranging from $\frac{1}{2}$ to 4 inches long.

Buds: Imbricate, greenish brown, sometimes tinged red, shiny, 2 loosely overlapping scales visible, essentially glabrous.

Stem: Green to brown on the current year's growth, developing rootlike holdfasts along the internodes; older stems develop an exfoliating character much like *Acer griseum* (paperbark maple); the bark color is a rich cinnamon-brown and unparalleled by any other hardy vine.

Flowers: Inflorescence a corymb, flat-topped, with sepals in clusters of 3 to 5 at the periphery, clusters 1 to $1\frac{3}{4}$ inches across, up to 12 clusters per inflorescence, entire inflorescence 6 to 10 inches in diameter; individual sepal clean white, rounded, entire to irregularly serrated on upper half, $\frac{1}{2}$ to $\frac{3}{4}$ inches high and wide; fertile flower dull white, petals united, falling as a cap, fragrant and greatly attractive to bees, with 15 to 22 stamens.

CHAPTER THREE

Hydrangea arborescens
Linnaeus

SMOOTH HYDRANGEA

Unsung, unknown, unloved, and unrecognized except in the large-flowered mophead forms, 'Annabelle' and 'Grandiflora', *Hydrangea arborescens*, smooth hydrangea, literally melds into the shadows of the eastern North American forests. The species is among the most common occurrences in my excursions, forays, and expeditions in the Southeast. On the Rabun Bald trail in northeast Georgia, *H. arborescens* forms thickets that are almost impenetrable, while isolated specimens are sprinkled throughout Turkey Run State Park, Marshallville, Indiana. In the native state, plants range from 3 to 10 feet, often forming large colonies as they sucker outward. In fact, division is an easy method of propagation if a few plants are desired (see discussion under "Cuttings and Selected Vegetative Propagation Approaches" in chapter 13).

In a garden setting, habit is more rounded-mounded with stiff, largely unbranched stems and quite compact when plants are sited in abundant sun. The remarkable attribute is the ability to flower on new growth of the season, thus ensuring a healthy dose of flowers every year. Old inflorescences can be removed to tidy the plant in late winter (or sooner) before leaf emergence. Leaves are evident in late March in Athens. Flowers are smaller on this regrowth. If the stems are cut to the ground, the new shoots produce larger inflorescences. *Hydrangea arborescens* will reliably produce flowers in gardens from Alberta, Canada, to North Florida.

Flowers are borne at the terminal (apex) of the shoot and initially appear as clusters of floral primordia that resemble the head of broccoli. As the last pair of leaves below the inflorescence unfolds, the small broccoli-shaped flower bud becomes visible. Be careful not to damage the tender growth because the floral extravaganza depends on the maturation of the entire shoot.

Hydrangea arborescens,
Crabtree Falls, North Carolina

Typically, 6 nodes, i.e., 6 leaf pairs, subtend each flower bud. By late April to early May (Athens), the developing inflorescences are evident at the ends of the shoots.

Flowers of *Hydrangea arborescens* develop on a compound inflorescence called a corymb (see flowers description under "Identification Characteristics"). Depending on the particular seedling, the inflorescence is composed of all fertile flowers, a mixture of fertile (in the center) with showy sepals (in

Hydrangea arborescens,
garden setting

3s or 4s) around the periphery (the lacecap configuration), or the predominantly sterile type with the showy sepals forming a solid globose to rounded shape. This last inflorescence also carries several fertile flowers under the sepals that, when pollinated, produce viable seeds.

Inflorescences range from 3 to 4 inches in diameter on the species to 10(12) inches on 'Annabelle'. Remember: from a gardening viewpoint, the more vigorous the shoot growth, the larger the inflorescence,

Hydrangea arborescens, lacecap

whether the species or cultivars. Many gardeners prefer the smaller inflorescences of the species because shoots remain upright and do not splay and flop like those of 'Grandiflora' and 'Annabelle'. However, 'Annabelle' is sold in astronomical numbers on a yearly basis.

The medium to dark green leaves, rather thinnish in texture, largely ovate to heart-shaped, strongly serrate, range from (2)3 to 6(8) inches long, 2 to 6 inches wide. The lower surface is pubescent on the veins and uniformly green. Subspecies *discolor* and *radiata* have gray and cottony white undersides, respectively. Their botanical, taxonomic, and horticultural merits are discussed in "Cultivars and Varieties." In fall (mid-November, Athens), leaves turn soft lemon-yellow with color persisting into early December. The mature leaves as well as the young leaves in the spring are more frost-resistant than those of *Hydrangea macrophylla* and *H. serrata*.

My garden success with the species and 'Annabelle' is predicated on consistent moisture and an organic-amended, acid, well-drained soil. The species is more adaptable to higher pH soils than *Hydrangea macrophylla*, but prefers acid soil. I studied numerous herbarium specimens of the species and the two subspecies, and the collection notes often refer to the three taxa growing on limestone (calcareous) as well as acid soils. 'Annabelle', even in full sun, at Griffin, Georgia, yet more at ease with sun further north, has prospered. At Orono, Maine, and Chanhassen, Minnesota, *H. arborescens* and cultivars thrive in full sun exposure. A sliding light scale should be applied, as plants are utilized from Florida to Minnesota: more shade in the South than in the North. Light shade is the best prescription for garden success, and, in the wild, plants grow on north slopes of mountains and under deciduous tree canopy, and never experience anything but heavily filtered light.

Hydrangea arborescens
'Grandiflora', splaying

Bonnie and I hiked to Crabtree Falls off the Blue Ridge Parkway under forest canopy so thick a flashlight was almost necessary. At the base of the falls, growing out of a crevice in the rocks, was a healthy specimen of *H. arborescens*.

Hydrangea arborescens, foliage

The species and cultivars are great choices for mixed shrub borders or combined with herbaceous perennials. In the Dirr garden, a large colony of 'Annabelle' grows at the base of a tall stewartia, *Stewartia monadelpha*, weaving its way through the stewartia's lower branches; from June until March when the tired heads of the 'Annabelle' are removed, the combination sparks interest. Jenny Purviance, Middleton, Rhode Island, has commingled *Hydrangea arborescens* with *H. macrophylla* and *H. paniculata*, a knockout spectacle in early July. In the median of Belle Meade Parkway, Nashville, Tennessee, enormous sweeps of 'Annabelle' control (slow) the flow of traffic. The late Buddy Hubbuch, horticulturist, Bernheim Arboretum, Clermont, Kentucky, sited a grouping of 'Annabelle' under pine trees. The effect was akin to a 500-watt lamp in a dark room.

The species is less obtrusive than the large sterile-flowered types and easily harmonizes with naturalistic plantings. Most of the seedlings I observe in

'Annabelle', Bernheim Arboretum

the wild have limited showy sepals and consist largely of fertile flowers. Bonnie and I have hiked the southern Appalachians and observed the full range of variation from fertile, to mixed, to perfectly rounded, snowball-flowered forms. In 2002, three, rich pink-flowered seedlings, one with large abundant sepals, were discovered at 3,600 feet elevation in Rabun County, Georgia. To date, 'Eco Pink Puff', 'Wesser Falls', along with 'Pink Pincushion' and

'Eco Pink Puff' seedling in bud

'Chestatee', are the only pink-flowered forms. They are wispy and slender-stemmed with small inflorescences, pink in bud, opening white. My hope is to develop a pink-flowered 'Annabelle' type. These strategies are discussed under 'Annabelle' in the "Cultivars and Varieties" section.

Hydrangea arborescens frequents ravines and rocky river banks from the southern part of New York to Florida and westward to Iowa and Missouri, primarily in the Ozark region of the latter state. In the southern Appalachians and Piedmont, it is as common as rocks. Garden adaptability is Zones 3 to 9.

Cultivars and Varieties

Subspecies *discolor* (ashy hydrangea) and subsp. *radiata* (snowy hydrangea) are recognized. In this author's opinion, the status of subsp. *discolor* is tenuous, with the identifying characteristic being the light gray underside of the leaf. In subsp. *radiata*, which occurs in abundance in the mountains of North Carolina, the leaves are silver-white on their undersides. Also, subsp. *radiata* is not as comfortable in the heat and drought as the typical *Hydrangea arborescens* and its cultivars. Subspecies *radiata* is more difficult to root from cuttings than the species and subsp. *discolor*. This has been a consistent trend in our shop. On several occasions, subsp. *radiata*, carefully sited in the Dirr garden, simply died, while a large colony of 'Annabelle' has thrived for over 20 years. Subspecies *radiata* produces more ray (showy) sepals than the wild *H. arborescens* and subsp. *discolor* (which produces more than *H. arborescens*), and on several occasions I have noticed seedlings of subsp. *radiata* in the wild that were extremely showy because of the dominant number of sepals. Hardy to Zone 4 and flowers early to mid July at the Morton Arboretum, Lisle, Illinois. I counted 4 leaf pairs (nodes) subtending each inflorescence (full flower, 14 June 2003) on a large plant at the North Carolina Botanical Garden, Chapel Hill. Remarkably, no variance from the four nodes was noted on the 20 inflorescences.

Hydrangea arborescens subsp. *discolor*

A day in the University of Georgia botany herbarium examining every specimen of subsp. *discolor* and subsp. *radiata* resulted in the following determinations. Subspecies *discolor* occurs over a wider range than subsp. *radiata*, although in the higher elevations of the southern Appalachians they overlap. Subspecies *discolor* specimens were collected in the wild from Kentucky, Indiana, Missouri, Tennessee, North Carolina, Arkansas, and Georgia from limestone bluffs, sandy limestone outcroppings, and moist, north-facing, wooded, rocky bluffs. The leaves had crooked unbranched hairs on the major veins above, with more prominent numbers below on the veins and interveinal areas. The pubescence was variable from specimen to specimen but imparted a grayish color to the lower surface. The hairs of subsp. *discolor* are covered with numerous tubercles (bumps), while subsp. *radiata* has none or few. McClintock (1957a, pages 182-183) shows the nature and distribution of the tubercles. Subspecies *discolor* grows at lower elevations than subsp. *radiata*.

Hydrangea arborescens subsp. *discolor*, habit

In subsp. *radiata*, the distribution is restricted to higher elevations, 2,000 feet or greater in Georgia, North Carolina, South Carolina, and Tennessee. Grows in cool, moist habitats in shade but also in sunny positions along the mountain roads. Occurrences in Georgia are restricted to Rabun County at elevations of 2,800 feet and above. As mentioned, this most beautiful plant languishes in the heat of the Piedmont and lower South. The Dirr garden is

Hydrangea arborescens subsp. *radiata*

Hydrangea arborescens subsp. *radiata*, habit

located at about 850 feet elevation, and the plant has never acclimated. I suspect the high night temperatures are partially to blame.

In subsp. *radiata*, the upper surface of the leaves has hairs along the veins. The lower is cottonmouth white, covered with a thick fabric of white hairs that microscopically appear woven like a carpet. The actual underside, i.e., lower epidermis, of the leaf is not visible because of the thick, cottony pubescence. Easy to identify as the undersides flash silver in the buffeting breezes.

McClintock's taxonomic treatment of *Hydrangea* legitimizes subsp. *discolor* (Seringe) E. M. McClintock and subsp. *radiata* (Walter) E. M. McClintock (see McClintock 1957a). Another taxonomist, R. E. Pilatowski (1982), rejected McClintock's treatment and keeps *H. cinerea* (subsp. *discolor*) and *H. radiata* as distinct species. He noted that the three taxa maintain their distinctness even when overlapping in geographical distribution. Pilatowski's rationale is discussed more lucidly in chapter 16. An as-yet-unpublished revision of the *Vascular Flora of the Carolinas* by Alan Weakley follows Pilatowski's taxonomy.

'**Annabelle**' was named and largely promoted by the late J. C. McDaniel, University of Illinois, for its extremely large corymbs (up to 1 foot across) and the fact it flowers 10 to 14 days later than 'Grandiflora'; individual sepals average 0.37 inches long, 0.33 inches wide; the clusters average 0.77 inches across and completely shroud the

Hydrangea arborescens subsp. *radiata*, foliage (silver-white underside, left)

fertile flowers; flowers about mid-June in the Dirr garden; heads are more erect on the stem with a more nearly symmetrical radius, and are usually larger in total diameter than those of 'Grandiflora' grown under the same conditions; has become one of the most popular hydrangeas and is commonly available from nurseries. This is definitely a superior plant and was introduced by a true plantsman and gentleman. The history of this selection is presented in *Proceedings of the International Plant Propagators Society* 12:110 (1962) and in *Legends in the Garden* (Copeland and Armitage 2001); plant

'Annabelle', flowers at peak

first observed in 1910 along a wooded trail in the hills of Union County, near Anna, Illinois; fifty years later McDaniel reported finding clumps of the original plant growing in the discoverer's garden in Anna, a testimonial to its longevity. Selected for the 1995 Georgia Gold Medal Award; garden cognoscenti say the flowers are too large, gauche, obtrusive; one person's favorite garden plant is another's bane; life is great. With plants cut to the ground, 7 to 9 nodes (leaf pairs) develop below the inflorescence. Flowering shoots from previous year's wood have approximately 6 nodes (leaf pairs) subtending each inflorescence.

'Annabelle' is unabashedly the queen of the *Hydrangea arborescens* cultivar bash. The flowers are immense and, when wet, splay and weep. My approach to improvement is to select for slightly smaller inflorescences and stronger stems. 'Annabelle' is self-fertile, meaning pollen from the same flower will effectively pollinate the female flower and produce viable seeds (see chapter 16). Most seeds of 'Annabelle' produce sterile-flowered, globose to round-shaped, white, mophead offspring. Several selections are currently under evaluation.

'Annabelle', inflorescences maturing to green

Another goal is to breed pink into an 'Annabelle' type. My optimism stems from the pink-budded and -flowered 'Eco Pink Puff' and 'Wesser Falls', both largely fertile-flowered forms. Controlled crossing using 'Annabelle' as the female will be necessary. With the quick time to flower, less than 12 months from seed sowing, many flowering generations are possible over a career.

'**Balsam**'. See Dirr Selections.

'Annabelle', fall color

'**Bounty**' is an enigma—its origin has been untraceable. The plant stood tall and firm, with a broad sterile-flowered dried corymb, when I first viewed it at Hillier Arboretum, Hampshire, England, in February 1999. The stout stems provided the significant ingredient lacking in 'Annabelle'. I hoped to secure a piece of the original plant but was given two small liners by Ian Hobbs, former propagator at Hillier Nurseries (separate from the arbore-

'Bounty', Hillier Arboretum

tum). Cuttings were rooted and passed to many nursery and gardening friends. Then came the refrain that the flowers and habit looked just like 'Annabelle'. Hillier Arboretum had true 'Annabelle' and 'Bounty' within 100 yards of each other. They *were* different as I viewed them.

Gene Griffith, Wilkerson Mill Gardens, Palmetto, Georgia, talked through the issue and said the 'Bounty' I gave him was similar to 'Annabelle'; but Keith Howe,

'Bounty', Keith Howe

Country Gardens, provided a 'Bounty' as described above. However, the inflorescence is somewhat lumpy and rounded, not at all like the Hillier 'Bounty'. Allen Coombes, botanist, Hillier Arboretum, found nothing in the records about 'Bounty'. Perhaps the plants I received from Ian could have been taken from the 'Annabelle' in the Arboretum instead of the 'Bounty'? I hope to secure material from the original Hillier 'Bounty' and take another look.

'**Chestatee**' is a pink-budded selection, flowers open white, few sterile flowers, 3- to 4-inch-wide inflorescence; leaves 4 to 5 inches long, no fall color; grows 3 feet high and wide; found by Richard Saul, Atlanta, Georgia.

Dirr Selections. My wife and I love this most widely distributed American hydrangea species and in June, July, and August, when hiking and riding through the Southeast, are always peering, prying, and hoping for unique variation. In the Balsam Mountains of North Carolina, we discovered a sterile form of *Hydrangea arborescens* with lacy flowers on strong stems, not as large or heavy as 'Annabelle'. Bonnie named this 'Highland Lace'. Thankfully, I gave this selection to several friends, for my plants perished. I called Don Shadow, Winchester, Tennessee, about retrieving a few cuttings; Don said his plants also died. The Atlanta Botanical Garden (ABG) had placed their plant in the collection, and Scott McMahan, horticulturist, wrote the following: "The habit is basically an 'Annabelle' type with much thicker stems that are better suited to holding the flowers up . . . we (ABG) have been very impressed with it." The real moral resides in the importance of sharing a new plant, not simply for preservation, but also evaluation. On three occasions Bonnie and I returned to the original location to secure cuttings. Never could the plant be located because the highway crews mowed it to the ground. The act of sharing almost always returns full circle. Also, ABG had no records of the plant's origin and called it 'Balsam'. When I heard the name through a third party, the hunt was again in motion with the results exciting to Bonnie and me. Another small, sterile, perfectly round-flowered seedling was discovered growing from the side of a cliff along Highway 106 in North Carolina. On 25 July 2002, we discovered three pink-flowered forms (all much pinker than the 'Eco Pink Puff', 'Pink Pincushion', and 'Wesser Falls' forms) one with abundant, showy pink sepals.

Subspecies *discolor* **'Frosty'** is described as a dwarf mound, 3 to 4 feet high, with shiny blue-green foliage throughout the growing season; myriads of white flowers bloom in rather flat sterile clusters during summer. Sun to part shade. This description is almost verbatim from Roslyn Nurseries. On 24 June 2003, a chance meeting with a fellow plant enthusiast, Clarence Towe, clarified the origin. Clarence discovered the plant near Clayton, Rabun County, Georgia. He said it was a sterile-flowered type with single sepals forming the mophead-type inflorescence.

Subspecies *discolor* **'Sterilis'**, often confused with 'Grandiflora', has a flatter-topped head, showing some areas of small perfect flowers not covered by the persisting sepals of the showy flowers; Paul Cappiello (formerly of the University of Maine) and I identified a planting on the Maine campus as 'Sterilis'; the flower corymbs appeared more uniform, i.e., not as lumpy. Have also studied a large planting of 'Sterilis' at Savill Gardens, England, fully 5 to 6 feet high, that parallels the above description. The old name that is occasionally used is *Hydrangea cinerea* 'Sterilis'.

Hydrangea arborescens subsp. *discolor* 'Sterilis'

Hydrangea arborescens subsp. *discolor* 'Sterilis', Savill Gardens

'Eco Pink Puff'

'**Eco Pink Puff**' is a light pink-flowered form composed of largely (all) fertile flowers from Don Jacobs, Eco Gardens, Decatur, Georgia. In the heat of Zones 7 and 8, buds are dark red-purple, but flowers open pinkish to white. A degree more pink than 'Wesser Falls'. Seedlings with deeper pink buds as well as showy pink fertile flowers and sepals have been selected.

'**Emerald Lace**' ('Green Dragon'). Leaves are jagged and incised like American holly, with some leaves resembling a compound pinnate leaf like an ash; flowers are lacecap types, with fertile flowers in center, white sepals on the periphery; discovered by Stan Tyson, in Illinois.

'**Grandiflora**' is often referred to as the Hills of Snow Hydrangea; the corymbs are 6 to 8 inches across with primarily sterile white flowers; the individual "sterile" showy sepals are larger than 'Annabelle', but the total number of flowers in a head is fewer; the heads are not so radially symmetrical, looking like four parts loosely pushed together, and soon becoming floppy in appearance. This cultivar, discovered growing wild in Ohio in the late 1800s, was planted throughout the Midwest, East, and upper South. Plants sucker and form large colonies, 10 to 20 feet across. In Maine, this cultivar and *Hydrangea paniculata*

'Grandiflora' are both common around older homesteads. Has fallen from favor with the ascendency of 'Annabelle', but is still a reliable and showy flowering shrub.

'Green Knight'. Described as unique and exciting with pure white, mophead globular inflorescences, which turn a rich dark green as they age; originally given to Louisiana Nursery by Mary Nell McDaniel, wife of Joe McDaniel, offered by Louisiana Nursery, Opelousas, Louisiana.

Hydrangea arborescens 'Grandiflora'

'Hayes Starburst' is a remarkable introduction with narrow, oval, shiny, sharply toothed, wavy margined, dark green leaves and sterile, multiple-sepaled white flowers that originated as a self-sown seedling in the garden of Hayes Jackson, Anniston, Alabama. The habit is more compact than the species, probably 3 to 4 feet high at maturity and rounded in outline. For me,

Hydrangea arborescens 'Grandiflora', habit

'Hayes Starburst'

it has been persnickety and may require slightly cooler conditions to maximize growth and flowering. Without debate, this is one of the most striking selections of *Hydrangea arborescens*. An interesting sidelight: the original plant died, but Jackson had shared the plant with friends. Had he not passed along his discovery, our gardens would be the poorer.

'Mary Nell'

'Mary Nell' is a wonderful species type with prominent showy sepals around the periphery of the inflorescence and scattered toward the center. The plant came from the garden of the late Joe McDaniel and is named after his wife. Phyllis Brussel of Urbana, Illinois, sent me photographs and a few plants. Her thinking was to share the plant with nurserymen who could evaluate and produce it commercially.

'Picadilly'. A largely fertile-flowered form with darker green leaves than the species. Flowers are not spectacular, and this name may not be legitimate. I witnessed the plant and name at the 2002 "Hydrangeas—Beginning to End" meeting in Thomson, Georgia.

'Pink Pincushion'. Introduced through Wilkerson Mill Gardens, Palmetto, Georgia, by Gene Griffith and Elizabeth Dean. Pink buds open pinkish white to white, primarily fertile-flowered, discovered by the owners on their property. Listed as a *Hydrangea cinerea* selection, i.e., subsp. *discolor*, by the Morton Arboretum, Lisle, Illinois.

Subspecies *radiata* 'Elkins Garden' is listed in the *Hydrangea International Index*.

Subspecies *radiata* **'Robusta'** is listed by Trelissick Gardens, England, without any supporting information.

Subspecies *radiata* **'Samantha'** is a sterile-flowered form with the inflorescence shape residing between 'Annabelle' and 'Grandiflora'. Inflorescences 4 to 6 inches diameter, emerge green, mature white, fading to green and finally parchment, sepals in (3s)4s(5s), 1 to $1^{1}/_{2}$ inches across, each sepal broad-ovate to rounded, entire, slightly overlapping, $^{1}/_{2}$ to $^{3}/_{4}$ inches long, $^{3}/_{8}$ to

'Picadilly'

$^{5}/_{8}$ inches wide. In Dearing, Georgia, under 55 percent shade and the same culture and care provided a large population of *Hydrangea macrophylla*, the cultivar simply pooped out. I suspect, like the subspecies, it requires cooler day/night temperatures than are available in Zones 7 and 8. Attractive flowers, combined with silver-backed leaves, make for a handsome garden plant. Starting to make its way into commerce.

Subspecies *radiata* **'Silver Flash'**, with silver/white-backed leaves, is mentioned by Don Buma (2002).

Hydrangea arborescens subsp. *radiata* 'Samantha'

Subspecies *radiata* **'Spring Grove'** is listed in the *Hydrangea International Index*.

Subspecies *radiata* **'Terry Greer'**, a double, sterile-flowered form, is slowly making its way into commerce. I do not believe it has the appeal of 'Samantha'. Clarence Towe, Walhalla, South Carolina, was responsible for introducing these subsp. *radiata* selections into cultivation.

'**Snow Cone**' is similar to 'Grandiflora'. I observed it in the *Hydrangea* trials at the Mountain Research Center, North Carolina State University, Fletcher, North Carolina, and without the label would have been unable to separate same from *H. arborescens* 'Grandiflora'. Richard Bir, horticulturist at the center, reported the inflorescence is more cone-shaped.

'**Visitation**' is a smaller, sterile-flowered form that I experienced for the first time at the 2002 "Hydrangeas—Beginning to End" meeting in Thomson, Georgia. The inflorescences were smaller than those of 'Grandiflora' and appeared more uniform in shape. The plant was container grown, and the resultant flowers may not be representative of garden performance. Introduced by Ryan Gainey, Atlanta, Georgia.

'**Wesser Falls**' is another pink-budded, opening white, fertile-flowered selection by Richard Olsen, former master of science student, University of Georgia.

White Dome™ ('Dardom') is advertised as a new introduction of the species type with largely off-white fertile flowers surrounded and occasionally interspersed with white sterile sepals in clusters of 3(4). Inflorescences are larger than those of the typical species and carried on strong stems. The leaves are more robust, larger, and thicker. I witnessed plants at a North Carolina garden center and immediately knew something was amiss. The above characteristics are more or less accurate; however, the selection is not from *Hydrangea arborescens* but either subsp. *discolor* or *radiata*. The leaves are white beneath. From an adaptability standpoint it will lack heat tolerance, particularly in Zones 7 to 9, where *H. arborescens* will thrive. Also, the flowers, as shown in advertisements, are similar to many subsp. *radiata* I experienced in western North Carolina. From Darthuizer Nursery, The Netherlands. On 1 June 2003, I saw the cultivar in flower in Hillsborough, North Carolina. The flowers were nothing like the photographs. The sepals were sparsely punctuated around the periphery of the inflorescence. Sepals were small, about $^1/_2$ to $^3/_4$ inches across the cluster. I evaluated about 40 plants, and the above floral comments applied across the group.

White Dome™

Others are seeking superior selections of *Hydrangea arborescens,* and in reviewing Arrowhead Alpines extensive hydrangea offerings, I read mention that the nursery hoped to offer a couple of wonderful new *H. arborescens* clones in the next few years (visit their Web site at www.arrowheadalpines.com).

Identification Characteristics

Leaves: Opposite, simple, elliptic, ovate, to heart-shaped, 2 to 8 inches long, 2 to 6 inches wide, acuminate, rounded or cordate at base, dentate, medium to dark green, glabrous often with hairs on major veins above, puberulous on veins below, often heavy, the hairs slightly crooked, and green beneath; petiole 1 to 3(6) inches long.

White Dome™, showing white leaf underside and sparse sepals

Buds: Imbricate, 4- to 6-scaled, greenish brown, divergent, $^1/_8$ to $^1/_4$ inch long, glabrous, much longer than *Hydrangea paniculata* buds.

Stem: Stout, gray-tan-brown, shiny, young branches are often pubescent, glabrous with maturity, smooth, without gray streaks; older stems exfoliating, called "sevenbark" because the bark exfoliates in layers; pith relatively large, roundish, continuous, whitish, second year pith brown, finally hollow.

Flowers: Corymb type, flattened inflorescence, typically 3 to 4(6) inches wide, sepals in 3s and 4s, each sepal rounded-orbicular, pubescent, $^2/_5$ to $^3/_5$ inches in diameter, typically on short pedicels (stalks) at the periphery of the inflorescence, sometimes scattered throughout, and in the sterile types like 'Annabelle' covering the entire structure to form a snowball-type flower, sepals emerge apple-green, mature white, fading to green, parchment and finally brown, remaining attached through fall and winter, color peaking in early to mid June (Athens), one month later in Boston. Fertile flowers fragrant, dull white, 5 petals, each 2 mm long, 1 mm wide, 10 stamens, erect to spreading, filaments white, anthers white, styles 2, white.

Hydrangea aspera, towering at Marwood Hill

CHAPTER FOUR

Hydrangea aspera
D. Don

This species and its many variants have yet to coalesce into an understandable whole or convert me to wholesale acceptance, primarily because of tenuous cultural adaptability. All taxa umbrellaed by this species have large fuzzy leaves and stems, lacecap inflorescences, typically blue or purple in the central fertile flowers, with an outer ring of white to lilac-pink showy sepals. Large, knobbily rounded bud clusters foreshadow the flowers. Depending on one's aesthetic bent, the bud clusters are somewhat attractive to rather scary. Bark on mature plants exfoliates in papery brown strips and sheets. Many an English garden have I traipsed in March, looking at the furry stems and bark, wondering why American gardeners would want this when *Hydrangea quercifolia* is part of the national heritage.

But . . . during my 1999 sabbatical in England at the great Sir Harold Hillier Gardens and Arboretum, Hampshire, I relentlessly pursued the *Hydrangea aspera* complex, observing, collecting data, and photographing. Indeed, they are confusing, and the same plant, or so it appeared, would have one name in one garden and another in the next.

In North America the species is, without question, best adapted to British Columbia, the Pacific Northwest, south to San Francisco; however, respectable plants grow in Philadelphia; Athens; Atlanta; JC Raulston Arboretum, Raleigh, North Carolina; and Aiken, South Carolina. I was informed that the species and cultivars will flower on new growth if cold injures flower buds and stems. I have yet to confirm this, however. All flower buds observed at the Atlanta Botanical Garden (18 May 2003) on

Hydrangea aspera subsp. *sargentiana*

Hydrangea aspera, pubescent stems

'Robusta' and subsp. *sargentiana* were derived from old wood. This means that pruning should be conducted after flowering. Also, at JC Raulston Arboretum on 3 June 2003, the flower buds of a Villosa Group member and 'Rocklon' were just visible at the terminals of the current season's shoots, which were derived from old wood. Subspecies *sargentiana* produced visible flower buds from old wood (only) as I viewed the lone plant at the JC Raulston Arboretum on 8 May 2003. The species is susceptible to late spring frosts (freezes), and my 1999 sabbatical notes state "flattened by frost," "frosted severely," and "melted to the ground." Hardiness is listed as Zone 5 by Bell Family Nursery, but my limited observations and reading of the literature suggests Zones (6)7 to 8(9 on West Coast). Scott Arboretum, Swarthmore, Pennsylvania, reported the species was tender in Zone 6b. Listed in living collections of the Holden Arboretum, Mentor, Ohio, Zone 6. Mike Hayman, Louisville, Kentucky, told me that subsp. *sargentiana* suffers some dieback but does flower from buds on old wood.

The *Hydrangea aspera* complex is extremely tolerant of high pH (chalky soils), and the flower (sepal) colors tend not to be affected by pH (i.e., aluminum). Shade is a requisite in the South, perhaps less so on the West Coast. Certainly in England plants prospered in full sun, such as it is. Penny McHenry reported that Japanese beetles eat the foliage, and from her observations this is the only *Hydrangea* taxon so impacted. She has grown members of the *H. aspera* complex since the late 1990s with no dieback. The subsp. *sargentiana* "types," approximately 9 feet high, were in full flower on 29 June 2003, when I visited her superb garden. Cutting propagation can be difficult because of heavy pubescence and the cuttings' penchant for rotting under mist.

The habit is almost always upright in youth; some plants maintain the configuration into old age. However, I observed many older specimens that had become broad mounds. In Europe, plants 15 to 18 feet high and wide crossed my path.

The flowers are configured as lacecaps, and I have yet to experience a sterile, mophead type, although at least two such types are described by Haworth-Booth. July is the peak window for floral expression with drift on either side. My photos of the *Hydrangea aspera* taxa in England were primarily taken in July to early August. The developing flower buds remind me of purple-brown cauliflowers at the stem ends. In 'Macrophylla', 'Robusta', and subsp. *sargentiana*, they are quite large and Martian.

The inflorescences, fully expanded, range from 4 to 6 inches to 10 inches in diameter. The fertile flowers are small, numerous, white, blue, pink, purple, each with 5 petals that abscise early; the flower stalks (pedicels) are

Hydrangea aspera, bud clusters

Hydrangea aspera, foliage

Hydrangea aspera, bark

hairy; the sterile flowers in clusters of typically 4, each sepal white, rounded, toothed or entire, the entire configuration 1 to 1½ inches across. The flowers are beautiful, lacking the glitz and glamour of *Hydrangea macrophylla* types, more restrained, and showing well against the large, fuzzy leaves.

Leaves . . . wow . . . warm, fuzzy, like bunny ears, dark green above, variably pubescent, yet below grayish and cloaked in velvet, waiting to be stroked. Foliage is typically not as thickly set as the *Hydrangea macrophylla* taxa, and plants, particularly at their bases, are without mass. However, the exfoliating bark is shown to perfection.

The great *Hydrangea* literature (Haworth-Booth, Lawson-Hall, Mallets, McClintock) ascribes the native range as the Himalayas, central and western China, Taiwan, Sumatra, and Java. Ernest Henry "Chinese" Wilson, the greatest plant explorer, introduced many of the associated taxa to cultivation. The nomenclature, as mentioned previously, is muddied with the numerous variants. Herein, *The Hillier Manual* (2002) categories provide guidance for the discussion.

Villosa Group

Shrubs are less coarse with narrower, more refined leaves. The leaves, stems, and flower stalks are densely villous; the spreading, curly hairs somewhat rust-colored. The leaf margins are fringed and minutely serrated with the lower surface grayish white. Leaves about one-half mature size by early April in Athens.

Inflorescences are lilac-blue to mauve-purple with white to pink-mauve sepals. Will grow 6 to 10 feet high, 6 feet wide. May grow 10 feet high by 15 feet wide. Flower buds just emerging (still small) on 3 June 2003, at JC

Raulston Arboretum. Five to seven nodes subtend each flower bud derived from old wood. Flowers fully open 10 July 2003, with mauve sepals and fertile flowers. Provide evenly moist, organic-laden soils. A singular plant growing in the garden of Mr. and Mrs. Vincent J. Dooley in Athens, Georgia, now 7 feet high, and has flowered and fruited. No frost damage or dieback have occurred. An 8-foot-high plant has flowered at the Atlanta Botanical Garden.

Hydrangea aspera Villosa Group

The following cultivars nest herein because of lack of clear understanding of their group affinity: **'Mauvette'** has 6-inch-wide flower heads, mauve fertile flowers, and increased numbers of sterile flowers, white to mauve; **'Rocklon'**, with slender green leaves, purple fertile, white ray flowers, was still in tight bud on 25 June 2003, at the JC Raulston Arboretum, buds green and still tight on 10 July, flowers open on 24 July, sepals white, serrated, few, fertile flowers dirty gray-white, not much to recommend this cultivar; **'Rosthornii'** with sepals in 4s and 5s, white, bluish purple fertile flowers; **'Sam MacDonald'** with abundant terminal and lateral

'Sam MacDonald'

flower buds on young plants, white to mauve sepals, mauve fertile flowers, fully open 28 June 2003, in Athens; and **'Velvet and Lace'**, a Hillier introduction, with corymbs to 9 inches wide, purple-blue fertile flowers, serrated, pale mauve-pink nodding sepals, in 4s and 5s, leaves to 8 inches long.

Kawakamii Group

Produces deep violet fertile flowers surrounded by white sepalous clusters (4s) measuring 1½ inches across. At Fillan's Plants, England, this type produced larger, later flowers than subsp. *sargentiana* with pinkish leaves and reddish petioles. My lone plant from Heronswood is intermediate in leaf characteristics between the Villosa Group and subsp. *sargentiana*. From Taiwan.

Hydrangea aspera
Kawakamii Group

Subspecies *sargentiana* (Rehder) E. M. McClintock

Hydrangea aspera subsp.
sargentiana

This taxon showcases 8- to 9-inch-long, rich velvety green pubescent leaves, grayish pubescent below, and bristly pubescent stems. The leaves are coarse-textured with an undulating surface. I noted horrendous Japanese beetle feeding on this taxon at Fletcher, North Carolina, on 10 August 2003; a large collection of *Hydrangea paniculata* growing in the same row were largely unaffected. Inflorescences are 5 to 6 inches in diameter, pale purple in the center, with white ray (sepal) flowers. A plant in full flower on 25 June 2003 at the JC Raulston Arboretum had white, pink, and mauve sepals, slightly bluish fertile flowers with faint fragrance. The sepals are grouped (3s)4s(5s) together, 1½ inches wide; each sepal ir-

regularly rounded and entire. Sepals reverse after pollination and fertilization, develop parchment color, and lose their effectiveness in the heat of Zone 7, even in shade. Apparently, develops flowers ahead of Villosa Group based on flower bud development at JC Raulston Arboretum.

Hydrangea aspera subsp. *sargentiana,* foliage

'Anthony Bullivant' is a robust broad-rounded form with flowers and leaves akin to subsp. *sargentiana*. From Stourton House and Garden, Wiltshire, England. Named after the late Anthony Bullivant who with his wife, Elizabeth, amassed a wonderful collection of hydrangeas.

'Macrophylla', as I viewed it at Knightshayes, England, although scarce, was less bold than subsp. *sargentiana*. 'Macrophylla' at Fillan's Plants, England, was deep purple in the center with white sepals. Flowers July to early August at Scott Arboretum, Swarthmore, Pennsylvania, where it is marginally hardy. Listed in the Living Collections of the Morton Arboretum, Lisle, Illinois. Habit is coarse and can be gaunt and leggy. Requires shade and even moisture.

'Peter Chappell', a selection with broad inflorescences of white fertile and sterile flowers in 6- to 8-inch-wide lacecaps, August, was named after the owner of Spinner's Nursery and Garden, Peter Chappell, by his friend, Maurice Foster. Leaves to 6 inches by 2 inches, hairy like all *Hydrangea aspera*. Listed as growing 5 feet high and wide. This fits, based on leaf shape, with the Villosa Group. Spinner's, located in Boldre, near Lymington, Hampshire, England, is a delight and should be visited by all garden travelers. One of my favorite rare plant nurseries.

Hydrangea aspera subsp. *sargentiana,* bark exfoliating in sheets

'Robusta' [subsp. *robusta* (Hooker f. and Thomson) E. M. McClintock], with leaves somewhat akin to subsp. *sargentiana*, resides herein. I observed 'Robusta' next to subsp. *sargentiana*, and the leaves of the latter were larger, otherwise differences were minimal. 'Robusta' leaves from a Heronswood plant were roughly 5 inches long, broadly heart-shaped, with more jagged serrations.

Other cultivars listed in the *Hydrangea International Index* (2002) include 'August Abundance', 'Bellevue', 'Farall', 'Highdown Form', 'Sapa', 'September Splendour', 'Stäfa', 'Taiwan Pink' ('Taiwan'), and 'The Ditch'.

Subspecies *strigosa* (Rehder) E. M. McClintock

Recognized by the strigose pubescence that covers the large, lance-shaped leaves and reddish stems. White, 1-inch-wide ray flowers, sepals broadly egg-shaped, entire or toothed, lilac fertile flowers open ahead of other *Hydrangea aspera* types. May be damaged by spring frosts. I have doubts about the validity of this taxon. The one plant in my collection, purchased as subsp. *strigosa*, has hairs that appear like bristles in a toothbrush, with 9-inch-long broad lance-shaped leaves held on strong red petioles and stout reddish purple stems. Wilson (1923) reported collecting wild specimens of subsp. *strigosa* with globose heads of sterile flowers.

From a pragmatic viewpoint, it makes everyday sense to mesh the various groups into one large melting pot, saving the subsp. *sargentiana* designation. As I cross-checked my notes on *Hydrangea aspera* from many gardens and hydrangea enthusiasts, I became more uncertain of the taxonomic pigeonholes ascribed. Gardeners will be able to identify *H. aspera*; however, any classifying beyond this (again, excepting subsp. *sargentiana*) is guesswork. McClintock's distribution map for *H. aspera* and related taxa shows the subspecies commingled from western to eastern China to Taiwan. With this type of distribution, variable degrees of leaf morphology and pubescence are givens. In the United States, *Acer rubrum* from North to South could be divided mercilessly into subspecies. Likewise, *Cercis canadensis* from the Northeast to Southeast to Southwest could be carved into worthless subspecies. Lumping is more logical than splitting.

CHAPTER FIVE

Hydrangea heteromalla
D. Don

Like *Hydrangea aspera*, *H. heteromalla* is a variable species in terms of growth habit, size (8 to 18 feet), foliage, and flower size and quality. Shrubs range from frail, weak growers to sturdy, 15- to 18-feet-high behemoths.

Foliage is dark green above, gray to white below, ranging from 3 to 8 inches long, 1 to 5 inches wide. Typically glabrous or with a few hairs on the upper surface, gray pubescent below, at least on the veins, toothed and bristly at the margins. The 1- to 2-inch-long, pubescent petioles are often rich red, a characteristic that facilitates separation from *Hydrangea paniculata*. Great variation in foliar colors in a seedling population that I grew: leaves ranged from green (petiole red) to bronze-green. Emerging leaves are extremely pubescent on the lower surface, often with a reddish margin. The grooved petioles are covered with hairs on the ridges of the upper side.

Flowers, lacecap in composition, appear in mid-May (Dearing, Georgia), June and later (Boston), in 3- to 12-inch-wide flattish corymbs, with 4(5) white sterile sepals, each cluster 1 to 2 inches wide, each sepal elliptic to oval-rounded, surrounding the numerous, small, white, fertile flowers. The fertile flowers provide a slight, sweet fragrance. The sepals, via maturation, develop pink, rose, to burgundy tints. The summer flowering effect is a slow evolution and provides a continuum after most shrubs have closed shop until the next spring floral cycle. The sepals turn toward the ground, presenting a semi-wilted appearance as they mature. Flower buds are formed on the previous season's growth. Emerging flower buds are evident by mid-April, open in mid to late May, in Zone 7b. Unfortunately, heat can cook the sepals gray-brown by late June.

Habit is upright, vase-shaped to spreading, higher than wide at maturity. The plant "fits" most accommodatingly in the shrub border, perhaps skirted with small shrubs. Full sun to partial shade and moist, organic-laden, well-drained soils provide the best opportunity for success. Appears to tolerate higher pH soils, based on splendid perform-ance in many English gardens.

Hydrangea heteromalla

Hydrangea heteromalla, foliage

Mature stems are stout, thickish compared to *Hydrangea paniculata*, gray-brown, glabrous with rounded, raised lenticels and large, cream-tan, solid pith, and bark that typically does not exfoliate. In 'Bretschnei-deri', the bark flakes; however, the flowers are not particularly showy, about 4 to 5 inches across, with 6 to 9 dull white ray flowers.

Native to the Himalayas, west-central and northeastern China; some of the original

Hydrangea heteromalla, inflorescence of a four-year-old seedling

Hydrangea heteromalla, mature inflorescence

Hydrangea heteromalla, habit

introductions were collected at 10,000 feet elevations, which should equate with reasonable cold hardiness. Described as growing in mixed forests, thickets, and open areas. Listed as Zone 6 (RHS), Zone 5 by Sandra Reed, and a handsome flowering specimen resides in the Arnold Arboretum, Jamaica Plain, Massachusetts. Also, has flowered outdoors in Minneapolis, Minnesota. Growing at Holden Arboretum, Mentor, Ohio. Four different accessions were 2, 3, 3, and 2 feet high after many years. Twice, once in the early 1990s, again in 2000, I grew large populations of *Hydrangea heteromalla* seedlings. Both populations, although vigorous in youth, suffered in the heat. A few survived and flowered in their fourth year. Parallel to this activity was a large population of *H. paniculata* seedlings of 'Brussels Lace' and Pink Diamond, all of which thrived, flowered, and produced 24 eye-catching variants.

Hydrangea heteromalla is considered by McClintock to be similar to *H. paniculata* in flower and fruit, the major differences being the paniculate inflorescence of *H. paniculata*, compared to the corymbs of *H. heteromalla*. I observed hundreds of seedlings of both and have never experienced doubt when separating the two species. Leaf characteristics work well, although McClintock mentioned that *H. heteromalla* ranges from glabrous to pubescent to tomentose throughout the range.

Cultivars and Varieties

'Bretschneideri' (aforementioned) is among the more cold hardy selections with exfoliating, chestnut-brown bark. Introduced from China around 1882. As I have observed this form: not as vigorous or showy in flower as 'Jermyns Lace' and 'Snowcap'. Flowers peak mid to late June at the Morton Arboretum, Lisle, Illinois.

'Crûg Farm' has a larger number of sterile florets.

'Fan Si Pan' has bronzy new leaves, red new stems and petioles, white flowers, on a 10-foot-high shrub. Seed collected by Crûg Farm on Fan Si Pan, the highest mountain in Vietnam.

Hydrangea heteromalla, doing splendidly at Hidcote

'Krista' grows to 5 feet with cream-white lacecap flowers in June and July.

'Jermyns Lace' is a large shrub, fully 15 feet tall, growing at Hillier Arboretum. Vigorous, with broad lacecap inflorescences, the white sepals turning pink. Flowered in late June 1999 at the arboretum. Grown originally as *Hydrangea heteromalla* var. *xanthoneura*. Named after Mr. Hillier's home, Jermyn's House.

'Morrey's Form' is less upright than 'Snowcap', vigorous, 10 to 15 feet, elliptic-oblong bright green leaves, with 8-inch-wide corymbs, sepals in 4s, each white, elongated, entire, and curly.

'Nepal Beauty' has white fertile flowers and sterile florets.

'Snowcap' is another Hillier introduction of a shrub that was for many years grown as *Hydrangea robusta*.

Stately shrub with large heart-shaped leaves and 8- to 10-inch-wide, flat-topped corymbs of white flowers. Sepals, in 4s, are oval, entire, and do not overlap. Flowers later than 'Jermyns Lace', and the sepals remain creamy white but may fade to purplish pink.

'Yalung Ridge' with rich red/crimson young leaves, the approximately 2-inch-long petioles are red; 7-inch-wide corymbs; flowers pale pink initially, fading to white; flowers early, often by May into June; introduced from Nepal by Tony Schilling.

In the Pacific Northwest, following the coast south, *Hydrangea heteromalla* would prove successful. Flowers occur on previous year's wood. Superb specimens are evident in the southern part of England. I suspect that high day and night temperatures reduce the opportunity for success in the South. Based on Arnold Arboretum and Minneapolis successes, northeastern, and midwestern gardeners should consider experimenting with the species.

Seeds and cuttings, preferably softwood, should be handled as described in chapter 13. Softwood cuttings collected 24 April 2003, treated with 3,000 ppm KIBA, and placed in peat:perlite, under mist, rooted 50 percent by 6 June.

Heronswood Nursery listed two taxa of *Hydrangea heteromalla*. Dan Hinkley, director of collections at Heronswood, is the most active American plant collector of the 21st century, and the Heronswood catalog reflects his many successes. He teams with Bleddyn and Sue Wynn-Jones for some of the expeditions. The latter two own Crûg Farm Plants, a wonderful nursery and a treasure trove of magnificent plants. Under *H. heteromalla*, the nursery describes 11 different types. There is no mail order at Crûg Farm Plants, so a trip to Wales is the only option. See Resources and Nursery Sources for addresses.

Be forewarned: *Hydrangea* are prohibited from immediate entry into the United States and must be quarantined until USDA-APHIS inspectors release them for propagation and eventual sale to the public. The quarantine period is typically about two years for hydrangeas. My understanding is that all *Hydrangea* taxa are included in the quarantine.

CHAPTER SIX

Hydrangea involucrata
Siebold

This smallish, 3- to 4-foot-high and -wide shrub, allied to *Hydrangea aspera*, receives streaming accolades in the avant-garde of horticultural literature but seldom (how about never) shows its floral face on the everyday commercial radar screen. Rarities are often exalted, at times without justification. My sightings, three long stares are necessary, have yet to incite the magical yip of the passionate plant enthusiast . . . Wow! In fact, almost every day while at Hillier Arboretum, I walked passed the 'Hortensis' specimen behind Jermyn's House and kept waiting for noble happenings. In late July, it stirred to leaf, with the scaly flower buds showing life. I wait for the second coming!

Hydrangea involucrata is often flattened to the ground and springs back to flower on the new growth. All the plants I have observed were under 3 feet high, which is probably about the maximum regrowth until the next freeze cycle occurs. Witnessed a suckering colony at Hawksridge Nursery, Hickory, North Carolina, that regrew to about 12 inches high with flower buds on 10 July 2003. Obviously, the original plant had been smooshed by cold on more than one occasion. This *sighting* attests to the ability of the plant to form flower buds on new growth of the season.

The slender-pointed, light to medium green leaves are broad-ovate to oblong, 3 to 6 inches long, 1 to $2^{1}/_{2}$ inches wide, finely serrated (bristle-tipped), rough above with short, $^{3}/_{4}$- to 1-inch-long petioles. The new emerging growth is covered with pale brown bristly pubescence. Leaves are hairy and gray on their undersides. The flower buds are covered with approximately 6, broad-ovate bracts, which open outward and persist with

Hydrangea involucrata

flattened, white hairs. The irregular corymbs, 3 to 5 inches wide, are composed of numerous, small, pink to blue fertile flowers and relatively few, long-pediceled, white, pale blue, or light pink, $^3/_4$- to 1-inch-wide, sterile flowers composed of 3 to 5 sepals. Flowers open late, typically late July, August. In Athens, flower buds were opening on 7 June 2003. Flowers in August at Scott Arboretum, Swarthmore, Pennsylvania. Bears a close resemblance to *Hydrangea aspera* in flower, fruit, and leaf characteristics except *H. involucrata* has tomentose capsules and involucral bracts.

Provide evenly moist, acid, organic-laden, well-drained soil in partial shade. English literature states its tolerance of chalky, i.e., high pH soils. Leaves anemic green even under the best culture. Hardiness approximates Zones 6(7) to 9. A reasonable specimen of 'Hortensis' grows at the Scott Arboretum, Swarthmore, Pennsylvania. Cornell Plantations, Ithaca, New York, has a plant in the collections. Noteworthy was its total absence from the gardens visited in the Southeast while cross-checking species and cultivars. The sepal color is affected by aluminum and on more acid soils will be bluer. Native to Japan and Taiwan.

Cultivars and Varieties

'Hortensis' ('Tama Danka') produces double, cream-white, sterile flowers that become rose-tinted with maturity. Leaves are bristly, broad-ovate to heart-shaped. Inflorescence is loose and open, the small sepalous clusters resembling miniature roses. Sepals turn green in fall. Flowers mid to late June in Athens. Introduced into England circa 1906.

'Plena' is a lacecap version of 'Hortensis' with pinkish fertile flowers surrounded by double, white ray florets. Grows 5 feet high and wide.

An uninspiring hybrid of *Hydrangea involucrata* and *H. aspera* is known. Flowers are white lacecaps, displaying no flash, plant compact with anemic green leaves more reminiscent of *H. involucrata*. For the collector who truly has everything.

Hydrangea involucrata 'Hortensis', foliage and dried inflorescence

'Hortensis'

Watercolor of *Hydrangea macrophylla*.

CHAPTER SEVEN

Hydrangea macrophylla
(Thunberg ex J. A. Murray) Seringe

BIGLEAF HYDRANGEA

This chapter is the longest and most important because herein resides the quintessential species on a worldwide basis. As a garden shrub, as a florist potplant, and as fresh and dried cut flowers, there are no equals. To most gardeners, the name "hydrangea" is synonymous with this species. Blue in the garden is a gift from the heavens, and no species of woody shrub provides the range from the softest blue, violet-blue, to purple-blue. Please note flowers will be pink in non-aluminum soils and media.

The plan is to lead the reader through the history, introduction, and improvement of *Hydrangea macrophylla*. Considerable detail is presented on the University of Georgia's breeding program and its approaches to improving the species, particularly emphasizing remontant (reblooming) flowering, mildew resistance, leathery lustrous dark green foliage, and compactness. Perhaps most useful will be the chart of cultivars, which concludes this chapter. The cultivars are cobbled from myriad sources, extracted from the literature, from visits to gardens, and from testing and evaluation in Athens, Georgia; they are presented in alphabetical order with cryptic descriptions and represent my best attempt to allow the reader to select the cultivars that are most appealing and available. The color descriptions are fraught with misgivings, representing as they do a continuum of changes mediated by stage of floral development and aluminum availability. The Notes sections present data, comments, and observations about the relative merits of the

'Nikko Blue', habit

'Preziosa', habit

cultivars. The chart checklist is not exhaustive but provides a ready reference to the vast pool of cultivars offered in American commerce.

Minimal variety is offered in most garden centers. On a visit to three garden centers in Chapel Hill, North Carolina (10 May 2003), I recorded 'Blue Wave', 'Cardinal Red', 'Dooley', 'Glory Blue', 'Mariesii Variegata', 'Merritt's Beauty'(?), 'Nigra', 'Nikko Blue', 'Pia', and 'Preziosa'. Only 'Blue Wave', 'Dooley', 'Nikko Blue', and 'Preziosa' were heavily budded and legitimately salable. The 'Cardinal Red', 'Glory Blue', 'Mariesii Variegata', 'Nigra', and 'Pia', although shipped to the garden centers, were injured by cold, full of dead stems and/or had minimal to no flower buds. Also, a description of 20 top *Hydrangea macrophylla* and *H. serrata* taxa (see "The Best of the Best") is advanced for those who wish to wade into the somewhat shallow but safe side of plant selection.

Characteristics and Uses

Hydrangea macrophylla typically ranges from 3 to 6 feet high and wide with exceptions to 10 feet. Time-weathered and -honored colonies have persisted around old homes for decades, surviving in spite of neglect. In my travels through the United States, I experience magnificent plantings that equate with indestructibility. Unfortunately, the cultivars' identities were lost to antiquity, and it is impossible to ascertain whether the survivors are 'Mousseline', 'Générale Vicomtesse de Vibraye', 'Nikko Blue', 'Souvenir du Pdt. Paul Doumer', ad infinitum. These self-perpetuating cultivars are the ideal choices for those who simply desire a reliable flowering hydrangea.

My passion for the genus, and certainly *Hydrangea macrophylla*, knows no bounds. I have been fortunate to visit and study hydrangeas in great gardens throughout the United States and Europe. These opportunities to accumulate field notes and photographs have provided the foundation for this book. Without equivocation, *H. macrophylla* has more tape recorder, notebook, and photographic consideration than the rest of the species combined. I counted the number of *H. macrophylla* taxa described and/or photographed from 1999. An astounding 222 was the result.

True *Hydrangea macrophylla* has a limited distribution in Japan (Honshu Island, Izu Peninsula, Bōso Peninsula, islands of Izu Archipelago). I used the map in Takeomi Yamamoto's *The Japanese Hydrangeas Color Guide Book* to delineate nativity (Yamamoto 2000). Photographs show the native plants growing, actually hanging, from the cliffs above the ocean. *Hydrangea macrophylla* is tremendously salt tolerant and is utilized often in coastal gardens on a worldwide basis. Wilson (1923) wrote, "It [*H. macrophylla*] grows right on the edge of the foreshore under the full influence of the sea and also inland among volcanic detritus, but all parts of the localities in which I know this plant to be wild are strongly influenced by the sea." In Cornwall, southwestern England, plants grow as hedges, masses, isolated specimens, in front and back yards, in sun and shade, seemingly without any care, yet flourishing with apparent neglect. If only this were the case in most areas of the United States.

Bailey (1989a) provides climatic data for the native habitat that explains *Hydrangea macrophylla* sensitivity to certain extremes. Honshu enjoys more that 5 months of frost-free temperatures. The mean low and high temperatures are 31 and 47°F in January and 72 and 85°F in August, respectively. Annual rainfall is between 70 and 90 inches, while mean relative humidities during January and August are 65 percent and 85 percent, respectively. The conclusions are obvious: *H. macrophylla* prefers moderate temperatures, moderate to high humidity, and plentiful moisture.

Hydrangea macrophylla forms a rounded-mounded shrub composed of erect, usually unbranched stems. The mature stems are light brown, thickish, with a large, white, central pith. Stems become grayish brown and weathered with age. The winter texture is quite coarse, and the best that can be said is that well-grown plants have the aura of bundles of sticks.

However, the classic garden look resurfaces with bud break and leaf development as the stems are reduced to support for the large, often glossy, thick-textured, cabbagy foliage. In Athens, fully mature leaves of all *Hydrangea macrophylla* taxa are present by mid-April. Buds often break with sneak peeks of foliage evident in late February. Estimate one month later for this in Boston.

Leaves are 4 to 6(8) inches long, two-thirds as wide, larger in more vigorous plants, coarsely toothed, ranging in color from flat matte green, light green, dark green, to lustrous dark green. Nutritional status affects the quality and color of foliage. The more nitrogen and iron, the darker green the foliage. Leaf texture can be quite thick, reminiscent of the waxy, shiny, squeaky feel of cabbage foliage. 'Nikko Blue' has a dull green, thinnish leaf; 'Veitchii' medium thickness, lustrous dark green leaf; and 'Ayesha', a more rounded, thickish, polished lustrous dark green leaf. Typically, fall color is inconsequential, although on occasion leaves die off yellow. 'Veitchii' developed shades of yellow-red-purple in November in our trials. Fall color equates with specific cultivars and not the species taken as a whole. I have read rather extensive lists of superior fall coloring cultivars based on European evaluations. Leaves are often killed by cold before having the opportunity to develop fall color. In November 2002, 25°F killed leaves of all taxa in the Georgia trials except 'Veitchii'. I have also noticed that 'Veitchii' foliage displays increased spring frost tolerance. However, gardeners do not plant *Hydrangea macrophylla* for foliage. The leaves are the photosynthetic apparatus that fuels the development of the magnificent flowers. The showy sepals and fertile flower petals and sepals are simply modified leaves. For full expression of the genetic potential for flower size and quality, foliage is the engine. About 6 to 8 leaf pairs subtending the inflorescence are necessary to support (photosynthetically) the development of the mature flowers.

Flowers occur in corymbs, lacecap in the wild types, fertile flowers in the center, sterile showy clusters composed of 3, 4, and/or 5 sepals in a homogeneous grouping (sometimes called ray florets). The sepals provide the show and are magnified in number in the mophead or hortensia types, forming a more or less solid dome or globe of white, pink, rose, red, blue, and purple. The individual sepals are oval to orbicular-rounded, entire or toothed, and range in size (the clusters) from 1 to 1½(2) to 3 inches and larger. 'Beauté Vendômoise', a lacecap, has immense sepals, up to 5 inches across, according to the literature; however, I have never observed this size. Fertile flowers are small, typically ¼ to ½ inch wide with 5 petals, 5 sepals, 10 stamens, typically pink, blue, to purple. They show better in the lacecaps when massed together in the center of the inflorescence. The fruit is a ribbed capsule, smallish, about ¼ inch high, containing small brown seeds, and matures in October and November.

'Beauté Vendômoise' just opening

Flower expression, i.e., maximum coloration, occurs from mid-May to mid-June in Athens; late June to early July, Boston; mid to late July in Vancouver, British Columbia. From budbreak (outdoors) to full flowering takes about 12 weeks. Plants forced in the greenhouse require approximately 10 weeks to flower, depending on day/night temperatures.

The sepals often transition through multiple colors during maturation. I think of 'Frillibet', a sport of 'Mme Emile Mouillère', opening cream-yellow with a touch of blue, to finally blue. Then when the flowers are pollinated, the sepals turn down in the lacecaps, and the colors regress, albeit beautifully, to soft, burnished green, blue, pink, rose, and burgundy on

'Frillibet' at emergence

their backsides. This sepal inversion occurs on most hydrangea species. To describe sepal color on any *Hydrangea macrophylla* in the absolute is impossible. The beauty resides in the sliding color scale. Also, aluminum wreaks havoc with sepal color, depending on concentration in the soil, and eventually the leaves and sepals. A guaranteed formula: the greater the available aluminum, the bluer the sepal color. See the discussion of flower color in chapter 12.

Inflorescences range from 3 to 4 inches wide to 10 inches, depending on cultivar, age and vigor of the plant, nutrition, and pruning practices. On a given plant, inflorescences will vary by 100 percent in size. On occasion, a single flower on a vigorous branch will be three times larger than "normal."

The essential information about cold hardiness, soils, fertilizer, pruning, propagation, flower color, and diseases is described in chapter 12.

I am probably the least qualified individual to discuss the use of *Hydrangea macrophylla* in the landscape. If planted next to a chicken coop, it would still be beautiful; see "Designing with Hydrangeas" in chapter 15. The flowers, in their prime and purity, are intrinsically magnificent. Beauty in any form, anywhere in the world, is easily recognized. So it is with this magnificent flowering shrub. Bonnie and I have placed *H. macrophylla* in groups, spotted them wherever holes exist in shady borders, used them in containers, and mixed them like jelly beans. What's not to love?! Great collections at Van Dusen Botanical Garden, Atlanta Botanical Garden, Norfolk Botanical Garden, Stourton House and Gardens, Savill Gardens, Marwood Hill, Maurice Foster's, Wisley, Abbotsbury, and finally Trelissick have inspired and educated. The latter, with approximately 360 cultivars planted inside the walled garden, brought tears of joy to my eyes. Need I elaborate more?!

Hydrangea macrophylla, Van Dusen Botanical Garden

Respectable Choices for Hardiness

Walled garden at Trelissick

The logical question that readers should ask is which are the most reliable *Hydrangea macrophylla* cultivars for cold hardiness (in all its manifestations, i.e., fall, winter, spring) and flowering potential. In Zones 6 to 9(10) on the West Coast, possibly coastal areas of the eastern seaboard, almost any cultivar will provide some measure of flower. In a series of papers, Richard Bir (2000a, 2000b) detailed the *H. macrophylla* and *H. serrata* survival and flowering data from the three-year evaluation at Fletcher, North Carolina, Zone 7a. Minimum winter temperatures were between 5 and 10°F during the study.

Hydrangea macrophylla or *H. serrata* cultivars that did not survive at least three winters under simulated landscape conditions in Zone 7a are listed below (Bir 2000a). Several inconsistencies are evident in the three lists, but I left the plant lists as they appeared in the articles. For example, 'Schwan' is in both the "*did not survive* 3 years" and the "*survived* 3 years" lists. Obviously, it cannot be both ways. All spellings per the *Hydrangea International Index of Cultivar Names* (2002) and not the original article.

'Alpine Glow'	'Pia'
'Altona'	'Pieta'
'Amethyst'	'Quadricolor'
'Benigaku'	'Regula'
'Blaumeise'	'Rose Supreme'
'Blue Billow'	'Rosita'
'Böttstein'	'Schwan'
'Bright Star'	'Soeur Thérèse'
'Enziandom' ('Gentian Dome')	'Tricolor'
'Kasteln'	'Wave Hill'
'Lemon Wave'	'White Wave'
'Leuchtfeuer'	'Winning Edge'
'Mme Faustin Travouillon' ('Peacock')	'Zaunkönig'

Hydrangea macrophylla or *H. serrata* cultivars that survived at least three winters under simulated landscape conditions in Zone 7a are listed next (Bir 2000a). Bir added that all survivors did not have problems with mites or powdery mildew despite conditions that favored development of the pests.

'Acuminata' *(H. serrata* subsp. *acuminata*)	Doneau')
'All Summer Beauty'	'Blue Prince'
'Ami Pasquier'	'Blue Wave'
'Ansley'	'Cardinal Red'
'Ayesha'	'Coerulea Lace'
'Beauté Vendômoise'	'Decatur Blue'
'Blau Doneau' (same as 'Blue Danube')	'Domotoi'
'Bluebird'	'Europa'
'Blue Boy'	'Geisha Girl'
'Blue Danube' (same as 'Blau	'Générale Vicomtesse de Vibraye'
	'Gertrude Glahn'
	'Goliath'

'Grayswood'
'Hadsbury'
'Hamburg'
'Harlequin'
'Heinrich Seidel'
'Holstein'
'Kluis Superba'
'La Marne'
'Lanarth White'
'Libelle'
'Lilacina'
'Mariesii'
'Masja' ('Sibilla')
'Mathilda Gütges'
'Merritt's Supreme'
'Mme Emile Mouillère'
'Niedersachsen'
'Nikko Blue'
'Oregon Pride'
'Otaksa Monstrosa'
'Paris'
Pink and Pretty™
'Preziosa'
'Red Star'
'Révélation'
'Rose Supreme'
'Schwan'
'Seafoam'
'Shishiva'
'Souvenir du Pdt. Paul Doumer'
'Teller Red' ('Rotdrössel')
'Tokyo Delight'
'Variegata'

In North Carolina, in the winter of 2000-01, 52 reblooming bigleaf hydrangea cultivars were killed to the ground. Twenty of 52 flowered in early summer and fall 2001 (Bir et al. 2002), as follows:

'All Summer Beauty'
'Altona'
'Blue Boy'
'Blue Danube'
'Blue Prince'
'Coerulea Lace'
'Decatur Blue'
'Europa'
'Geisha Girl'
'Kluis Superba'
'La Marne'
'Lanarth White'
'Lilacina'
'Maréchal Foch'
'Mme Emile Mouillère'
'Nikko Blue'
'Révélation'
'Souvenir du Pdt. Paul Doumer'
'Veitchii'
'White Wave'

In our evaluations and those of Bir, 'All Summer Beauty', 'Coerulea Lace' ('Coerulea', 'Caerulea'), 'Decatur Blue', 'Frillibet', 'Geisha Girl', 'Lilacina', 'Mme Emile Mouillère', 'Nikko Blue', 'Souvenir du Pdt. Paul Doumer', 'Veitchii', and 'White Wave' were consistently identified as the most reliable for cold hardiness and flowering.

Extremely fascinating is the omission of other *Hydrangea serrata* cultivars, except for 'Geisha Girl', which are considered more reliable than the *H. macrophylla* taxa. The safest and most logical answer to these literature anomalies is that plants never read books. When researchers and gardeners actually test the plants, *in situ*, performance evaluations may be diametrically opposite. Certainly not always the situation, but worth thinking about.

'All Summer Beauty'

The Best of the Best

If I were to make a garden, specifically one with *Hydrangea macrophylla* and *H. serrata* taxa as the centerpiece, those featured below—the tried, true, recommended, and available—would be the first choices. The new wave of remontant introductions, except for Endless Summer™ and 'Penny Mac', are not in the mainstream marketplace. I believe these are the future of *H. macrophylla* in the United States.

Somewhat disappointing are the newer *Hydrangea macrophylla* cultivars like the Japanese Lady series, Hovaria® series (Kaleidoscope® in the United States), and the 26 Teller series lacecaps (1952-1992). Although the flowers are magnificent, the lack of cold hardiness and/or high mildew susceptibility are garden liabilities. Anything is worth trying to satisfy the persistent gardener's curiosity. Simply do not allow the hype to consume the aesthetic desires and common sense.

'Altona'

'Ami Pasquier'

'All Summer Beauty'. Mophead, pink to blue; frequently listed as remontant, not so in Georgia trials; lustrous dark green foliage; mildew susceptible; all seedlings from 'All Summer Beauty' had lustrous leathery dark green foliage and, in September and October, mildew to match, 51 to 75 percent mildew on 18 September 2001. Obviously develops many flower buds lower on the stem. Shows up at many nurseries in the North, i.e., Zones 4 and 5.

'Altona' ('Althone'). Mophead, rose-madder to vivid deep blue, ethereally stunning, serrated to entire sepals; excellent as dried flower; medium green leaves; burnished red fall color; stout stems; listed as rebloomer by Bir and Haworth-Booth; absolutely smooshed by April freeze in England, froze to ground at Wisley and Saville; in our evaluations at the Hydrangea Shade Garden at the University of Georgia, dieback after two years, on 9 April 2003, but regrowth; unfortunately, with only three expressed inflorescences by late May 2003; grows to 7 feet; H. Schadendorff, 1931.

'Coerulea Lace'

'Ami Pasquier'. Mophead, crimson to purple, sepals entire; leaves turn red in autumn; abundant flowers on 27 July 2002, at Fletcher, North Carolina; this and 'Preziosa' ('Pink Beauty') were the only two of 52 taxa with significant flowers; dwarf to moderate size, 5 feet; 1 to 25 percent mildew on 18 September 2001; at the UGA Hydrangea Shade Garden, after two years, on 9 April 2003, dieback, but regrowth and respectable flower production; E. Mouillère, 1931; a seedling of 'Maréchal Foch'.

'Dooley'

'Coerulea Lace' ('Coerulea', 'Caerulea'). Lacecap, pink to blue, entire sepals; not flashy but reliable, true remontant taxon that is integrated into our breeding program; appears consistently on lists of cold hardy/reblooming taxa; listed as *Hydrangea japonica* var. *caerulea* by Hooker; an ancient Japanese hybrid of *H. serrata* and *H. macrophylla*; reliable and delicate; in full flower on 15 May 2003.

Endless Summer™, blue

'Dooley'. Mophead, pink to rich blue entire sepals, cold hardy, laboratory tests showed stems hardy to -11°F; medium to dark green leaves; mildew susceptible; robust, 6 feet high; introduced in 1996 by author from the garden of Coach Vincent J. Dooley; 51 to 75 percent mildew on 18 September 2001; at the UGA Hydrangea Shade Garden, after two years, on 9 April 2003, dieback, but regrowth with abundant flower buds; actually was

'David Ramsey'

'Europa', pink

'Freudenstein'

the impetus to initiate the *Hydrangea macrophylla* improvement. See "Cold Hardiness Evaluations, Breeding History, Georgia Breeding Program" later in this chapter for the rationale.

Endless Summer™ ('Bailmer'), 'Decatur Blue', 'David Ramsey', 'Oak Hill', 'Penny Mac'. Remontant types; quite similar; intensely researched at the University of Georgia; greenhouse, nursery, and field data unequivocally showed their ability to flower on new growth; foliage flat medium green; moderate mildew susceptibility; estimating 3 to 5 feet high and as wide; have suffered cold damage in my trials but the new shoots develop flower buds and fully expressed inflorescences; all five laden with flowers on 17 May 2003 in our trials; most floriferous taxa in our tests on 5 June 2003; I walked the entire collection and was overwhelmed with the magnitude of flowers.

'Europa'. Mophead, pink to blue-purple, sepals etched; dries well; listed by Bir and Haworth-Booth as reliably flowering; light to medium green leaves; leaf spot susceptible; tall and vigorous; 5½-feet-high plant at Saville Garden; susceptible to late spring freeze(s); H. Schadendorff, 1931; could be replaced by 'Goliath', 'Gentian Dome', 'Souvenir du Pdt. Paul Doumer' or 'Westfalen'.

'Freudenstein'. Mophead, reddish pink, Persian-rose, to blue; entire, occasionally serrate sepals, lustrous dark green leaves; strong stems; flowered heavily at Hillier Arboretum on 17 July 1999, after devastating April freeze; at the UGA Hydrangea Shade Garden, after two years, on 9 April 2003, dieback, but regrowth; worth seeking although not common in U.S. commerce; dense and compact, 3 to 4 feet high; 26 to 50 percent mildew on 18 September 2001.

'Frillibet'. Mophead, cream-yellow-blue upon emergence, finally blue; serrated (frilly) sepals, sepals show their backsides in late summer and fall like the lacecaps; lustrous dark green leaves; branch sport of 'Mme Emile Mouillère' introduced by Haworth-Booth; 5-foot-high plant at Maurice Foster's; exceptionally beautiful, abundant flowers in Georgia trials; 1 to 25 percent mildew on 18 September 2001; at the UGA Hydrangea Shade Garden, after two years, on 9 April 2003, dieback, but regrowth with abundant flower buds.

'Geisha Girl' (*Hydrangea serrata*). Lacecap, white to pink, rose, burgundy; serrated sepals; inflorescence small like 'Veitchii', about 4 inches across; medium green foliage; one of five in our trials with no injury after spring freezes; flowered heavily on 8 June 2001, in Athens; at the UGA Hydrangea Shade Garden, after two years, on 9 April 2003, strong growth with no dieback; upright grower; mildew susceptible, 1 to 25 percent mildew on 18 September 2001; introduced by Bill Barnes, Lorax Farms. 'Tokyo Delight' and 'Rosalba' are similar.

'Générale Vicomtesse de Vibraye'. Mophead, opening soft cream-yellow, finally pink to blue; entire to serrated sepals; reliable doer; have measured 8-foot-high plants with 10-inch-wide inflorescences; one of the early French hybrids; stems spotted (speckled) wine-red; medium green leaves; mildew susceptible, 26 to 50 percent mildew on 18 September 2001; at the UGA Hydrangea Shade Garden, after two years, on 9 April 2003, strong growth with no dieback; abundant flowers on 17 May 2003; Mouillère, 1909, using 'Otaksa' x 'Rosea'.

'Grayswood' (*Hydrangea serrata*). Lacecap, white aging to pink, rose; sepals toothed; inflorescences borne from lower buds along shoots; flat medium green leaves; observed plants 3$^1/_2$ to 6 feet high; delicate and beautiful in flower; mildew susceptible; April 1999 freeze at Hillier Arboretum flattened the plant, although most *H. macrophylla* and *H. serrata* were doomed by that frost, normally considered robust and frost tolerant.

'Lanarth White'. Lacecap, white with pink to blue center (eye); sepals entire and showy; dries well; impressive lacecap for size of inflorescence; sepals are abundant and occasionally inflorescence resembles the mophead type; leaves lustrous light green, thick-textured; Bir et al. (2002) reported it killed to ground and then flowering in early summer and fall of the same year; 4$^1/_2$

'Frillibet'

'Geisha Girl'

'Générale Vicomtesse de Vibraye'

feet high at Wisley, to 7 feet; considered the best of the whites for a sunny, dry, or coastal site; excellent in full sun at JC Raulston Arboretum 25 June 2003, when in the same vicinity 'Dooley', 'Goliath', 'Schwan', 'Générale Vicomtesse de Vibraye', and 'Beauté Vendômoise' were wilting; from Lanarth, Cornwall, England in the 1940s.

'Grayswood'

'Lilacina'. Lacecap, pink to phlox-pink, lilac to blue, imperial purple; sepals serrated; fertile flowers a good blue; extremely reliable; reblooming; dries well; lustrous dark green leaves; 4 to 6 feet high; slight mildew susceptibility, 1 to 25 percent mildew on 18 September 2001; at the UGA Hydrangea Shade Garden, after two years, on 9 April 2003, strong growth with no dieback; excellent for breeding, also displays drought and sun tolerance; stems with red nodes; French hybrid, V. Lemoine, 1904.

'Lanarth White'

'Mme Emile Mouillère'. Mophead, butter-cream to white, pinkish with age, center eye pink or blue; sepals serrated; extremely reliable; the best white mophead for general use; tall and vigorous; appears on all lists for cold hardiness; consistent flowering; no cold damage in Georgia trials; at the UGA Hydrangea Shade Garden, after two years, on 9 April 2003, strong growth with no dieback; fully expressed flowers on 17 May 2003; glossy medium to dark green leaves; mildew susceptibility, 26 to 50 percent mildew on 18 September 2001; French hybrid, E. Mouillère, 1909, 'White Wave' x 'Rosea'.

'Lilacina'

'Mousseline'. Mophead, pink to light blue; sepals entire; flowers early, fairly consistently, remarkably freely, lasting well; much akin to de Vibraye; not well known in the United States but showed superb frost tolerance in 1999 in England when most cultivars were mush; my field notes indicate excellent flowering at Hillier (7 July), Saville (24 July), and Wisley (10 July); in fact at Wisley the hydrangea collection was sited in a frost pocket of the garden where 'Mousseline' was one of the few flowering stalwarts; medium green leaves; French hybrid, Lemoine, 1909, seedling of 'Rosea'.

'Nikko Blue'. Mophead, pink to blue; an enigma as to origin; the true taxon, consistently listed as a cold hardy and remontant cultivar, confused in trade; in Georgia trials three different plants came disguised as 'Nikko Blue', the one outplanted in the trials froze to the ground in 2001-02 via late spring frosts; flowered well in Bir's Fletcher, North Carolina, trials; at the UGA Hydrangea Shade Garden, after two years, on 9 April 2003, dieback, but regrowth with abundant flowers expressed on 17 May 2003; English hydrangea authorities Mark Fillan and Maurice Foster cited the reblooming potential of the cultivar; Foster noted that his 'Nikko Blue' was flattened to the ground in 1998 and 1999, grew back and flowered both years, this indicates true remontant nature; leaves are medium green, mildew susceptible, 51 to 75 percent mildew on 18 September 2001. Will the real 'Nikko Blue' please stand!

'Mme Emile Mouillère'

'Preziosa' (*Hydrangea serrata* × *H. macrophylla*). Mophead, smaller than typical *H. macrophylla*; leaning more toward *H. serrata* in leaf, stem, and habit characteristics; pale cream, white, pink-rose to red, lilac, violet; colors many and vivid; leaves red-green, developing good autumn color in reds and purples; beautiful reddish stems; have grown this for years, and on occasion it is spectacular, usually not so; one of the worst for mildew, 51 to 75 percent mildew on 18 September 2001; used in our breeding program, the intensity of the Persian-rose-fuchsia flowers is neon; unfortunately every seedling is a mildew farm; to 5 feet high; introduced by G. Ahrends, 1961.

'Mousseline'

'Veitchii'. Lacecap, white aging to pink, essentially entire sepals in 3s(4s), beautiful blue-violet fertile flowers; inflorescence about 4 inches across; reliable and bulletproof; always a good doer in the Dirr garden; lustrous dark green leaves; often with yellow-red-purple fall color; frost and mildew resistant; no mildew on 18 September 2001; without equivocation our best breeding genotype for quality foliage characteristics; 6 to 8 feet tall; old Japanese cultivar; introduction date variable, possibly 1880.

'Nikko Blue'

'White Wave' ('Whitewave'). Lacecap, white aging to pink, sepals serrated; fertile flowers pink or blue; side shoots produce flowers indicating buds lower on the stem are floral; lustrous dark green leaves; mildew resistant, no

'Preziosa'

'Preziosa', foliage

'Veitchii'

mildew on 18 September 2001; has been a good breeding line; strong, vigorous constitution, 5 feet high and wide; French hybrid from V. Lemoine, 1904, from open-pollinated seed of 'Mariesii'; original name 'Mariesii Grandiflora'.

For reference, the major greenhouse forcing or potplant cultivars are also listed here. They typically show up in florists, grocery stores, and corner markets, but are also offered as garden plants. They were bred and selected for the greenhouse forcing trade and are usually not cold hardy. Often they are not labeled as to cultivar, but are offered as white, pink, red, or blue hydrangeas. They are beautiful but generally are not sufficiently rough and tumble for sustained, long-term garden culture. According to Bailey (1989a), principal cultivars are 'Merritt's Supreme', 'Tödi', 'Rose Supreme', 'Kasteln', 'Mathilda Gütges', 'Böttstein', 'Gartenbaudirektor Kühnert', 'Soeur Thérèse', 'Red Star', 'Schenkenberg', 'Wildenstein', 'Brestenburg', 'Stratford', 'Enziandom' ('Gentian Dome'), 'Merveille', 'Regula', 'Blue Danube', 'Rosita', 'Gerda Steiniger', and 'Charme'. All are mopheads. In recent years, more lacecaps have been produced as potplants. Primarily, I see the Teller series, which was bred for greenhouse production, being offered in American commerce.

Cold Hardiness Evaluations, Breeding History, Georgia Breeding Program

Everblooming, billowy, blowsy, celestial, cumulus clouds of cerulean blue on a terrestrial plant . . . am I dreaming or has hydrangea fever taken hold? Certainly the dream of gardeners worldwide is the successful culture of *Hydrangea macrophylla*. In the real garden world, low winter temperatures, 10°F and lower, and early fall and late spring freezes often reduce or eliminate the flowering potential. Money-back guarantees for consistent flowering are nonexistent, for the vagaries of temperature often eliminate flowers from Massachusetts to the Gulf Coast. Flower buds are formed in summer and fall in response to short days and cooler temperatures. The species requires 1,000 to 1,200 chill hours to satisfy bud dormancy. Then when provided warmer temperatures, the buds break, shoots emerge, and flowers develop.

Unfortunately, *Hydrangea macrophylla* is slow to develop cold hardiness in fall, and rapidly deacclimates in spring. Emerging leaves are evident as early as late February in Zone 7b. This is an anathema, for temperatures in the mid-teens to twenties often return in March, thus killing most flower buds and stems. Weather data in the Athens-Atlanta area reflected this pattern from 1996 to 2002. In 1996, the June hydrangea garden tour in Atlanta was canceled because of the devastation caused by 9 consecutive days (from 20 to 28 February) above 60°F, 5 of which were above 70°F, followed by 28, 17, 12, 21, 27, 27, and 27°F on 7 through 13 March, respectively. Temperatures of 26 to 28°F will injure young leaves. (On 30 March 2003, with leaves approximately 80 percent of full size on 'Grayswood' seedlings, 'Veitchii', 'Ayesha', 'Lady in Red', 'White Wave', 'Mousmée', and others in the Dirr garden, the temperature dipped to 30°F, and no foliar injury occurred.)

And yet, in 1996, in the garden of Mr. and Mrs. Vincent J. Dooley, I discovered a large colony frothing with blue mophead flowers. Its origin was lost to antiquity, but for tracking purposes I asked Coach Dooley (athletic director at the University of Georgia) if it could be named. In brief, it was christened 'Dooley'. Word spread and several growers put it into production. Authenticity was questioned. 'Nikko Blue', 'Générale Vicomtesse de Vibraye', 'Penny Mac', and 'Souvenir du Pdt. Paul Doumer' were equated with 'Dooley'. All were field, laboratory cold hardiness, and/or DNA tested (Lindstrom et al. 2003), and indeed 'Dooley' proved unique. 'Dooley' also developed some late-season flowers, indicating the ability to initiate flowers on new growth. In winter of 2002-03, the original colony of 'Dooley', 6 feet high, was mistakenly pruned to 3 feet. The regrowth produced flowering shoots by early June, reflecting the taxon's ability to set flower buds the length of the stem.

This 1996 serendipitous discovery under the cloud of the disastrous climatic umbrella triggered abundant questions about potential breeding strategies. In the past, I grew seedlings of *Hydrangea arborescens*, *H. paniculata*, and *H. quercifolia* with nothing better than the maternal parents. What would 'Dooley' yield? Cold hardiness and remontant (reblooming) character in this taxon might generate garden-worthy seedlings. To answer

'Veitchii', habit

'White Wave'

'Enziandom'

these questions, seeds were germinated and grown to flowering as described in the chapter 16.

When the first 'Dooley' seedlings flowered in 1999, all were mopheads. A larger population (59) in 2000 were all mopheads. No other hydrangeas grew near 'Dooley', and the seeds resulted from self pollination. Copious records were taken of growth habit, flower color, size, leaf and stem characteristics, and mildew resistance. Unfortunately, every 'Dooley' seedling contracted mildew. At this juncture, the pieces of the breeding puzzle started to come together.

Our initial approach to selection and evaluation was excessively loose. With the large numbers of seedlings in the mill, the process needed focus and restraint. In 2000, 3 selections were made, 69 in 2001, and 104 in 2002. Each selection is coded, i.e., Veitchii-02-00, meaning the second plant selected in 2000. Digital photographs are taken of flower and leaf along with data on habit, leaf qualities, flowers, etc. The original selection is propagated by cuttings, then four replicates of each are grown in 3-gallon containers side by side with the mother plant, and evaluated one to two additional years. In 2002, six to eight evaluations were made for each selection. Ruthlessly, any seedling selection with even moderate mildew is rogued. The three selections from year 2000 were eliminated and two of the 69 selections from year 2001 made the final cut. When The University of Georgia's name is attached to the new introduction, the goal is to offer a pedigreed hydrangea with superior aesthetic qualities and high disease resistance.

In concert with the breeding activity, over 100 cultivars of *Hydrangea macrophylla* and *H. serrata* were purchased, traded, and propagated for evaluation. A new shade garden area was developed, and plants were established in ground with duplicate container-grown plants in the shade house. Data were taken as mentioned for 'Dooley' with the goal of utilizing the best in a controlled breeding program. To date, no perfect hydrangea has emerged. Under Zone 7b climatic conditions, 'Ayesha', 'Lilacina', and 'Veitchii' were "best" for foliage characteristics, while 'Lilacina', 'Mme Emile Mouillère', 'Générale Vicomtesse de Vibraye', 'Geisha Girl', and 'Veitchii' exhibited the greatest cold hardiness. In laboratory cold hardiness tests, Adkins et al. (2002) showed that stems of 'Dooley', 'Générale

Vicomtesse de Vibraye', and 'Mme Emile Mouillère' were hardy to -11°F, followed by 'Veitchii' at -6°F. 'Veitchii' consistently produced seedlings with the most lustrous dark green foliage, highest mildew resistance, and greatest cold hardiness and vigor. The leaves of many 'Veitchii' seedlings also showed excellent frost resistance into November, remaining lustrous dark green after exposure to 25°F. This is a white lacecap with blue fertile flowers that, according to Haworth-Booth, was introduced from Japan in 1902, although 1880 was listed by Hillier. I have observed large, robust, heavily flowered shrubs in European collections. 'Veitchii' received the Award of Garden Merit from the Royal Horticultural Society in 2002. Most pertinent to gardeners in the United States is its persistence and tenacity: 'Veitchii' is more robust, suffers less dieback, and flowers more consistently than any standard lacecap cultivar.

To fully, actually more like partially, appreciate the unbelievable past and present activities with *Hydrangea macrophylla*, thorough reading (and digestion) of the popular and research literature is required. Throughout my career, I have attempted to understand the flowering response, or lack of same, among the various cultivars of *H. macrophylla*. One researcher's strong-growing, heavy-flowering cultivar is another's herbaceous perennial. My roots were grounded in Cincinnati (home, formative years). Along life's journey—Columbus, at The Ohio State University, and Amherst, at University of Massachusetts (education); The University of Illinois, Urbana, Illinois, and for the past 25 years, The University of Georgia, Athens, Georgia (profession)—I witnessed few glorious billowy spheres of blue on *H. macrophylla* because of cold—early fall, winter, late spring. Where were the cold hardy types?

The amazing answer to this question is that until 1995, limited extensive trials of *Hydrangea macrophylla* to assess cold tolerance and remontant flowering had been undertaken. Recent field testing of known cultivars by Sandra Reed (2002a) utilizing New Franklin, Missouri (Zone 5b), and McMinnville, Tennessee (Zone 6b), sites; Richard Bir (2000a, 2000b), North Carolina State University, Fletcher, North Carolina (Zone 7a), and David Creech, Mast Arboretum, Stephen F. Austin University, Nacogdoches, Texas (Zones 8b to 9a), provided incongruous information on cold hardiness and flowering potential. Reed's evaluation of 21 commercially available cultivars, in Zones 5b and 6b, including the purportedly hardy and/or remontant taxa 'All Summer Beauty', 'Blue Billow', 'Générale Vicomtesse de Vibraye', 'Mme Emile Mouillère', 'Nikko Blue', and 'Preziosa', showed that none of the cultivars flowered well during the three years of the study nor exhibited the remontant ability. Dieback occurred on all plants at both locations and regrowth (along with flowers) came from buds located at the base of the stems. Reed commented that the lack of reliable flowering from any of the cultivars tested pointed to the need to develop plants adapted to fluctuating fall and spring temperatures.

Bir et al. (2002) reported that 20 of 52 cultivars that flowered produced new flowers in early summer and fall 2001 in Fletcher, North Carolina, Zone 7a (see "Respectable Choices for Hardiness" earlier in this chapter for the results of the three-year test). I visited the evaluation tests on 27 July

'Ami Pasquier', Fletcher, North Carolina

2002 and, except for 'Ami Pasquier' and 'Preziosa' ('Pink Beauty'), noted that flowers were largely absent. No plants exhibited the remontant flowering characteristic of producing flowers on the new growth. I speculate that the flowers that occurred in early fall 2001 resulted from pre-existing basal/crown flower buds.

All this translates to minimal advances in the improvement of *Hydrangea macrophylla* for remontant flowering, cold hardiness, and mildew resistance. About the only consistency in the literature relative to cold hardiness and flowering potential of *H. macrophylla* cultivars is the inconsistency. The earliest efforts to "improve" *H. macrophylla* were engineered by French nurserymen, Lemoine of Nancy and Mouillère of Vendôme. 'Mme Emile Mouillère' (white mophead, 1909), 'Générale Vicomtesse de Vibraye' (blue mophead, 1909), 'Blue Wave' (blue lacecap, 1904), 'Lilacina' (blue lacecap, 1904), and 'Mousseline' (blue mophead, 1909) are still in commerce.

Many Belgian, German, Dutch, Swiss, and English hybridizers also worked in the early to mid 1900s. Starting in 1952, and over a 40-year period, the Teller series (with bird names like 'Blaumeise', 'Fasan', 'Libelle', 'Rotdrössel', and 'Taube') was released (Bell and Bell 1997). See the cultivar chart that concludes this chapter for their specifics. They were all lacecaps, bred for potplant use, but are common in gardens. A wild white lacecap was crossed with the red mophead 'Tödi' to produce the 26 cultivars. My attempts to grow 'Teller Blue' ('Blaumeise') and 'Teller White' ('Libelle') proved futile as late winter and early spring freezes decimated the plants. All have large sepals and thick-textured medium to dark green foliage. Unfortunately, they are mildew susceptible. 'Blaumeise' is considered the hardiest by most hydrangea experts but did not survive Bir's three-year test. However, it grew 4 feet high in the Atlanta Botanical Garden and flowered (18 May 2003).

More recent breeding programs in the Netherlands (Hovaria®) and Japan (Japanese Lady series) spawned new cultivars with exquisite colors and inflorescence shapes. Our early tests indicate the cultivars of both series lack cold hardiness and are mildew susceptible. In the United States, Hovaria® is marketed under the name Kaleidoscope®. Cultivars released to date include 'Hobella' (soft pink, 1994), 'Homigo' (blue, 1996), 'Hopaline' (soft pink, 1997), 'Fireworks White' (white, double, 1998), 'Hobergine' (aubergine, 1999), 'Hilibel' (white, 2000), 'Fireworks Pink' (pink, double, 2001), 'Mirai'/'Love You Kiss' (white with pink margin, 2001), and 'Ripple' (white with lipstick rose-red margin, 2003). This improvement work was initiated 1980-90 by Koos Hofstede and his son Wilko, Huissen, The Netherlands. The "Ho" in Hovaria® comes from Hofstede. They are protected. More testing is essential in the United States. They are beautiful in flower. Photographs, with history and text, are available at www.hovaria.com

In the 1970s, Hiroshi Ebihara bred the Japanese Lady series. In June 1999 I first laid eyes on these remarkable mopheads, pink, blue, and purple, each sepal with a lighter (white) margin producing a picotee effect; their consumer appeal was phenomenal, and the customers at the Wisley Plant Center were loading them on their wagons. Hydrangeas possess that eye-candy (impulse) appeal. In fact, I out-maneuvered several mesmerized hydrangea gawkers and purchased three that were then given to Hillier Arboretum. 'Lady Katsuko' (red), 'Lady Fujiyo' (peach-pink), 'Lady Taiko Blue' (blue), 'Lady Taiko Pink' (pink), 'Lady Mariko' (lilac-blue), and 'Lady Nobuko' (purple) have been released. In our test plot they are not frost tolerant. 'Lady Fujiyo' produced only

'Lady Taiko Blue'

a single flower in 2002, and every leaf was covered with mildew by October. Three flowers developed in 2003, a non-serious frost year in Athens. Several are now patented in the United States with slightly different names ('Frau Machiko', 'Frau Fujiyo', 'Frau Katsuko', 'Frau Reiko', 'Frau Nobuko', 'Frau Taiko', and 'Frau Kinue') and are available in general commerce. For detailed descriptions of the patented Frau series, visit the U.S. Patent and Trademark Office Web site: www.uspto.gov

To punctuate the above history, a detour to France and the Shamrock Hydrangea Collection is essential (see "Associations" in Resources and Nursery Sources). Here the Mallets, Robert and Corinne, are assembling the largest collection of species and cultivars in the world. My understanding is their collection now encompasses over 1,000 different species and cultivars of *Hydrangea*. Their work is scholarly, with purposeful documentation of taxa, via books and checklists. Their *Hydrangea International Index of Cultivar Names* (2002) includes approximately 785 *H. macrophylla* and 121 *H. serrata* taxa. Corinne has traveled to Japan on several occasions to study hydrangeas in the wild. Their collection will serve as the holy grail for breeders and gardeners who hope to understand the genetic plasticity of the species and improve on the current palette of cultivars. Shamrock also publishes a terrific newsletter, offering some of the best and most current legitimate information. It is a great read, and I eagerly anticipate each issue.

Also in France, the Institut National d'Horticulture (see "Associations" in Resources and Nursery Sources) houses a national collection of hydrangeas. Hélène Bertrand, the registration authority for new cultivars of the genus, is responsible for compiling a preliminary checklist of known cultivar epithets and establishing an International Registry. She also encourages breeders to register their new cultivar(s); the INH's registration form is shown on page 94.

I should mention that Bertrand's responsibilities are sanctioned by ISHS, the International Society for Horticulture Science. The idea is to bring nomenclatural order to hydrangeas (as well as to all cultivated plants) by following the *International Code of Nomenclature for Cultivated Plants*, 1995. The INH *Preliminary Hydrangea Checklist*, issued 26 October 2001, is a tremendous resource for cross-checking authenticity and spelling of cultivar names.

I have also been in touch with Luc Balemans of Hydrangeum vzw, Belgium (again, see Resources and Nursery Sources for contact info). Their collection contains over 300 different botanical species and cultivars of *Hydrangea*. My communications with Balemans, as I attempted to comprehend the variation within *H. aspera*, *H. scandens*, and *H. macrophylla*/*H. serrata*, have been extremely helpful. His thinking was that until someone undertakes a credible botanical study, the taxonomy should be kept simple by lumping, rather then splitting.

Does the garden world need another pink to blue mophead or lacecap? Not really, unless the cultivar is remontant, has superior leathery lustrous dark green foliage, fall color, mildew resistance, compact habit, and/or increased flower bud/stem cold hardiness. Haworth-Booth (1984) listed 42 single or double-starred remontant types. He writes,

> The double-starred varieties 'Altona', 'Enziandom' = 'Gentian Dome', 'Europa', 'Fisher's Silverblue', 'Générale Vicomtesse de Vibraye', 'Hamburg', 'Heinrich Seidel', 'Imperatrice Eugenie', 'Kluis Superba', 'Mme Emile Mouillère', 'Niedersachsen', 'Preziosa', 'Violetta', 'Vulcan', and 'Westfalen' are so free-flowering that every branch usually carries several corymbs (inflorescences) and new shoots will often flower in the same season, like a herbaceous plant. Thus if the top is killed by frost, flowers may still be had, provided that any excess numbers of new shoots are removed and frost-damaged wood is carefully cut back to healthy growth.

'Europa', blue-purple

APPLICATION TO REGISTER *HYDRANGEA* CULTIVAR NAMES

Cultivar name submitted for registration:_____

Parentage (species, hybrid, un-named selection, other):_____

Origin (chance seedling, controlled pollination, mutation, other):_____

Location of original plant:_____

Selector or discoverer:_____

Address:_____Date:_____

Namer: _____

Address:_____Date:_____

Introducer:_____

Address:_____Date:_____

Year of introduction:_____

Collector number:_____

Has the name, accompanied by a description, appeared in a dated publication? If so, please indicate the first such publication

giving author, publication and date._____

Copy of such publication submitted for reference file?_____

Plant patent?_____PCVO?_____

Trade name?_____Trademark?_____

If so, specify, and date._____

This plant has been compared with and may be distinguished from related cultivars by following characteristic features,

and to the best of my knowledge represents a new and distinct cultivar:_____

Brief description of the inflorescence type, sterile flowers (sepal shape, colour, etc.), foliage and growth habit (include

measurements where significant; indicate colour chart used for colour designation):_____

Awards received and dates:_____

Cultural requirements (zone of hardiness, propagation, soil, etc.):_____

Please consider providing one or more of the following: herbarium specimen; photographs; plant.

Signed:_____Date:_____

Name:_____

Address:_____

Return to Hélène Bertrand, Institut National d'Horticulture, 2 rue Le Nôtre, 49045 Angers cedex, France.

My *in situ* evaluations at Athens and travels to numerous hydrangea collections in the United States and Europe identified no *true* remontant types. I want to mention that the word "remontant" is interpreted differently by various researchers. My narrow definition includes reflowering sporadically or continuously from new vegetative regrowth of the season, not preexisting floral primordia, i.e., flower buds.

Then . . . on 11 September 1998, during a visit to Bailey Nurseries, Inc., St. Paul, Minnesota, a horticultural miracle unfolded. Rod Bailey, Terry Schwartz, and Don Selinger were showing me Bailey's new plant trials. I asked about a row of *Hydrangea macrophylla* in full flower. St. Paul experiences Zone 4 winters (-20 to -30°F). No *H. macrophylla* without protection is sufficiently cold hardy to survive and flower unless flowers are produced on the new growth of the season like petunias, geraniums, and marigolds. The original plant was found in a garden in St. Paul by Vern Black, a Bailey employee. I suspect it is an old potplant (greenhouse) cultivar, purchased by the homeowner, outplanted to the garden where this remontant (reblooming) trait was recognized. Cuttings were requested, provided, rooted, and grown to flowering in Athens. Remarkably, small cuttings kept developing flower buds and fully expressed inflorescences in the greenhouse throughout the fall and winter of 1998–99. Was this the plant that could advance hydrangea breeding to the fail-safe flowering stage?

On the trip home to Athens, my legal pad was scribbled with breeding strategies. Can this genetic trait for remontancy be incorporated via hybridization into seedling populations? As mentioned, the ongoing evaluation and breeding with approximately 100 cultivars indicated 'Ayesha', 'Veitchii', and 'Lilacina' offered many desirable foliage and mildew resistance traits. This Minnesota discovery needed a name and, mixed among my notes, was "Endless Summer." Now for the rest of the story.

Critical testing by Jeffrey Adkins, then a University of Georgia master's student, showed Endless Summer™ was truly remontant. Several articles and lectures spurred enthusiasm from growers and gardeners. Bailey Nurseries, Inc., decided to protect Endless Summer™ ('Bailmer') and applied for a plant patent. Bailey's also engineered a first-class marketing program to promote Endless Summer™. A consortium of growers across the United

States had one million plants in production for partial release in 2003, fully so in 2004. Of all the plants that have passed through the Georgia program, Endless Summer™ has generated the most volcanic enthusiasm. In Georgia, Endless Summer™ flowers May and June, with a second full-blown flush in October and November. Our greenhouse research showed that when flowers are removed, it takes 10 to 12 weeks before the new shoots develop full-size inflorescences. For continuous color, the gardener might remove one half the inflorescences, allowing the remainder to dry on the plant while the new shoots are producing flower buds for the later show.

Endless Summer™ is as good as advertised (actually better), but there is more to this everblooming hydrangea saga. As I spread the gospel, gardeners and plant friends mentioned hydrangeas with similar attributes. Again plants and cuttings were shared, tested, and documented for remontancy. 'David Ramsey', 'Decatur Blue', 'Oak Hill', and 'Penny Mac' proved remontant. In fact, all are similar to Endless Summer™, so much so that I questioned their uniqueness. My first thought was this same cultivar, grown as a greenhouse potplant, and sold throughout the United States, was simply showing up in different locations.

This trepidation was mitigated with the involvement of an academic colleague, Jon Lindstrom, Department of Horticulture, University of Arkansas, Fayetteville, who extracted the DNA from the five and did RAPD analysis which "chops up" the DNA via enzymes. The bands that develop for each cultivar are compared and contrasted. A dendrogram (cultivar tree) is statistically developed that categorizes the similarities between and among the cultivars. In brief, Endless Summer™ and 'David Ramsey' are quite similar, the others different from each other and the first two. Since plant numbers (except for Endless Summer™) are small, mildew resistance and cold hardiness differences have yet to be determined, although all will contract some mildew. Since all are remontant, the goal is to determine the cultivar with the best traits for sustained, energetic, controlled breeding.

To date, seedlings of open-pollinated Endless Summer™ lacked vigor, and died. Of two open-pollinated seedlings of 'Penny Mac' (the first remontant type with seedlings that flowered), one was remontant. Tentatively named 'Mini Penny', it is 16 inches high, 36 inches wide, after two years, with leathery lustrous dark green leaves and moderate mildew resistance. Thirty-three flowers were fully expressed in May and June 2002, removed on 25 June, with 34 developed terminal buds and/or inflorescences on 14 November. Most exciting was that the remontant trait was expressed in this first-generation seedling. Often, it is necessary to backcross from this first-generation (F1) seedling to one or the other parent to incorporate more of the desired characteristics.

Controlled crosses in 2001 (in greenhouse) of 'Veitchii' (♀) x Endless Summer™ (♂) yielded six seedlings, five of which flowered in 2002. The seedling, 'Veitchii' x Endless Summer™-03-02, a beautiful white mophead that ages to pink, was named 'Blushing Bride'. The mophead characteristic was expressed in the maternal 'Veitchii' seedling, which indicates introgression (gene flow) from both parents since 'Veitchii' is a white lacecap, Endless Summer™ a pink to blue mophead. Young rooted cuttings of 'Veitchii' x Endless Summer™-03-02 developed fully expressed flowers in the greenhouse (January 2003). Lindstrom plans to examine DNA of each parent and the seedling to verify the hybridity.

In March 2002, using flowers of 'Decatur Blue' (♀), 'David Ramsey' (♀), Endless Summer™ (♀), and 'Veitchii' (♂), controlled crosses (in greenhouse) were consummated. Viable seeds resulted and seedlings of the three maternal parents have been transplanted. If remontancy was transferred to the seedlings, a percentage will flower in the summer of 2003. In March and April 2003, 2,500 controlled crosses were constituted, utilizing primarily the remontant types as maternal parents. Fruit development exceeded expectations, and 2004 will prove a banner year. Each seed is a genetic gold mine on the road to self-expression. Based on our early successes, I believe a new generation of repeat-flowering hydrangeas with improved foliage and habit is in the making. Endless Summer™ provided the genetic foray into this elusive world. From Maine to Florida, hydrangeas will reliably flower, regardless of the vagaries of climate. 'Tis a dream come true.

Identification Characteristics

Leaves: Opposite, simple, elliptic, broad-ovate, to obovate, 4 to 8 inches long, two-thirds as wide, acute or short-acuminate, broad cuneate at base, coarsely serrate with triangular obtusish teeth, flat matt, lustrous medium to dark green above, often rather fleshy texture and greasy to the touch, reminds of a cabbage leaf, glabrous or slightly puberulous beneath; petiole stout, $^1/_2$ to 2 inches long, leaving large scars, the opposite one contiguous.

Buds: Vegetative, small, sitting on top of leaf scar; flower, $^1/_2$ to $^2/_3$ inch long, rather plumpish, appressed to stem, green to brown, seemingly valvate with the 2 outer scales gently overlapping or touching; larger buds are not always floral in composition; terminal bud is typically a flower bud and represents the hope for flowering, if not killed by cold.

Stem: Light brown, scarcely branched, glabrous, round, stout; pith, large, white.

Flowers: Corymb, lacecap or mophead, with sterile florets, i.e., ray flowers, 1 to 2 inches across, composed of 3 to 5 sepals, entire or toothed, ovate to rounded, white, pink to blue; fertile flowers small, 5 short triangular sepals, 5 narrow ovate petals, pink or blue, 10 stamens.

Hydrangea macrophylla Cultivar Chart

Hydrangea macrophylla taxa were collected from the literature, Internet, nursery catalogs, and observations. This tabular format allows for easy cross-referencing of names and characteristics. These taxa were referenced and/or offered in American commerce from 2000 to 2003. Unfortunately, a given taxon with a legitimate cultivar name may be relabeled for commercial purposes. 'Pia' is 'Pia', a dwarf pink mophead, and should always be such. Unfortunately, the names 'Comet', 'Winning Edge', 'Piamina', and Pink Elf™ are also ascribed to this plant. The crazy aspect is the nurseries who sell the same plant with two names. I hope this chart serves as a guide to *H. macrophylla* cultivars that the reader will be able to obtain from American nurseries (see Resources and Nursery Sources). Happy hunting.

Data from the UGA Hydrangea Shade Garden collected 17 May 2003 and from Atlanta Botanical Garden on 18 May 2003. Based on these windows (flower, foliage, habit, vigor), the following—all remontant taxa (numerous flowers)—were afforded the Dirr seal of garden approval: 'All Summer Beauty', 'Altona', 'Ami Pasquier', 'Dooley', 'Frillibet', 'Fuji Waterfall', 'Générale Vicomtesse de Vibraye', 'Hillier Blue', 'Lilacina', 'Mme Emile Mouillère', 'Nikko Blue', 'Souvenir du Pdt. Paul Doumer', 'Veitchii', and 'White Wave'. All plants in the UGA garden were planted in mid-June 2001.

Colored pencil drawing of *Hydrangea macrophylla* 'Alpenglühen.'

'Beauté Vendômoise'

'Blaumeise'

CULTIVAR	FLOWER TYPE	COLOR (-AL)	(+AL)	FLOWER NOTES	FOLIAGE & HABIT NOTES
'Adria'	mophead	pink	rich blue		semi-dwarf; 3' tall, small shiny lustrous dark green leaves
'All Summer Beauty'	mophead	pink	blue	flowers summer and fall; flowers on new wood	3 to 4' tall; hardy; dark green foliage; abundant flowers on 17 May 2003, fully open
'Alpenglühen' ('Alpenglow', 'Alpenglühn', 'Glowing Embers')	mophead	crimson-red	blue-purple	flowers start out with a white eye; 10 to 12 inches across, dry well; serrated sepals, broad-ovate, overlapping, turning up at the margins	shiny, dark green leaves; compact growing, 3 to 4' tall; late flowering; mildew on plant in lath 28 June 2003 every leaf smothered
'Altona' ('Althone')	mophead	rose-madder	vivid deep blue	serrated, overlapping sepals; large head; flower with attractive autumn tints, flowers for 4 to 5 months; red, blue, and green sepaled autumn colored head; great for drying	moderately tall; 4 to 6' stout growth; semi-lustrous dark green leaves; stems heavily spotted or stained purple-black, 3 flowers on 17 May 2003, from just opening to full
'Amethyst'	mophead	soft pink	pale violet	double serrated sepals; flowers with white centers in early stage of blooming; best flowers in early autumn; small corymbs	shoots stout; leaves thick and deep green; 3 to 4' tall; 8 flower buds just emerging 17 May 2003; flowers from terminal buds only; seedling of 'Europa'
'Ami Pasquier'	mophead	pink to crimson	blue to wine-purple	flowers heavily until frost; inflorescence 4 to 5" wide; prolific flowering	glossy green leaves; strong growing; 3 to 4' tall; seedling of 'Maréchal Foch'; abundant flowers, Atlanta Botanical Garden, 18 May 2003; can be confused with 'Westfalen'
'Atlantica' ('Atlantic')	mophead	pink to red	blue		similar to 'Floralia'; compact late bloomer
'Ayesha' ('Uzu Ajisai', 'Silver Slipper', 'Flieder')	mophead	pale pink or mauve	light lilac-blue	sepals like cupped spoons; faint but distinct fragrance; late flowering	lustrous dark green leaves have a waxy consistency; 4 to 6' tall; flower buds just showing 17 May 2003, 5 to 6 buds; no color to sepals on 3 June 2003; 7' tall on 29 June 2003 at Penny McHenry's with numerous flowers, one of the best specimens I've seen outside of Europe

CULTIVAR	FLOWER TYPE	COLOR (-AL)	(+AL)	FLOWER NOTES	FOLIAGE & HABIT NOTES
'Beauté Vendômoise'	lacecap (pseudo-mophead)	white sterile; pink fertile	white sterile; blue fertile	age green-cream to pink; large, crowded corymbs; mid to late season, large sepals, 10" wide flowers; sterile florets scattered about the entire head	5 to 6' tall, 4½' at Atlanta Botanical Garden; abundant flowers 18 May 2003; large lustrous green leaves; spectacular in flower; almost full on 3 June 2003 at JC Raulston Arboretum
'Bethany Beach'	lacecap		light blue	long flowering	robust growing, 5' tall, glossy deep green leaves
'Big Daddy'	mophead	pink	blue	inflorescences 8 to 12" across; thin sepals	glossy thick large leaves; yellow fall color; grows 5 to 6' high, thick stems; perhaps a seedling of 'Otaksa'
'Blauer Prinz' ('Blue Prince')	mophead	rose, red	cornflower blue with touch of purple	late-flowering; flower heads stay in perfect condition and turn green, red, and purple in autumn; pointed sepals, overcrowded corymb	dark green leaves; 4 to 6' tall
'Blauer Zwerg'	mophead		blue/purple	heavy bloomer	dwarf
'Blaumeise' ('Teller Blue', 'Blue Tit', 'Blue Sky', 'Armore')	lacecap	rose red	deep blue	sterile florets reverse as they age, eventually showing their undersides; flowers dry well; inflorescences up to 9" across	luxuriant rounded shiny green leaves; stout stems; 4 to 6' tall stout growth; large shrub; protect from late frosts; winter protection recommended; possibly the most cold hardy of the Tellers; 4' tall plant with strong old stems has persisted at the JC Raulston Arboretum and is sited in sun
'Blue Danube' ('Blau Donau', 'Danube Bleu')	mophead	pink	deep metallic blue	striking color, greenhouse type	compact to 3'; dark green leaves; 6' tall at Atlanta Botanical Garden, abundant flowers; similar to 'Mathilda Gütges' in flower color at Atlanta Botanical Garden on 29 June 2003
'Blue Wave' ('Bluewave', 'Mariesii Perfecta')	lacecap	pink	lilac to pale blue sterile; dark blue fertile	numerous, large ray florets; sepals entire and toothed	unusually strong and hardy grower; lustrous dark green leaves; rounded, 4 to 6' tall; weak and without flower buds 17 May 2003 in Georgia garden; leaves reminiscent of 'Lilacina'

'Blue Danube'

'Blue Wave'

CULTIVAR	FLOWER TYPE	COLOR (-AL)	(+AL)	FLOWER NOTES	FOLIAGE & HABIT NOTES
'Blushing Pink'	mophead	blushing pink	blue	cut flower	sport of 'Merritt's Beauty'; lustrous medium green leaves; cold sensitive; flower buds green 17 May 2003
'Bodensee' ('Bon Cuse')	mophead	pretty pink	blue	heavy bloomer; will typically bloom twice in one season	lustrous green leaves; 4 to 6' tall; not particularly cold hardy, no flower buds 17 May 2003
'Böttstein'	mophead	red	violet deepening to a royal blue	normal greenhouse hydrangea	robust, large, dark green leaves; scarlet fall color; medium size, to 4 to 5' tall; also described as 2 to 3' tall
'Bouquet Rose'	mophead	pale pink	clear blue	free flowering; over-sized flowers are great for cut and dried flowers; florets float above the head on long pedicels	3 to 4' tall; weak stems
'Brestenburg'	mophead	pink	true blue	cupped sepals; early flowering	medium size
'Bridal Bouquet'	mophead	wedding white			
'Brunette' ('Sanguine(a)', 'Folis Purpurea', 'Verdun', 'Colour Fantasy')	mophead	red	violet blue to purple	color is unbelievably intense	weak grower at Penny McHenry's; considered same as' Merveille Sanguine(a)' by Mallets; different by Wilkerson Mill Gardens

'Brympton Mauve' is similar to 'Beauté Vendômoise' except with more sterile florets, which give it a mophead appearance.

CULTIVAR	FLOWER TYPE	COLOR (-AL)	(+AL)	FLOWER NOTES	FOLIAGE & HABIT NOTES
'Burg Königstein' ('Königstein')	mophead	red		serrated sepals	
Buttons 'n Bows®	see 'Harlequin'				
'Cardinal Red' ('Cardinal')	mophead	vibrant red	blue-purple		lustrous dark green leaves; minimal cold hardiness; no flowers on 3 June 2003 at JC Raulston Arboretum
'Carmen'	mophead	deep pink	blue	large heads; reliable bloomer	deep green foliage; turns orange-yellow in fall; medium sized shrub; vigorous grower
'Charme' ('Charm', 'Charm Red')	mophead	deep pink, red	blue	large flowers	dark green leaves; cold sensitive
'Coerulea Lace' ('Caerulea', H. japonica)	lacecap	pink to mauve	blue	delicate flowers, always consistent	medium growth habit; abundant flowers 17 May 2003

CULTIVAR	FLOWER TYPE	COLOR (−AL)	(+AL)	FLOWER NOTES	FOLIAGE & HABIT NOTES
'Compacta' ('Monink', Pink and Pretty™)	mophead	deep pink		3" heads, sepals do not droop	3' tall plants; sturdy grower
'David Ramsey'	mophead	pink	blue	remontant type	flat medium green leaves; 4' tall; abundant flowers on 18 May 2003
'Decatur Blue'	mophead	pink	blue	remontant type	flat medium green leaves; robust grower to 5' tall; numerous flowers on 18 May 2003
'Deutschland'	mophead	cream center with rose/ purple border	purplish blue	mid to late season	attractive fall foliage
'Domotoi' ('Domotoi Rosea', 'Yae', Sekkayae')	mophead	pale pink	blue/mauve	double, large florets	attractive glossy dark green foliage; 5 to 6' tall
'Dooley'	mophead	pink	blue	flowers formed the length of the stem	5 to 6' tall, stems cold hardy to −11°F; 27 flowers tight to full 17 May 2003; loaded with flowers 3 June 2003, at JC Raulston Arboretum, sited in full sun
'Eisvogel' ('Teller Purple', 'Kingfisher')	lacecap	pink	purple	heavy blooms	
'Elster' (Teller series, 'Magpie')	lacecap		lavender-white	very large, to 8" across, very graceful; cut flower	shiny dark green leaves, compact 3 to 4' shrub, sensitive to spring frosts
Endless Summer™ ('Bailmer')	mophead	pink	blue	remontant, flowers on new growth	medium green foliage, probably 3 to 4' tall; 29 flowers, green buds to full, 17 May 2003
'Enziandom' ('Gentian Dome')	mophead	vivid pink, reddish pink	deep blue	sepals overlapping and entire; a favorite among florists and landscapers; dries well; mid to late season	dark green foliage; leaves turn dark red to copper in autumn; 3 to 4' tall
'Europa'	mophead	deep pink	vivid blue, purple	sepals serrated, overlapping, and cupped; a favorite among florists for forcing and cutting; makes a great dried flower; large heads	4 to 6' tall; vigorous
'Fasan' (Teller series, 'Pheasant', 'Twilight')	lacecap	bright red sterile; crimson fertile	dark lavender with purple overtones	July to frost; large blooms; double row of sterile florets	dark green, coarse leaves; stout stems; 4 to 6' tall

Endless Summer™

CULTIVAR	FLOWER TYPE	COLOR (-AL)	(+AL)	FLOWER NOTES	FOLIAGE & HABIT NOTES
'Forever Pink' ('Draps Wonder')	mophead	bright pink	blue	flowers all summer and into fall; 3 to 4" flower heads	lustrous dark green leaves; vigorous dwarf plant; 3 to 4' tall; cold sensitive; not a single flower 17 May 2003
'Freudenstein'	mophead	vivid pink	mauve to purple	early to mid-summer flowering	4 to 5' tall; stout stems; lustrous dark green leaves
'Frillibet' ('Ardtornish')	mophead	cream-yellow, white, with blue tips	ages blue	blooms early and lasts well into fall; very frilly sepals; sepals flip upside down late in the season	lustrous dark green leaves; 4 to 6' tall
'Fuji Waterfall' ('Fujinotaki'; listed as *H. serrata*, but appears to belong here)	mophead (loosely configured)	white suffused with pink with aging	white suffused with blue with aging	double, cascade effect around the flower head; 12" wide head; will repeat flower into the fall; a knockout spectacle	dark glossy green leaves; full flower on 17 May 2003
'Gartenbaudirektor Kühnert' ('Nursery Director Kuhnert')	mophead	pink	vivid French blue	mid-July to August; excellent for drying; not very free-flowering	moderate to strong growth; 5' by 5'
'Générale Vicomtesse de Vibraye'	mophead	pink	light blue	overcrowded heads; free-flowering; flowers on terminal and side shoots; entire, overlapping sepals; one of easiest for drying; if picked pink, they'll dry lime green; if picked blue they'll turn blue-green	tall, slender stems; flat medium green leaves; speckled stems; reddish nodes; hybrid of 'Otaksa' and 'Rosea'; abundant flowers 17 May 2003; pink to rich blue on the lone plant
'Gentian Dome' see 'Enziandom'					
'Geoffrey Chadbund' (actually a Teller, 'Möwe')	lacecap	red	purple, violet, fuchsia	perfect for cutting and filling vases; sometimes will bloom while still very young	rich, dark green foliage; 4 to 6' tall, not very cold hardy; 4' and abundant flowers at Atlanta Botanical Garden, 18 May 2003
'Gerda Steiniger'	mophead	bright pink	blue	strong bloomer; early	
'Gertrude Glahn'	mophead	deep pink	blue to purple	numerous, firm heads; flowering from mid-season to late; superior for drying	strong stems; lustrous medium green leaves; 4 to 6' tall
'Glory' ('Glory Blue', 'Glory Pink')	mophead	pink	rich blue	large inflorescences	common in southeastern nursery trade; probably a rename, no clear origin; 4' tall; lustrous dark green leaves
'Gold Dust'	lacecap	pink to mauve	blue	large, flat heads; prolific flowering	gold-dusted leaves; vigorous; medium sized shrub; yellow with a tinge of red in fall

'Fuji Waterfall'

'Goliath'

CULTIVAR	FLOWER TYPE	COLOR (-AL)	(+AL)	FLOWER NOTES	FOLIAGE & HABIT NOTES
'Gold Nugget'	lacecap	white to mauve-pink		medium sized, flat heads; prolific flowering over a long time period	dwarf habit; leaves have large golden yellow center with green edging
'Gold Strike'	lacecap	pink to mauve	blue		foliage variegation of gold stripes and blotches; vigorous growing, medium sized to 3 to 4' tall; sport of 'Gold Dust'; yellow to red in fall
'Goliath'	mophead	deep pink	purplish-blue, French blue, royal blue	large flowers; serrated sepals; popular for forcing in Europe; free-flowering; good dried; mid-season	4 to 6' tall; vigorous and tall; dark green leaves; one of the finest for seaside gardens; not particularly cold hardy; although 7 flowers tight to fully open 17 May 2003
HC 970642 (Heronswood, 2003)	lacecap	pink	light blue		collected from upper elevational limit and may prove hardier; leaves lighter green, not strong growing
'Hadsbury'	lacecap	pink	blue		cold sensitive, no flowers; literally flattened to ground when first observed on 8 May 2003 at JC Raulston Arboretum, by 3 June 2003, regrowth to 3' with blue lacecap flowers showing color; flowers developed from basal crown buds
'Hamburg'	mophead	deep pink	purplish or deep blue	boldly serrated sepals; flowers last an unusually long time, maintaining an intense pigment in their dried state; flowers turn red in autumn	massive growth and fine foliage; 4 to 6' tall
'Hanabi' ('Fireworks', 'Sumida-no-'Hanabi', Hanabi-Ajisai')	lacecap	white initially, dark pink sterile; light pink fertile		double sterile florets, darker rose-burgundy with age	lustrous dark green leaves; 4' tall; not very hardy
'Harlequin' ('Monrey', 'Sensation 75', 'Harlekijn', Buttons 'n Bows®)	mophead	red with white margins	purple with white margins	serrated, picotee; later flowers are often solid color	lustrous dark green leaves; more tender, semi-dwarf, 3'; abundant flowers at Atlanta Botanical Garden 18 May 2003; many colors in aging (drying) inflorescences on 29 June 2003 at Atlanta Botanical Garden
'Haworth Booth'	mophead	red	pinkish purple	small inflorescences	lustrous dark green leaves

'Hadsbury'

'Hanabi'

CULTIVAR	FLOWER TYPE	COLOR (-AL)	(+AL)	FLOWER NOTES	FOLIAGE & HABIT NOTES
'Heinrich Seidel' ('Glory of Aalsmeer')	mophead	cherry-crimson	purple	fringed; free-flowering; mid-season; overcrowded with sepals giving it a "frilly" look	moderate to tall; sturdy stemmed; vigorous grower; 4 to 6' tall; cold sensitive; seriously wounded at JC Raulston Arboretum, i.e., no flowers 3 June 2002
'Hillier Blue'	mophead	pink	blue		flat dark green leaves; flowers almost full on 17 May 2003; similar to 'Générale Vicomtesse de Vibraye'; survived April freeze in 1999 and was the most floriferous taxon at Hillier
'Hobella' (Hovaria® series)	lacecap	soft pink		substantive heads	5' by 5', weak growing; no flower buds 17 May 2003; heavy insect damage; one of the worst for mildew susceptibility
'Holstein'	mophead	salmon pink	sky blue, rich saturated blue	serrated sepals; rounded head; flowers mid-season	stately stems and strong growth; 4 to 6' tall; flat dark green leaves, susceptible to frosts; no flower buds 17 May 2003
'Homigo' (Hovaria® series)	mophead	pink	blue	serrated sepals	flat dark green leaves; 2 flower buds 17 May 2003
'Horben'	mophead	mauve to pink		cupped crowded sepals	
'Hörnli'	mophead	bright red	purple	small flower heads, however can reach 5" in diameter	dwarf; to 18" (3'), light green leaves, contracts heavy leaf spot
'Ice Blue'	mophead	light blue to near white			strong stems hold flowers upright even when wet; yellow fall color
'Izu-no-Hana'	lacecap	pink	lavender-blue to blue	semi-double, not particularly showy	flat dark green leaves; 2 flower buds 17 May 2003; many inflorescences, mostly fertile, on 29 June 2003, at Penny McHenry's
Japanese Lady series: See page 91.					
'Jennifer'	?	magenta	royal purple	early to mid-summer	3 to 4' tall
'Jōgasaki'	lacecap	silvery pink sterile, pink to white fertile	rich blue-purple sterile; blue-purple fertile	large, double sterile florets	5' tall; semi-lustrous dark green leaves

'Hobella'

'Izu-no-Hana'

'Jōgasaki'

CULTIVAR	FLOWER TYPE	COLOR (-AL)	(+AL)	FLOWER NOTES	FOLIAGE & HABIT NOTES
'Kardinal' (Teller series)	lacecap	pink-red (red)	mauve sterile; medium pink fertile	flowers develop late	lustrous dark green leaves; stout stems; 3 to 3½' tall; cold sensitive
'Kasteln'	mophead	deep pink		large head; prolific flowering; dries well; good for arrangements	medium sized shrub
'King George'	mophead	cherry pink	blue	dries well; flowers late	apple-green foliage; 5 to 6' tall
'Kluis Superba'	mophead	deep pink	violet or blue/purple	covered in masses of wide, rounded flower heads; good for drying	stout growing; 4 to 6' tall
'La France'	mophead	phlox pink	mid-blue	slightly serrated sepals; massive heads; free-flowering; mid-season and lasts into fall	tall growth; 4 to 6' tall; apple-green leaves
'La Marne'	mophead	pink	pale blue	serrated sepals; very large heads	tall, massive grower; handsome, glossy foliage
'La Tosca'	mophead	pink		double flowers	dark green foliage; yellow fall color; large-sized shrub; robust, 4½' tall at Atlanta Botanical Garden, 18 May 2003
'Lady Fujiyo' ('Frau Fujiyo') (Japanese Lady series)	mophead	rose with white picotee margin	purple-blue		lustrous dark green leaves; strong stems; one open flower, several buds 17 May 2003
'Lady in Red'	lacecap	pinkish white sterile; blue-purple fertile	light blue	ages to burgundy-rose; 4" across, 5 to 10 sepalous clusters; sepals rounded and overlapping	dull dark green leaves; red veins, petioles, stems, and fall color, high mildew resistance
'Lanarth Lavender'	lacecap	white-lavender	light blue		large grower at Atlanta Botanical Garden 29 June 2003
'Lanarth White'	lacecap	white with pink fertile flowers	white with blue fertile flowers	late season; flowers reaching peak 3 June 2003, at JC Raulston Arboretum; sepals ovate, entire, scarcely overlapping	compact growth; 3 to 4' high and wide; revels in full sun and wind; lustrous dark green leaves, one of the best lacecaps for gardens
'Le Cygne' ('Alberta')	mophead	white, sometimes tinged pink	white	prolific, vigorous; cut flower	tall shrub
'Lemmenhof'	mophead	pink with white eye	blue	serrated sepals	dwarf

'La France'

'Lady in Red'

'Lady in Red', foliage

'Lanarth White'

'Lemon Zest'

'Leucantha'

CULTIVAR	FLOWER TYPE	COLOR (-AL)	(+AL)	FLOWER NOTES	FOLIAGE & HABIT NOTES
'Lemon Wave' ('Tricolor')	lacecap	white/ cream	light blue sterile; gentian blue fertile		bright yellow splotches on variegated green/white leaves; more colorful than 'Mariesii Variegata', no doubt derived from 'MV' as flowers are similar; like all variegated types, it reverts—terribly
'Lemon Zest' ('Ogonba', Sun Goddess™, 'Yellowleaf', possibly others)	mophead	pink	blue (requires high aluminum)	pink flowers against foliage remind me of a golden spirea	golden-yellow foliage throughout the spring and summer; frost sensitive; in Georgia trials not vigorous or persistent; one flower bud 17 May 2003, heavy insect damage
'Leucantha'	lacecap	white sterile; white fertile	white sterile; white fertile	sepals rounded, entire, overlapping, 1½" across; inflorescence averages 7" across	strong stems, lustrous medium green leaves with deeply impressed veins; leaves reminiscent of those of 'Lilacina'; high mildew susceptibility; from Hines Nursery
'Leuchtfeuer' ('Firelight', 'Hermann Dienemann')	mophead	bright pink	blue-purple	sepals overlap; largely entire; 6" in diameter	strong stems; lustrous dark green almost rounded leaves; 3 to 3½' tall; cold sensitive
'Libelle' ('Teller White', 'Dragon Fly', 'Snow', 'Hermine')	lacecap	white		rounded sepals; sepals loosely arranged among the multi-colored center fertile flowers	glossy green tapered leaves; 4 to 6' tall; not very cold tolerant
'Lilacina' ('Mariesii Lilacina')	lacecap	phlox pink sterile; blue fertile	lilac to pure blue	sepals generally not overlapping,, strongly serrate, although also entire; mid to late season; produces flowers an exceptionally long time	strong growing; large, pointed, lustrous dark green leaves; 4 to 6' tall; late, sepals just showing 17 May 2003, 57 flower buds
'Luvumama'	mophead	pink	blue (good, rich)	repeat (remontant); different from other remontants	flowers abundant on 26 June 2003 (McHenry); lustrous dark green leaves, 7' tall
'Mme Baardse'	mophead	deep rose			
'Mme Emile Mouillère' ('Sedgewick's White')	mophead	white with pink eye	white with blue eye; have observed sepals with a blue tint	repeat displays; petals become dotted with pink as they age; serrated sepals; free flowering; the classic white hydrangea	vigorous, cold resistant; luxuriant glossy foliage turns red, orange and green in autumn; 58 flowers opening 17 May 2003, best of show
'Mme Faustin Travouillon' ('Peacock')	mophead	crimson-pink	mid-blue	fairly free-flowering; early and late	vigorous growth, 3½', loaded with flowers at Atlanta Botanical Garden, 18 May 2003

CULTIVAR	FLOWER TYPE	COLOR (-AL)	(+AL)	FLOWER NOTES	FOLIAGE & HABIT NOTES
'Mandschurica' ('Nigra', 'Kurojiku')	mophead	pink	sickly blue, rather uninspiring	mid-season; flowers form at terminal buds; have observed clear blue in high Al soils	ornamental stems of glossy black; lustrous medium green foliage; rounded shrub 5' by 5'; often injured by cold; no flowers 17 May 2003
'Maréchal Foch'	mophead	rich rosy pink	purple to deep gentian blue	numerous, strong flowers; free-flowering; grown for forcing	4 to 6' tall
'Mariesii'	lacecap	white to rosy pink	pale blue (lots of aluminum)	sepals touching at edge to barely overlapping, entire; wide, flat corymbs; florets very large; mid-season	very hardy; the real 'Mariesii' doubtfully exists in commerce, original plant introduced in 1879 from Japan by Charles Maries, 4' tall, with narrow, evenly tapered leaves
'Mariesii Variegata' ('Maculata')	lacecap	pinkish-white	blue		green leaves with white margins; not stable and apt to revert; cold sensitive; dieback, no flowers 17 May 2003; I have doubts about the validity of this variegated form, i.e., is it truly a sport of 'Mariesii'?
'Masja' ('Sybilla', 'Sibilla')	mophead	vivid red	rich blue-purple	ball-shaped flowers	dark glossy green leaves; 3 to 4' tall; not particularly cold hardy
'Mathilda Gütges' (same as 'Royal Purple'?)	mophead	pink	blue or violet to rich blue	mid to late season; a plant may have pink, blue, or violet flowers or a combination of all three; sharply dentate sepals to entire	4 to 5' tall; lustrous dark green leaves
'Merritt's Beauty'	mophead	carmine-red		globe-shaped	mounded; 4 to 6' tall
'Merritt's Supreme'	mophead	pink to carmine	pink, touch of purple	sepals serrated; flowers as a young plant; flower heads stay in perfect condition turning green, red, or purple tinted in fall; greenhouse forcing type	3 to 4' tall; hardiness is suspect
'Merveille Sanguine(a)' ('Brunette', 'Folis Purpurea', 'Verdun', 'Colour Fantasy')	mophead	vivid rosy crimson	rich sky blue turning cobalt blue	medium heads with mid-sized flowers; early to mid-summer	4 to 5' tall; foliage dark green with wine-red overtone; has produced a number of branch sports; unbelievably rich sepal coloration

'Mathilda Gütges'

CULTIVAR	FLOWER TYPE	COLOR (-AL)	(+AL)	FLOWER NOTES	FOLIAGE & HABIT NOTES
'Miss Belgium'	mophead	carmine, rosy crimson	purple	mid-season; flowers age to deep wine colors; free flowering	sturdy stems; dark glossy green leaves; good in containers; 3 to 4' tall
'Miss Hepburn' ('W. J. Hepburn')	mophead	pink	deep purplish		
'Mousmée' ('Mousmé')	lacecap	rose, vivid hot pink	violet-blue	flowers June through September; turn antique colors or purplish blue in autumn	dark green leaves; good vigor; 4 to 6' tall; heavy stem with red streaks; zapped in Dirr garden
'Mousseline'	mophead	pale pink	light blue	sepals ovate, entire; flowers early and fairly continuously; lasting well	tall, stout growth; good autumn color; one of the more cold hardy types, similar to 'de Vibraye'; seedling of 'Rosea'
'Möwe' (Teller series, 'Seagull', same as 'Geoffrey Chadbund'?)	lacecap	red stronger tints of red	purple	lacecap version of 'Ami Pasquier' type and color	5' tall
'Niedersachsen'	mophead	pale pink	blue	late-flowering, long-blooming	5 to 6' tall
'Nightingale' ('Nachtigall', 'Teller Purple')	lacecap	red	indigo blue to purple	side buds bloom; inflorescences to 6" in diameter	stout, strong growth; lustrous dark green leaves; needs extra protection from the last blast of winter; to 5 to 6' tall; late, just showing color 18 May 2003 at Atlanta Botanical Garden; mildew ridden in lath, 29 June 2003
'Nigra' see Mandschurica'					
'Nikko Blue'	mophead	pink	blue	free-flowering; sepals always entire; dependable quantities of flowers; flowers start cream with blue margins; early flowering	4 to 6' tall; flat dark green leaves; considered one of the more cold hardy taxa; difficult to know what is true 'Nikko Blue'; flowers abundant, green-cream to blue; 60% full 17 May 2003
'Oregon Pride'	mophead	rich Persian rose to red	purple	powerful flower effect when right	sport of 'Merritt's Supreme'; dark green leaves; dark red strong stems; not very cold hardy
'Otaksa'	mophead	pink	blue	extremely large flower; free-flowering; excellent for drying	vigorous grower; glossy light green foliage; leaves orbicular-rounded; 4 to 6' tall; introduced from Japan in 1862

'Mousmée'

'Oregon Pride'

CULTIVAR	FLOWER TYPE	COLOR (-AL)	(+AL)	FLOWER NOTES	FOLIAGE & HABIT NOTES
'Paris'	mophead	deep pink	purple	massive flowers, 8 to 9" wide; individual florets 2 to 2½" wide; florets curly; a dried flower head looks like a bouquet all by itself	sturdy framework; 4 to 6' tall
'Parzival' ('Parsifal', 'Parsival')	mophead	rose-madder to crimson-pink	purple to deep blue	serrated sepals; numerous small heads; last well in shade	moderate growth; attractive fall tints
'Patio White'	mophead	pure white	pure white	long-flowering; medium sized, compact flower head	small to medium sized shrub; yellow fall color in shade; reddish purple fall color if planted in more sun
'Paw Paw Pink'	mophead	pink		large, round heads	dwarf to semi dwarf; vigorous; dark green leaves
'Penny Mac'	mophead	pink	mid-blue	age to tones of aquamarine; flowers on current season's growth	from the garden of Penny McHenry (AHS founder), Atlanta, Georgia; strong grower; 5 to 6' tall; possibly the most cold hardy of the remontant types; flat medium green leaves; abundant flowers 17 May 2003; received as a gift in April 1975, probably a florist type
'Pia' ('Piamina', 'Comet', 'Winning Edge', Pink Elf™)	mophead	red with white eye	blue, blue-violet	denticulate sepals of different sizes; slightly irregular flattened corymbs to 4" wide; 3' tall plant had all blue-purple flowers; I mention this because 'Pia' is often advertised as a pink-flowering form	dark green foliage; dwarf, 2 to 3' tall; minimal cold hardiness; often devastated by spring frosts; weak, 2 green flower buds 17 May 2003; heavy insect damage; leaf spot susceptible; have read cautionary notes that it may revert to tall-growing type
'Pieta'	mophead	rich pink		large flower heads; extremely floriferous	strong and durable plant; rich green foliage; dense, compact habit
'Pink Lace'	lacecap	bright pink		huge flower; cut flower	1 to 2' shrub; good for container or tiny corner
Pink and Pretty™ ('Monink', 'Compacta')	mophead	pink		abundant flowers	mounded, 4 to 6' tall, 3 to 4' wide
'Pink Reverse'	lacecap	pink to rose	rich blue	sterile florets stained rose at their centers and have rose veining; cobalt fertile florets; reverse of sterile florets stained rose and are revealed after pollination; 6 to 7" heads	dark green foliage; 8' by 5'

'Pia'

CULTIVAR	FLOWER TYPE	COLOR (-AL)	(+AL)	FLOWER NOTES	FOLIAGE & HABIT NOTES
'Président R. Touchard'	mophead	pink to red, cherry-pink	blue	free-flowering	
'Preziosa' see *H. serrata* chart in chapter 10					
'Princess Beatrix' ('Prinses Beatrix')	mophead	crimson-pink	purple	blooms held high above the foliage; free-flowering; blooms turn red in fall	4 to 6' tall; lustrous dark green leaves
'Princess Juliana' ('Juliana')	mophead	white		great cut	
'Quadricolor'	lacecap	pink to pinkish white		late summer flowering	foliage of four distinct colors: pale green, cream, deep green, and yellow; highly unstable and will revert; not cold hardy; a dog, 12" high, no flowers at Atlanta Botanical Garden 18 May 2003
'Red Star'	mophead	red	purple	mid-season	
'Regula' ('White Bouquet')	mophead	white		blooms prolifically; 7 to 8" heads; florets 2"; early to mid-summer	3½' tall; strong-stout growth
'Renate Steiniger' ('San Marcos')	mophead	rose	blue to purple-blue	large heads; early flowering; flowers age to green tinged purple with touches of blue	clear green foliage with uneven teeth; reddish purple fall color; 4 to 5' tall
'Révélation'	mophead	brick red	blue-purple	large heads; excellent for drying	moderate size, compact; lustrous dark green leaves
'Rose Supreme' ('Suprême')	mophead	rose to rosy lavender	rich blue	cupped florets; 7 to 8" heads; early to mid-summer	stems streaked in rose; 4 to 5' tall
'Rosita'	mophead	pink to rose	blue	bunches of rose flowers crowd the plant	strong growing; medium green leaves, significant cold damage at JC Raulston but regrowth with four flowers
'Rotdrössel' ('Red Wing', 'Teller Red')	lacecap	red	deep blue	two rows of sterile flowers surround the fertile flowers	lustrous dark green leaves; have observed heavy leaf spot
'Rotschwanz' (Teller, 'Red Start')	lacecap	red to magenta	blue-purple	mid-sized heads; florets with distinct white star in centers when young; early to mid-summer	foliage with brilliant autumn display; 4' by 4'

'Rosita'

CULTIVAR	FLOWER TYPE	COLOR (-AL)	(+AL)	FLOWER NOTES	FOLIAGE & HABIT NOTES
'Royal Purple' ('Mathilda Gütges')	mophead	rose	deep purple	darker flower heads than most	dense, compact
'San Vito'	mophead	pink, lavender, and white		large, round heads	dark green leaves; yellow fall color; dwarf, compact shrub
'Sara' ('Sarah')	?		dark cobalt fading to inky purple	florets stay partially open instead of flattening; early to mid-summer	shorter, compact habit, 4' by 4'
'Schadendorff's Perle'	mophead	pink	blue	vigorous blooms; large sepals; early	tall growth
'Schenkenberg'	mophead	red	blue-purple	large, mid-July to October	
'Schwan'	mophead	white	white	large flower, mid-season to late	lustrous green leaves; not cold hardy
'Seafoam' ('Sea Foam', 'Maritima')	lacecap	white	mauve-violet		older variety; gray/green leaves; tall to 6'
'Sensation' (see 'Harlequin', 'Monrey'; same as 'Sensation 75'?)	mophead	pink	violet purple with white picotee	summer flowering; bicolor effect stays when dried	medium-sized, lustrous dark green foliage; 4 to 5' by 4 to 5'
'Skips' (same as 'Ayesha'?)					
'Snowcap' ('Snow Cap')	lacecap	mauve-pink	blue		variegated leaves with white center surrounded by green border; low growing to 2 to 2½' tall
'Soeur Thérèse' ('Sister Theresa', 'Petite Soeur Thérèse de l'Enfant Jésus')	mophead	paper white	white	flowers become green tinted with red when ready to dry; delicate	healthy dark green leaves; slender-stemmed; delicate looking; 4 to 6' tall; not cold hardy; inferior to 'Mme Emile Mouillère' for garden culture; died in our Trial Garden
'Souvenir du Pdt. Paul Doumer'	mophead	intense neon pink to dark velvety red	purple to dark blue	mid-season	5 to 6' tall; lustrous dark green foliage; broad rounded leaves, abundant flowers 17 May 2003, half open
'Stene's Pink'	mophead	light to medium pink	blue	large heads; ages to green; can be dried at any stage	small to medium size shrub; yellowish fall color
'Stratford'	mophead	pink	blue		compact plant

'Schwan'

CULTIVAR	FLOWER TYPE	COLOR (−AL)	(+AL)	FLOWER NOTES	FOLIAGE & HABIT NOTES
var. *stylosa* (listed as subsp. *stylosa* by McClintock; see discussion in taxonomy chapter)	lacecap	pink	blue		5' tall; from southerly distribution in Japan and also China that will potentially exhibit more heat tolerance as well as evergreenness; not for cold climates; narrow, light green, hairy leaves and thin, hairy stems
Sun Goddess™ see 'Lemon Zest'					
'Sunset' ('Zeisig', or 'Grasmücke')	lacecap	red	sky blue fading to lavender	early to mid-summer	4' by 3'; appears to be a rename of a Teller selection
'Sybilla', 'Sibilla' see 'Masja'					
'Taube' ('Teller Pink', 'Dove')	lacecap	rich pink	darkest royal blue	large, flattened heads; nearly round sepals; late July through August; ring of sterile florets is always changing as ages	stout growing; 4 to 6' tall
'Tödi'	mophead	rose red with white speckled centers	blue	flowers from May to frost	dark green foliage; good vigor; cold hardy; 3 to 4' tall
'Tokyo Blue'	mophead	pink	blue		strong growth, 4' tall; lustrous dark green leaves; thought it might be 'Nikko Blue', but foliage is different
'Tovelit' ('Tofeelil', 'Tovelil')	mophead	rose to mauve with little white eyes		perfect for cutting; inflorescences to 5" wide, have frizzy effect	rich, dark green foliage; leaves narrow; compact, 3 to 4' tall; weak growing
'Tricolor'	lacecap	soft cream sterile; pink tinged fertile	soft pale blue sterile; blue tinged fertile		vigorous growing; variegation of three colors: deep green, light green, cream; 3 to 4' tall; subject to reversion
'Trophée'	mophead	rich pink	medium blue	vigorous bloomer; double flower	dwarf to medium-sized, 3 to 4' tall
'Trophy'	lacecap	soft cream subtle blue with hint of primrose		described as flowering from May to September; double on the first flush of flowers, possibly single later; inflorescence 8 to 10" across	branch sport of 'Libelle'; found in the garden of Tony Owens; marketed through Pride of Place Plants
'VanHoose White'	lacecap	white ages pink almost immediately after opening			

'Taube'

CULTIVAR	FLOWER TYPE	COLOR (-AL)	(+AL)	FLOWER NOTES	FOLIAGE & HABIT NOTES
'Veitchii'	lacecap	white sterile; pink fertile	white sterile; blue fertile	sepals age to pink; sepals in 3s, sometimes 4s; in shade sepals age to green at Atlanta Botanical Garden, 29 June 2003	dark green foliage; among the hardiest; great breeding parent; frost tolerant foliage; high mildew resistance; flower buds green 17 May 2003; 6' tall at Atlanta Botanical Garden; spectacular in flower; most robust lacecap *H. macrophylla*
'Wave Hill'	lacecap	white sterile; pink fertile	white sterile; blue fertile	minimal flower production; have observed whole plantings with not a single flower while every other hydrangea was loaded; consider for foliage; flowers are bonuses	silvery margined and blotched foliage; sport of 'Tricolor'; variegation is obtrusive; not stable; no flowers 17 May 2003
'Wayne's White'	lacecap	white ages to delicate pale pink		cupped sepals open to large flowers that all but cover the fertile flowers; flowers early and lasts all summer	dark green leaves; 4 to 6' tall
'Westfalen'	mophead	rich rose-red, vivid crimson	blue-purple, violet	beautifully shaped flowers	dwarf to moderate growth; flat medium green leaves; abundant flower buds just showing color on 17 May 2003; spectacular colors
'White Swan' see 'Schwan'					
'White Wave' ('Whitewave', 'Mariesii Grandiflora')	lacecap	pearly white with pink fertile	pearly white with blue fertile	reliable; sepals age light green	medium shrub; 5' high at Atlanta Botanical Garden; robust; one of the more durable lacecaps; abundant flower buds develop from lower on the stems; buds just expanding 17 May 2003, numerous
'Wildenstein'	mophead	pink	blue	flowers early; repeat flowers; large, round heads	
'Winning Edge' see 'Pia'					
'Woodworth White'	mophead	white		prolific flowering	dwarf, compact shrub; yellow fall color
'Zaunkönig' (Teller series, 'Teller Pink')	lacecap	deep pink, almost fluorescent	blue-purple, violet; white to pink fertile flowers	inflorescences to 7" in diameter	handsome foliage; 3 to 4' (5') tall

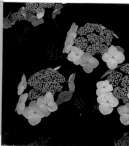

'Veitchii'

'Wave Hill'

Colored pencil drawing of *Hydrangea paniculata* Brussels Lace-17-01.

CHAPTER EIGHT

Hydrangea paniculata
Siebold

PANICLE HYDRANGEA

I refused to allow *Hydrangea paniculata*, particularly 'Grandiflora', into our Midwest garden. In Illinois, few people shared my sentiments, for it was as common as grass. In winter, the large, brown inflorescences are reminiscent of dirty, brown, inflated socks. Ugh! Over the years, the negativity has vaporized with the great number of newer cultivars, and a plant or two have taken residence in the Georgia garden. 'Praecox' was the first but has lost its lease.

Why change, you ask? First, *Hydrangea paniculata* is as easy to culture as crabgrass and—depending on the cultivar—flowers from June ('Praecox') to August and September ('Tardiva'). Second, the stimulus for the change of heart evolved from a 1994 visit to the Stockbridge, Massachusetts, home and studio of Daniel Chester French (1850-1931), sculptor of the Minute Man statue, Concord, Massachusetts, and Abraham Lincoln, Lincoln Memorial, Washington, D.C. *Hydrangea paniculata* lined either side of the walk leading from his studio to the natural area. This seemed the perfect plant for the space and temperament of the site.

The species and cultivars (except 'Praecox') flower on the new growth of the season. Ideally, prune in winter to remove old inflorescences, to improve structure, and to open the plant. Do not massacre the plant by reducing it to stubs. Attempt to develop an architectural framework that deports itself with dignity throughout the seasons. In Athens, leaves emerge

Hydrangea paniculata

between 20 and 30 March. This will occur approximately one month later in Boston. Try to prune before leaf emergence.

The species is typically 10 to 15 (sometimes 20) feet high and can be trained single- or multi-stemmed. The natural propensity is toward the latter. Charles S. Sargent, director of the Arnold Arboretum, reported plants to 30 feet in Japan. Since the species flowers on new growth, it is often stubbed back and produces extended, long shoots, which, under the weight of the flowers ('Grandiflora'), wind, and rain, cascade to the ground.

In early August, Bonnie and I visited the Highlands-Cashiers, North Carolina, region and witnessed more *Hydrangea paniculata* 'Grandiflora' in flower than any two travelers could visually digest. Most were hacked back and flopped to form cascading, white blobs. My primary objection to the typical 'Grandiflora' is the placement, too often prominent, and the general oafishness, clumsiness, and gaucheness of the flowers. Used in a shrub border or mixed (herbaceous and shrub) border, it can prove elegant. The creamy white sepals (showy part of flower) read well in the early morning and late evening light.

The species is variable in all characteristics over its extended native range from Japan, Sakhalin peninsula, and eastern and southern China, Taiwan (disagreement over its presence, although I witnessed a small plant at Maurice Foster's derived from wild-collected Taiwanese seed). McClintock (1957a) mentioned that *Hydrangea paniculata* was a fairly uniform species, showing no particular variation in any of its parts throughout the geographical range. Again, her interpretation was based on herbarium specimens. Horticulturally, significant variation exists based on the great number of cultivars. Also, Crûg Farm mentions a large, heavily flowering form derived from seed collected from Taipingsham north of Taiwan. In botanical literature, the species is described as a lax shrub to 6 feet or of tree stature to 25 to 30 feet. The inflorescences may consist of predominantly fertile (non-showy) flowers, but most of the introductions into cultivation include the showy, sepalous types.

I suspect cold hardiness would vary depending on provenance (seed source location), but almost all cultivars in the United States are adaptable in Zones (3)4 to 8. Rose et al. (2001) place cold hardiness for the species and nine cultivars between -30 and -35°F. I checked four Florida landscape plant references and found no mention of the plant. In Zone 7b, Athens, Georgia, the species and cultivars perform admirably if ample moisture is available into the summer flowering season. I have observed many dog-eared (wilted) *Hydrangea paniculata* after a summer's drought. Without equivocation, the species and cultivars are best suited to Zones 4 to 7, 8 to 9 on the West Coast. Species, 'Grandiflora', 'Limelight', Pink Diamond, 'Ruby', and 'Tardiva' flower reliably in Minneapolis, Minnesota.

The medium to dark green leaves average 3 to 6 inches long and may develop a hint of yellow to reddish purple. Never have I witnessed spectacular fall color, although yellow to muted rose-purple is cited. This is often a difficult species for gardeners to identify. One telltale sign is the presence of three leaves at a node (whorled), particularly on vigorous shoots.

The bark on older branches is gray-brown and develops a ridged and furrowed composition. When limbed up, the bark is quite respectable.

Flowers of the cultivated taxa are a mixture of fertile and sterile (showy sepals) parts in a 6- to 8-inch-long paniculate inflorescence. Fertile flowers are slightly fragrant. The cultivar and pruning practices influence inflorescence size, resulting in 6- to 18-inch-long panicles. Flowers last 4 to 6 weeks, sometimes 8, depending on temperature and moisture. The showy sepals are white and, with maturity, often color pinkish to purplish pink. The cooler the climate, the longer persisting and more showy the flowers. The sepals do not brown as fast in cooler climates and the pink coloration is enhanced and long persistent. Sepals are in clusters of 4s, each entire, and elliptic, ovate, to rounded in shape. Flowering times depend on cultivar with 'Praecox' the earliest, 'Tardiva' about the latest. In Athens, inflorescences of most cultivars and our seedling selections peak around 1 to 15 July. August is the peak month in the Chicago, Illinois, area.

Fruit is a small capsule that houses extremely small seeds. The seeds require no pretreatment and germinate 2 to 4 weeks after sowing. Flowering occurs on seedlings during the second growing season.

Hydrangea paniculata

Hydrangea paniculata is extremely adaptable and will grow in acid and alkaline, moist, and dry soils (once established), as long as drainage is respectable. The species has naturalized as the dominant shrub in a clearing in a red maple swamp, Lincoln, Massachusetts. I have never witnessed a stray seedling. The species prospers in the heavier clay and clay loam soils of the Midwest. During my 1991 sabbatical to the Arnold Arboretum, the summer was dry and the species and cultivars were less than vigorous. This is the most drought tolerant of the major landscape species: *H. arborescens*, *H. macrophylla*, *H. quercifolia*, and *H. serrata*. Flowering is reasonable in partial shade, particularly pine shade in the South, but full sun produces the most floriferous specimens.

I have not observed any serious insects or diseases. Deer will eat the foliage (see chapter 14).

Cuttings are easy to root; our standard procedure is softwood (April through July, Athens) and greenwood (August) material, 1,000 ppm potassium indolebutyric acid, 3 peat:1 perlite and intermittent mist. Cuttings are easily overwintered and grow off quickly when transplanted. Cuttings flower the first growing season after shifting to containers. See chapter 13 for propagation specifics.

Cultivars and Varieties

The cultivars have increased in recent years, with most originating in Europe. The de Belders, Kalmthout Arboretum, Belgium, have introduced more cultivars than all the other hybridizers combined. Many of their introductions are open-pollinated seedlings from their best introductions, like 'Unique' (1968). In 2000, I grew large seedling populations of 'Brussels Lace' and Pink Diamond, with 24 targeted for continued evaluation in 2001. My initial reaction was cautious and subdued because of the numerous cultivars already in commerce. Continued evaluation by nursery friends focused on three that were better than anything on the market. Strong stems, as large as the small finger, white sepals that completely cover the fertile flowers, large inflorescences that do not splay, and disease-free, dark green foliage are hallmarks of these clones.

An Internet and nursery catalog search identified 'Grandiflora' and 'Tardiva' as the most available in American commerce. In addition to the primary cultivars described, another 37 named selections, without supporting literature, were discovered and are listed at the end of the chapter.

'Barbara'

'Barbara' (The Swan™) develops the largest sepals (to 3 inches diameter) I have observed on any *Hydrangea paniculata* selection. The sterile florets, primarily in 4s, are composed of spatulate, concave, white sepals that do not overlap. Panicles are 10 inches long, 6 inches wide, dry well, and are useful for flower arrangements. Full flower 11 July 2003, JC Raulston Arboretum, inflorescences large, loose and floppy, sepalous clusters 3 inches across. Will probably grow 8 to 10 feet high, 5 to 8 feet wide. From the de Belders.

'Bridal Veil' is a supple-branched shrub with thinnish stems and small inflorescences. The sepalous clusters measure about 1½ inches across. Flowers are produced in succession over time. A seedling of 'White Moth' introduced by the de Belders in 1990.

'Brussels Lace' has large panicles, as high as wide, when pruned to a few buds. At Hillier Arboretum in the Centenary Border, panicles measured 10 inches by 10 inches when in full flower on 17 July 1999. Ray flowers are composed of 4 white sepals. Sepals rounded, overlapping, at JC Raulston Arboretum, 25 June 2003. Overall effect of the inflorescence is open and lacy. This is one of the first cultivars (after 'Praecox') to flower. On 3 June 2003, I evaluated the *Hydrangea paniculata* taxa at the JC Raulston Arboretum, and the 'Brussels Lace' sepals were about half developed and still cream-green. Full flower on 25 June 2003. True to form, only 'Praecox'

'Brussels Lace'

showed greater sepal development. The sepals become spotted with pink as they mature. Not as large growing, perhaps 6 to 8 feet high. Seedling of 'Unique' selected by the de Belders in 1975. Has been suggested that 'White Lace' is the same as 'Brussels Lace'.

'Burgundy Lace' is a de Belder selection from seedlings of 'Unique'. When grown in full sun, the white, sterile flowers become beautiful pink, and mature to mauve and light violet. Individual sterile florets are 1.2 to 1.6 inches wide. Inflorescences have an average length of 10 inches and an average width of 6 inches. The plant grows 10 to 14 feet high. The photograph I saw was spectacular and sufficient reason to at least test this form. I suspect high summer heat may reduce the intensity of the pink coloration.

'Chantilly Lace'

'Chantilly Lace' is a seedling of 'Tardiva' selected by the author and Kay Bowman, former director of the Center for Applied Nursery Research. In the heat of the South, the inflorescences are held on strong stems and do not "flag." Even mixture of showy, glistening white sepals and off-white, fertile flowers. Sepals become pink in September. A brief horticultural description follows per the release from the University of Georgia and the Center for Applied Nursery Research, Dearing, Georgia.

Habit: To date (six years old), tallest plant is 6 feet high and wide, with strong ascending branches that hold the flowers upright without the splaying of 'Grandiflora'.

Leaves: The darkest green of any *Hydrangea paniculata* cultivar.

Flowers: Inflorescences average 9½ inches high and 6½ inches wide. The combination of showy sepals and fertile flowers produces a balanced inflorescence, neither too sparse nor too heavy. Flowers open in mid-June and are still white in July, turning pink with the advent of cooler weather in September, remaining colorful into November.

'Dharuma'

'Dharuma' ('Daruma', 'Darlido'). A smaller plant and inflorescences with fewer sterile florets; witnessed in England and was not impressed; a different form with bigger, more abundant sepals is being grown by several southeastern nurserymen; as I witnessed the plant, the sparks did not fly; noticed the white sepals age to rose; listed at 4 feet high; appears to flower earlier, for sepals had aged to rose by 10 July 2003, at Hawksridge Nursery, Hickory, North Carolina.

'Floribunda', an older (1867) Japanese cultivar, was introduced to the St. Petersburg Botanical Garden in Russia by Maximowicz. The conical inflorescence is a mixture of primarily fertile flowers with a sprinkling of showy flowers. The inflorescences may grow 18 inches long and 6 inches wide at the base; typically about 12 inches long. Each showy floret is composed of 4 to 5, ⅝- to ¾-inch-long, elliptic to rounded, overlapping sepals. White sepals age to pink. Later flowering, often late July to early August. Grows to 15 feet high. Just coming into flower on 24 July 2001 at RHS Garden Wisley, England.

'Floribunda'

'Grandiflora' ('Minazuki') is the granddaddy of the group with massive panicles of white, primarily sterile, flowers with sepals that age to pink and purple-pink. The primary form in cultivation, it was introduced in the 1860s by von Siebold from Japan. Haworth-Booth (1984) writes, "By pruning and thinning, enormous lumps of flower can be produced. The panicle, almost entirely composed of the large, sterile flowers, sometimes attains 18 inches high and 12 inches through at the base." Typical inflorescences average 8 to

'Grandiflora'

12 inches long and 4 to 6 inches wide. Size of the inflorescence depends on pruning and plant vigor. Peaks in late July and remains effective to early September at the Morton Arboretum, Lisle, Illinois. Plants left to their own devices have smaller flowers, often broad-conical with length equaling width. Typically grows 8 to 10 feet tall, although I have witnessed many 15-footers in Maine, where the plant is highly recommended by moose for landscaping cabins. Bonnie and I visited Portland, Maine, in mid-October 2002 and noticed beautiful, large 'Grandiflora', the flowers rich rose-red to burgundy-rose.

'Greenspire' ('Green Spire', Green Fantasy™) produces pale greenish white showy sepals, turning white then green at end of flowering season. Somewhat similar to 'Kyushu', which produces a mixture of fertile and showy flowers. The long conical inflorescences reach 12 inches long and 8 inches wide. Sepals were small and sparse on the lone plant I observed. Full flower 11 July 2003 at JC Raulston Arboretum. Listed by Mal Condon, Nantucket, Massachusetts, as a strong upright grower and one of his favorites. Late July to September. A seedling of 'Unique', selected by the de Belders in 1975.

'Kyushu'

'Kyushu' is an upright selection with lustrous, dark green foliage and panicles mixed with fertile and sterile flowers. Touted by many as one of the better forms. I saw it for the first time at the Arnold Arboretum and, though beautiful in flower, it had suffered from the drought. My overall landscape impression is minimally enthusiastic: the number of ray flowers is limited compared to the fertile, and the sepals are relatively small. Full flower 11 July 2003, JC Raulston Arboretum. Originated from cuttings collected by Captain Collingwood Ingram in Kyushu, Japan. Distributed by the de Belders.

'Limelight' ('Lime Light') is promoted as producing bright lime-green flowers, however, as I observed it at Dudley Nursery, Thomson, Georgia, the flowers simulated those of 'Grandiflora'. Sepals are white with smaller, more uniform inflorescences; I suspect the heat of Zone 7 results in the expression of white. Condon confirms the white color in his Nantucket, Massachusetts, garden. Stems were weak with inflorescences, producing a weeping willow effect on the container-grown plants. Promos state flowers are fresh green in 10- to 12-inch-long, 6- to 7-inch-wide panicles, held on strong stems, grows 6 to 10 feet, 5 to 6 feet wide, rounded shrub, moderate grower. Hybridized by Pieter Zwijnenburg.

'Limelight'

'Little Lamb' ('Klein Schaapje') produces small inflorescences, the sepals largely covering the fertile flowers. The name is derived from the "appearance of little lambs," contrasting with the foliage. Grows 6 to 8 feet high. Another de Belder introduction.

'Meehanii' is listed by Arrowhead Alpines, Fowlerville, Michigan, without a horticultural description.

'Melody' produces roughly 14-inch-long, 7- to 8-inch-wide inflorescences in early summer. Mixture of sepals and fertile flowers. Fertile flowers dominate the inflorescence. Plant grows 12 to 15 feet high. A seedling of 'Unique'. Introduced by the de Belders in 1985.

'Mount Everest' ('Everest') is a large shrub, 12 feet and higher, with late-season large dense panicles composed of cream-white sepals turning pale pink in late summer and fall. Condon reported the large panicles were particularly attractive and similar to 'Barbara' (The Swan™). The fertile flowers are described as pale pink. Foliage is dark green. A stronger habit than 'Grandiflora'. Introduced circa 1989 by Hillier Arboretum.

'**Papillon**' is yet another 'Unique' seedling introduced by the de Belders in 1985. A strong grower, 12 feet and more, with an abundance of sterile florets with raised sepals, producing the effect of a cloud of white butterflies. Flowers from August until frost.

'**Pee Wee**' produces small inflorescences similar in constitution and shape to 'Grandiflora'. I have grown this for several years in the Georgia trials, and it is more shrublike, with smaller leaves and finer-textured branches. Probably 6 to 8 feet high at landscape maturity. Not as obtrusive and obnoxious as big sister. This grows next to 'Grandiflora', and together they remind me of Dr. Evil and Mini Me.

Pink Diamond ('Interhydia'). The large conical inflorescences are composed of fertile and showy flowers with the showy sepals turning rich pink. Many gardeners have been disappointed with the lack of pink sepal coloration. Forms a large plant. Confused in American commerce. A seedling of 'Unique'. Introduced by the de Belders.

'**Pink Wave**' produces long shoots with 8-inch by 8-inch panicles, the fertile flowers greenish white, the sterile florets concave up to 1 inches across. Sepals pure white, then greenish white, finally pink; the fertile flowers also change to reddish pink. Grows 8 to 10 feet high. Introduced by Edouard d'Andeew, circa 1980.

'Praecox'

'**Praecox**' is the earliest to flower (mid-June in the Dirr garden) with smaller inflorescences with a mixture of fertile and showy flowers. The sepals (4) of ray flowers, about 1 inch across, are elliptic to ovate and scarcely overlapping. The inflorescences are smaller, perhaps to 6 inches long, than some of the other forms. This selection flowers on last season's growth and should not be pruned until after flowering. The sepals are prominently toothed, an obvious difference from those of the species. The leaves are larger, more rugose and undulating than those of the species.

The original plant, still growing at the Arnold Arboretum, is more than 100 years old, a testimonial to its inherent landscape adaptability. From the literature I surveyed, the origin is attributed to Charles S. Sargent of the Arnold Arboretum, who discovered this form in the wilds of Japan. He collected seeds in 1893, from which the Arnold's current specimen in derived. The parent plant was about 12 to 15 feet tall and 18 to 20 feet wide in 1991.

'Praecox', Arnold Arboretum

'Ruby' (Angel Blush™). A seedling of Pink Diamond with white sepals deepening to pink and deeper colors later in the season. Introduced by the de Belders in 1990. I have grown 'Ruby' for several years in our garden, and it has never lived up to this description. Actually has proved a weak shrub with rather insignificant flowers.

'Tardiva' extends the flowering season into late August and September (October and November on Nantucket). The inflorescences are a mixture of fertile and sterile flowers. Sterile flowers are composed of primarily 4 sepals. Depending on weather conditions (cooler), the sepals turn pinkish. Just developing inflorescences on 25 June 2003, at JC Raulston Arboretum. This selection has gained momentum in the nursery and landscape trades.

'Tardiva'

'Unique' was grown and introduced in 1968 by the de Belders for its large, pure white, sterile florets (about 2 inches across) and rounded sepals. The showy sepals almost completely conceal the fertile flowers. The inflorescences may reach 16 inches long by 10 inches wide. This selection resulted from seedlings of 'Floribunda'. The seedlings were uprooted by birds, and the one plant that remained was properly termed 'Unique'. The plant will grow 10 to 14 feet high. Later flowering, approximately mid-July in Zone 7b.

This cultivar is horribly confused in nursery commerce, and seldom is the true form, as described, provided. I have grown three so-called 'Unique',

'Unique'

none true-to-description. A great plant friend, Ted Stephens, Nurseries Caroliniana, North Augusta, South Carolina, and I commiserated about the almost total confusion. Ted was able to secure the *true* 'Unique' from Mike Buffin, curator at the Hillier Arboretum, and now offers same as True Unique.

'Vera' produces large quantities of small inflorescences, the white sterile florets on long stalks. Flowers develop in August and September.

'Webb's' is most aptly described as an improvement of 'Grandiflora' with primarily sterile flowers and a uniform, broad-conical head. The sepals are pure white and age to a purplish pink. Photos I took in mid-October at Byers Nursery, Inc., in Huntsville, Alabama, attest to its late-season staying power. It was selected by J. A. Webb of Huntsville. This would make a good cut flower as, in fact, many of the *Hydrangea paniculata* selections do. Has grown for many years in the Dirr garden. Inflorescences are heavy and do initiate branch sway. Later flowering with green flower buds just emerging on 11 July 2003 at JC Raulston Arboretum.

'Webb's'

'White Moth' is a seedling selection from 'Unique' that was raised by the de Belders at Kalmthout. It flowers over a longer period than 'Unique' and produces new flowers that are intermingled with faded inflorescences. The inflorescences are irregular spheres and average 14 to 16 inches diameter. The flowers age to soft pink and invert as they mature. The sepals are ovate to ovate-rounded and occur in 4s and 5s, essentially covering the fertile flowers. Have counted up to 7 sepals per cluster. Average height is only 6 to 7 feet. At Wisley (26 July 2001) this cultivar was in full flower before 'Brussels Lace' and 'Burgundy Lace'. Weak growing at JC Raulston Arboretum; better at Atlanta Botanical Garden. Open, loose inflorescences, lustrous dark green leaves on 29 June 2003.

Readers should remember that the majority of these selections were evaluated in a cool, continental European climate that seldom experiences high heat, day and night, or the high humidity of the United States. Many gardeners have been overwhelmed by the hyperbole of performance, only to be disappointed.

The literature revealed many *Hydrangea paniculata* cultivars about which information is scant or nonexistent. They are listed herein for information only.

'White Moth'

'Akazukin'

'Big Ben'

'Boskoop'

Dart's Little Dot®

'Degudo' (correct name for 'Perle d'Automne')

'Dolly'

'Dwarf'

×*paniculata* 'Excelsior'

'Ezo Nori Utsugi' = 'Praecox'?

'Goliath'

'Great Escape'

'Lamette'

'Little Belgium'

'Little Dot' = Dart's Little Dot®

'Martinvast'

'Mathilde'

'Mega Pearl'

'Mid Late Summer'

'Mini K'

'Mont Aso'

'Mustila'

'National Arboretum'

'Nori-utsugi' ('Daruma Nori Utsugi')

'October Bride'

'Perle d'Automne' = 'Starlight Fantasy', 'Degustar', 'Degudo'

'Phantom'

'Pink Cloud'

'Pink Lady'

'Pinky Winky'

'Silver Dollar'

'Skylight'

'Super Pink'

'Tender Rose'

'Utsuri Beni'

'Velutina' [f. *velutina* (Nakai) Kitamura]

'White Lace' = 'Brussels Lace'?

'White Lady'

Identification Characteristics

Leaves: Opposite, sometimes whorled, especially on flowering and vigorous shoots, simple, 3 to 6 inches long, $1\frac{1}{2}$ to 3 inches wide, elliptic or ovate, acuminate, rounded or cuneate at base, serrate, medium to dark green and sparingly pubescent or nearly glabrous above, setose pubescent beneath, particularly on the veins; petiole, $\frac{1}{2}$ to 1 inch long. About the latest for leaf emergence among the major species. New leaves emerge green, typically without any red pigmentation, although petioles may be red. Also, pubescence is minimal compared to *Hydrangea heteromalla* and *H. aspera*. In 'Praecox', the leaves emerge soft yellow.

Buds: Imbricate, rounded, globose, 4- to 6-scaled, glabrous, brownish in color, sometimes with whorled character.

Stem: Emerging shoots, green to reddish, pubescent, later glabrous, stout, grayish to reddish brown, bark showing gray vertically streaked areas; older wood, 1 to 2 inches or greater, becomes gray-brown, ridged-and-furrowed; often quite handsome especially when lower branches are removed.

Flowers: Panicle, conical, pyramidal, in some cultivars like 'White Moth' blockily rounded, (3)6 to 8(10) inches long, 4 to 5 inches wide at base, numerous yellow-white fertile flowers, sterile flowers in 4s and 5s, white to pink, $\frac{3}{4}$ to $1\frac{1}{4}$ inches wide, each sepal elliptical, ovate, to rounded, entire; flowers originate on new growth of the season, flowers open from the base to apex.

CHAPTER NINE

Hydrangea quercifolia
Bartram

OAKLEAF HYDRANGEA

A March day in the garden, feverishly picking and shoveling to create enough holes (notice I did not say "planting spaces") to empty winter's accumulation of 30 or so 3-gallon containers. Occasionally, I raise up, to a chorus of snap, crackle, and pop, and across the grass, small, gray-gloved leaves, clasped in prayer, motion me to slow down and enjoy the garden. Pretty clever plants, these oakleaf hydrangeas! Divine intervention is truly manifested in remarkable ways.

Consider for a brief moment *Hydrangea quercifolia*, this most beautiful native shrub. Texture, flowers, fall color, exfoliating bark, and unusual cultivars are the great attributes. Fussiness under container culture, sun-shyness (particularly in the South), and disheveled winter habit might be considered liabilities. Once ensconced in the garden, all is forgiven—as for the puppy who chewed the slippers—because there is much to love.

The late J. C. McDaniel at the University of Illinois schooled me in the variation and intrinsic beauty of this southeastern native. Joe grew a number of clones in his Urbana, Illinois, garden, but 'Harmony' is the one I most remember. It was discovered by his father, Thomas Arthur McDaniel, in the Harmony Baptist Church Cemetery in Attalla, Alabama. The large, predominantly sterile inflorescences weighed branches to the ground.

Joe mentioned that in certain years the species did not flower due to winter kill of flower buds. During my seven years in Urbana, the lowest temperature was -20°F. The foliage alone is exquisite and provides justifiable reason to grow the plant in northern gardens (Zone 5). The Morton Arboretum, Lisle, Illinois, reported some dieback in winter but flowering every summer from late June through July.

Hydrangea quercifolia

From the southern perspective, I have observed plants in Charleston, South Carolina; Lee and Bristol (wild), Florida; Savannah and Pine Mountain (wild), Georgia; and in supra abundance (garden and wild) in Birmingham, Alabama, performing well in shade. In Athens, *Hydrangea quercifolia* is sited in full sun to heavy shade situations. Best long-term performance is always realized in partial to significant shade settings in the Southeast. In the Boston area, the species adapts to sun and shade environments as long as moisture is provided during severe drought. Dan Hinkley mentioned in the Heronswood Nursery catalog that the species performs best in more open, sunny conditions in his Washington garden.

A check of herbarium specimens revealed a range of habitats in Georgia and Alabama from slopes above the Chattahoochee, Catoosa, Coosa, and Coosawatte rivers, consistently in the understory and often in calcareous or limestone-rock soils. Frequently, it is found growing in the company of *Hydrangea arborescens*. Moist, rich woodlands, slopes, stream banks, and ravines, consistently well drained, provide the normal habitat in the wild. However, the extended droughts in the Southeast from 1997 to 2002 did not appear to reduce native populations. The range extends from Georgia (18 western counties), northwest Florida, to Louisiana, north to central Tennessee, Alabama, and Mississippi. Alabama may hold the largest native stands for along I-20, about 20 miles east of downtown Birmingham, the understory is rife with seedlings. In late May 2002, the forest floor was illuminated by 10,000 Soft White Light Bulbs. In late March 2003, the soft gray leaves were just emerging. In late December 2002, Bonnie and I hiked Torreya State Park, Bristol, Florida, where 10-foot-high seedlings were present on slopes above the Apalachicola River. I enjoy, enormously, observing plants in their native habitats while mentally extrapolating to their potential adaptability in garden settings. Sometimes extrapolation correlates closely with native conditions; often not.

In Europe, the species is greatly prized; however, the quantity and quality of flowers are less formidable than what I observe on garden plants in the United States. Most authorities attribute this to lack of summer heat. However, *Hydrangea macrophylla*, *H. serrata*, *H. arborescens*, and *H. paniculata* flower with reckless abandon in the cool European climate.

Hydrangea quercifolia, mature rosy sepals

Bonnie and I grow seedlings, 'Alice', 'Alison', 'Back Porch', 'Dayspring', 'Late Hand', 'Pee Wee', 'Sikes Dwarf', 'Snowflake', and Snow Queen® in the garden. The species and cultivars mesh well with *Loropetalum chinense* var. *rubrum*, *Michelia figo*, *Kerria japonica*, *Illicium* species, *Osmanthus* species, *Helleborus orientalis*, *Sarcococca* species, and bulbs. The broadleaf evergreens, as background and groundcovers skirting the branches, highlight the flowers and bold-textured leaves.

On 22 March 2003, tidying, pruning, and raking our garden, I reflected for sufficient time to appreciate the beauty of an understory planting of abelia, camellia, viburnum, anise, Japanese maples, tea-olives, and oakleaf hydrangea. The decidedly picturesque and stalwart performer was the *Hydrangea quercifolia*. Might note that the species is more persistent than *H. macrophylla* and *H. serrata*, possibly not up to the staying power of *H. arborescens* and *H. paniculata*. Tremendously old colonies in Athens, no doubt planted when the houses were built, attest to the longevity of the species. I estimate some are 100 years of age.

Oakleaf hydrangea is now a commodity item in nursery production and garden centers. I surveyed four Georgia growers, and all indicated that sales were through the roof. Dudley Nurseries, Inc., in Thomson, Georgia, produces about 7,000 *Hydrangea quercifolia* encompassing 'Alice', 'Snowflake', and seedlings. Monrovia Growers at Wight Nurseries in Cairo, Georgia, grows 10,000, 5-gallon 'Alice'; 20,000 seedlings in 5s; and 20,000 seedlings in 1s. McCorkle Nurseries, Inc., in Dearing, Georgia, produces 30,000 to 40,000 'Alice' in 3-gallons. Griffith Propagation Nursery in Watkinsville, Georgia, produced and sold 10,000 'Alice' liners with calls for another 10,000. Commerce is booming in the land of the oakleaf hydrangea.

Typically, growth habit is irregular rounded with a colonizing tendency. I measured two old colonies in Athens, one 10 feet by 15 feet, another 9 feet by 15 feet. 'Alice', which was discovered on the Georgia campus, is now more that 12 feet high. 'Pee Wee' in the Dirr garden is about 3 feet high after six years. Typical species sizes range from 4 to 6(8) feet. Plants in shade are always more loose than those grown in full sun. Branches will layer naturally when leaves and organic materials accumulate around the plant. I noticed the 'Alice' oakleaf in our garden continues to enlarge as the new rooted branches send out more disciples.

A remarkable attribute is the ability to flower in dense shade. Oakleaf hydrangea, *Aesculus parviflora* (bottlebrush buckeye), and *A. sylvatica* (painted buckeye) are three of the best native shrubs for shady borders. In the Dirr garden, the various cultivars of oakleaf hydrangea grow under *Quercus falcata* (southern red oak) and *Q. nigra* (water oak) and prosper. Supplemental water is a requisite when extended drought occurs.

Hydrangea quercifolia, fall color

Leaves, reminiscent of those of red oak, *Quercus rubra*, lend credence to the common name. Dark green, sometimes glossy above, grayish pubescent lower surfaces, turn muted burgundy to reddish purple in fall. 'Alison' has consistently produced outstanding red-purple fall color in our garden. I might add that even seedling-grown plants produce respectable autumn color. Leaves, emerging and mature, are remarkably frost tolerant. In Athens, temperatures between 15 and 20°F did not kill young leaves (March) or mature leaves (November).

Winter habit is a tad scary with flaying cinnamon-brown stems jiggling in all directions from the crown. The papery, sheathing bark, polished with moisture after a winter rain, softens the elegant entropy of the wandering stems.

Hydrangea quercifolia, bark

Insect problems are practically nonexistent. Leaf spots occur, particularly with overhead water in production settings. Shoots exhibit dieback, akin to rhododendron wilt. This occurs in container-grown plants, particularly under excessive moisture. My approach is to prune dead branches and remove old inflorescences, usually in late March when the leaves emerge. See chapter 14 for specifics.

Flowers, glorious panicles of white to cream-white, rising above the mature foliage in mid-May to mid-June (Athens), induce increased heart rates. To afford some concept of flowering date differentials, I experienced the species in flower on 22 April 2003, in Thomasville, Georgia, 200 miles south of Athens. Mid-May and later are typical peak times for Athens, while late June and July are optimal for the Chicago, Illinois, area. This flowering profile can be applied with some variation to other hydrangeas described herein. When garden books state that a particular plant flowers in June, the timeline has limited meaning. Panicles range from 4 to 12 inches long, 3 to 4(6) inches wide, with a mix of fertile flowers and showy sepals. Sepals occur in 4s and are typically rounded and entire. Sepals overlap at their edges, creating a singular-unit effect. Often, as sepals mature, they color pink, rose, to burgundy. One particular clone I found had the most beautiful burgundy-wine coloration that persisted even on cut and dried panicles. Bonnie considered this selection one of the most beautiful and named it 'Amethyst'. Technically this name is illegal under the rules of nomenclature for cultivated plants since the same cultivar name cannot be given to two separate species within the genus, and a *Hydrangea macrophylla* 'Amethyst' also exists. Stock is now being increased for eventual release. Flower buds are formed the year before opening, and pruning should be accomplished after the floral extravaganza.

Flowers develop on old wood and pruning should take place after flowers are spent. In our Georgia work, pruning one-half of the plant as late as mid-August allowed for flower bud development and expression the next year. Remember that plants still have $2\frac{1}{2}$ months of temperatures conducive to growth and flower bud development in the Athens area.

Fruit is a bell-shaped, strongly 8- to 10-ribbed, dull brown capsule that dehisces by a pore between the persistent styles. The dull brown seeds are strongly ribbed and less than $\frac{1}{25}$ inch long. Most cultivars have many to few perfect flowers that, if pollinated, develop capsules of no ornamental significance. The tiny brown seeds can be sprinkled on top of a seeding mix, not covered, placed under mist, and will germinate in 2 to 4 weeks. Seedlings are small and require careful attention to moisture until $\frac{1}{2}$ to 1 inch high. At this time, they can be transplanted to cells. In our shop, numerous seedlings have been grown to flowering in two years. Seeds sown in January 1997, flowered in summer 1998.

Hydrangea quercifolia, buds

Cuttings root readily, and in the old days I always focused on firm wood cuttings. At the Center for Applied Nursery Research, Dearing, Georgia, 16 April 1998, softwood cuttings (treated with 1,500-ppm KIBA, direct stuck, 3 per 3-gallon container) rooted and, with proper pruning, produced marketable plants by late July. This work was carried into mid-August (last prune), and flowers were produced in almost equal numbers the following spring on plants left unpruned or pruned in mid-June, mid-July, and mid-August. Pruning improved plant form; at least two prunings are recommended. Tissue culture has been a source of liners, and several laboratories are producing significant numbers.

Cultivars and Varieties

Cultivars have mushroomed, and many nurseries are striving to improve upon the species. In England, while on sabbatical in 1999, I experienced a soft yellow leaf form (branch sport) of 'Pee Wee' discoverered by Peter Catt, Liss Forest Nursery, England (see discussion of this selection, 'Little Honey', at 'Pee Wee'). More recently, from North Georgia nurseryman Vaughn Billingsley, a seedling selection with compact habit, ball-like sterile flowers, and deep burgundy fall color was brought to my attention. This selection, named 'Vaughn's Lillie' after Billingsley's wife, is patented (PP 12,982). The following list is significant considering that in the first edition of my *Manual* (1975), three were listed, and Toni Lawson-Hall and Brian Rothera (1995) describe the same number in *Hydrangeas: A Gardener's Guide*; in the 1998 *Hillier Manual of Trees and Shrubs*, two cultivars are described, and in the 2002 edition, five are presented.

'Alice'. In the 1990 edition of *Manual of Woody Landscape Plants*, I was reticent about this selection, but the industry, particularly McCorkle Nurseries, Inc., Dearing, Georgia, brought this cultivar into commercial production. The parent plant was 12 feet high and wide, with

'Vaughn's Lillie'

'Alice'

10- to 14-inch-long inflorescences on vigorous shoots, about 8 to 10 inches long on less active growth. Cream-white sepals, almost halfdollar-size, cover the fertile flowers and age to pink-rose as they mature. The dark green summer foliage turns burgundy-red in autumn. Has proven easier to grow in containers, quite vigorous; more sun tolerant and is grown in full sun at Monrovia Growers at Wight Nurseries, Cairo, Georgia, all other seedlings and cultivars in shade. I selected this cultivar from a seedling plant on the Georgia campus and named it after former Georgia horticulture student and research technician Alice Richards. Serendipity is amazing, and 'Alice' is on the fast track to becoming the volume leader in nursery production. Diane Dunn, propagator, Greenleaf Nursery, Park Hill, Oklahoma, reported the company is growing almost 100,000 'Alice' per year.

'Alison'. This clone was discovered and named at the same time as 'Alice'. Again, found by the author on the Georgia campus. Flowers are 10 inches long, some up to 12 inches, equal distribution of fertile flowers and showy sepals, pyramidal inflorescence held more upright than 'Alice'. Grows 8- to 10-feet high and is broader spreading than 'Alice'.

'Alison', fall color

Foliage is lustrous dark green with stunning almost fluorescent red-burgundy fall color. I told most people to grow 'Alice' after the feedback from McCorkle but am enthusiastic about both cultivars. In November, Bonnie and I were touring the garden and commented on how spectacular the fall color appeared. Both clones flower in late May to early June in Athens. Easy to root from cuttings. 'Alison' was named after Alison Arnold, one of my master of science students.

'Amethyst'. Smaller statured and more compact, to 6 feet high and wide. Flowers average 6 inches in length, sepals cream-white, turning wine-red and holding the color when dry. Flowers are held upright and remind me of those of Snow Queen®. Fall color is red to reddish purple. Selection by the author.

'Applause'. With deeply cut leaves and wine-red fall color. From the Netherlands.

'Back Porch'. Early-flowering, vigorous, with pretty, large, white flowers that mature pink. Louisiana Nursery introduction.

'Amethyst'

'Burgundy'. With shiny leaves and wine-red fall color. From the Netherlands.

'Camelot'. Vigorous, large, upright conical inflorescences, deep red fall color. From Mary Nell McDaniel, Urbana, Illinois.

'Cloud Nine'. Handsome, large, showy, white flowers. Louisiana Nursery introduction.

'Dayspring' ('Day Spring'). With large, white flowers; deep green foliage turns red-bronze in fall. Have grown this in the garden and see no great difference between this and better seedlings. Flowerwood Nursery introduction.

'Amethyst', mature sepals

'Ellen Huff'. Vigorous selection from Gulf Coast with good heat tolerance. Flowers large with a mix of showy sepals and fertile flowers.

'Emerald Lake'. See 'Wade Mahlke'.

'Gloster Form'. Vigorous, with 5 sepals in each cluster. It does exceptionally well in the South. Louisiana Nursery introduction.

'Harmony'

'Harmony'. Mostly sterile, large paniculate inflorescences, 12 inches long and 8 inches wide, white; will develop pink tinge; will weigh down the branches. Interesting and unusual but not as elegant as 'Snowflake' and Snow Queen®. Inflorescences a bit lumpy and bumpy, aesthetically difficult to digest. A large shrub to 10 feet. One of the best plantings is housed at Cedar Lane Farms, Madison, Georgia.

Hovaria® 'Quercifolia'. A selection from the Hofstedes, breeders of the Hovaria® *Hydrangea macrophylla* series. Have only seen a photograph of this rather compact form with abundant inflorescences.

'Joe McDaniel'. Vigorous with large showy white flowers. Collected in the South by McDaniel himself; offered by Louisiana Nursery.

'John Wayne'. Large showy white flowers. Does well all over the South. Excellent reddish purple fall color in the Dirr garden. Selected from Florida; offered by Louisiana Nursery.

'Late Hand'. Choice late-flowering clone with large "hand-like" lobed leaves and pretty white flowers. It extends the flowering season about one month. Louisiana Nursery introduction.

'Little Honey'. See discussion under 'Pee Wee'.

'Luverne Pink'. An attractive, bushy, medium-sized clone with pretty white flowers aging to a deep pink. Louisiana Nursery introduction.

'Lynn Lowrey'. Superior form introduced by Tom Dodd III and named after the late Lynn Lowrey. Large-growing type selected from a Louisiana provenance. Should show increased heat tolerance because of southern origin. Flowers are a mixture of fertile and sterile, like the species. Full flower on 3 June 2003 at JC Raulston Arboretum, with 8- to 10-inch-long inflorescences, the sepals covering 80 percent of the fertile flowers. Inflorescences arching due to their weight. Large shrub, 8 feet or more at maturity. 'Angola Prison' is possibly the same.

'Montmorenci Rose'. With flowers opening white, turning deep pink a week later. Found in a garden in Montmorenci, South Carolina, by Paul Crosby. Offered by Nurseries Caroliniana, North Augusta, South Carolina.

'Patio Pink'. Vigorous, early flowering, white flowers age pink, large leaves, good fall color. Louisiana Nursery introduction.

'Lynn Lowrey'

'Patio White' is listed in the *Hydrangea International Index*.

'Pee Wee'. Compact form, 2 to 3 feet tall and wide with leaves and flowers more refined. Has received rave notices from Atlanta gardeners. Have heard

'Pee Wee'

sizes to 3½ to 4½ feet high by 6 feet wide; in six years in the Dirr garden it has reached 3 feet tall and wide. The inflorescence is 4 to 5 inches long, somewhat broad-pyramidal shaped, almost appearing 4-sided. Sepals are delicate, small, abundant, and almost hide the fertile flowers. An excellent form for small gardens. Rose to red-purple fall color has occurred on plants in the Dirr garden. It suffered slight tip dieback in Orono, Maine—of course, it may have had snow cover. Peter Catt's soft yellow leaf sport of 'Pee Wee' is still under evaluation. Yellow supposedly holds into

summer with leaves turning red in fall. Briggs Nursery, Olympia, Washington, has produced this selection via tissue culture, and the name will be 'Little Honey'.

'Picnic Hill'. A vigorous bushy form with short internodes and handsome flowers. Louisiana Nursery introduction.

Pink Forms. Pink sepal color when opening, rather than aging to pink and rose. Know of one in Alabama, another in Pennsylvania. If the pink holds under nursery production, these selections will have great consumer appeal.

'Roanoke'. Loose and more open inflorescence than 'Harmony'. Actually the differences are minimal. Flowers will weigh down the branches. A massive planting at Bernheim Arboretum is 10 feet high, 30 feet wide, and spectacular as I viewed it on 24 June 1997.

'Roanoke'

'Semmes Beauty' is a more heat-tolerant selection suitable for planting in the Gulf Coast and lower South. The plant is vigorous and has large inflorescences with showy sepals and fertile flowers interspersed.

'Shannon' is a double with up to 20 sepals per cluster, double clusters not densely borne, open inflorescence, compact habit, 4 feet high, wider than tall. Introduced by the late Theodore Klein, Crestwood, Kentucky. Paul Cappiello, Yew-Dell, Crestwood, Kentucky, discussed this cultivar at the 2003 Southern Plant Conference; his slides show flowers held more upright than those of 'Snowflake'.

'Sikes Dwarf'. A dwarf clone, described as 2 to 2½ feet high, up to 4 feet across. It has pretty white flowers and attractive leaves. A plant in the Dirr garden is 3 to 4 feet high and supersedes published sizes. Inflorescences are larger than those of 'Pee Wee'. Sandra Reed is utilizing this, 'Pee Wee', and

'Snowflake', maturing
inflorescences

Snow Queen® to breed for compact types with improved foliage and fall color. Paul Cappiello related that plants he purchased as 'Sikes Dwarf' from different sources were variable.

'Snowflake'. Multiple sepals emerge on tops of older ones, creating a double-flowered appearance. Panicles are 12 to 15 inches long. It is actually the most beautiful of the sterile-flowered forms. Grows to 7 to 8 feet at maturity. As is true with 'Harmony' and 'Roanoke', the heads are heavy and the branches may be weighed down, but never to the degree of those two. It prefers moist soil and partial shade. A staple in the Dirr garden for over 15 years. Flowers slightly later than the single types, and flowers hold and age more gracefully. Usually mature parchment color without traces of pink. I toured the new Aldridge Gardens, Hoover, Alabama, dedicated in 2002 and which promises to collect and display extensive hydrangea collections; here

Snow Queen®

at Eddie Aldridge's former home, I witnessed gigantic plantings of 'Snowflake', over 10 feet high, growing in pine shade. Aldridge Nursery introduction.

'Snow Giant'. Large, lightly fragrant, snow-white flowers in early to midsummer. Leaves crimson-red in fall. This is the description provided by Piroche Plants in Pitt Meadows, British Columbia. Plants grown at the University of Georgia and the Center for Applied Nursery Research produced flowers similar to 'Snowflake'. I believe 'Snow Giant' is a rename.

'Snow Hill' is listed in the *Hydrangea International Index.*

Snow Queen® ('Flemygea'). An improvement of the species with larger and more numerous sterile florets that provide a more dense, solid appearance. Six- to 8-inch long inflorescences are held upright and do not bend or arch like many seedling plants. Leaves are dark green and hold up in the sun better than seedlings. Leaves turn deep red-bronze in fall. Flowers turn a good pink as they mature. More compact grower, possibly 6 feet high at landscape maturity. It is slower growing than 'Alice', particularly in containers. No damage at -22°F. A Princeton Nursery introduction. Not as robust in the Southeast and has fizzled out over the years in the Dirr garden while 'Alice', 'Pee Wee', 'Sikes Dwarf', and 'Snowflake' have persisted.

'Summit'. Produces narrow, conical inflorescences, shaped like ice-cream cones, 7 inches by 2 inches. Plant is 4 feet high, wider than tall. Introduced by the late Theodore Klein.

'Tennessee Clone' ('Tennessee'). Flowers listed to 10 inches long, 8 inches wide. A great abundance of 4 to 5 wavy sepals, white with hint of pale green, turning green at maturity. It grows 6 to 7 feet high, from seed collected in Tennessee, introduced in 1974 by Jelena and Robert de Belder.

'Turkey Hill'. A rounded form like 'Harmony' with the inflorescences more rounded and less floppy compared to that cultivar. Introduced by Hayes Jackson, Anniston, Alabama.

'Vaughn's Lillie'. See discussion at the beginning of this "Cultivars and Varieties" section.

'Wade Mahlke'. Compact flowers of sterile constitution intermediate between those of 'Harmony' and 'Roanoke'. In full flower 18 May 2003 at Atlanta Botanical Garden with large, 8- to 12-inch-long inflorescences, composed of largely sterile florets. Somewhat weepy under the weight. I am not sure the

'Wade Mahlke'

correct name for this taxon. *Hydrangea International Index* lists 'Wade Malke' clone (note absence of "h"). Also listed as 'Emerald Lake'.

Via our seedling and the tissue-culture work of Hazel Wetzstein, several variegated forms have materialized. Most are sectoral chimeras with yellow and/or cream coloration. Unfortunately, none have been stable. A tissue-culture mutation with uniform speckled green and white leaves is promising and has been multiplied in the laboratory while maintaining its unique variegation. Tissue-cultured plants often display different growth characteristics than cutting-produced plants. I have seen 'Pee Wee' from tissue culture with deeply lobed, undulating leaves. Also, Snow Queen® grows like a telephone pole for a time from tissue culture. Eventually these uncharacteristic traits are left behind and the normal patterns emerge. This discussion is not meant to alarm, only to advise that the plant purchased as 'Pee Wee' (or other tissue-cultured hydrangea) may not look quite authentic. Mark Griffith, former student and now owner of a large liner nursery, has used some of these tissue-cultured 'Pee Wee' in his garden. Several are now 5 feet high.

Identification Characteristics

Leaves: Opposite, simple, ovate to suborbicular in outline, sinuately 3- to 7-lobed, 3 to 8 inches long, two-thirds to fully as wide, usually truncate at base, sometimes subcordate and decurrent into the petiole, lobes broad, serrate and often slightly lobed, dark green and glabrous above, except on veins, whitish, grayish to brownish tomentose beneath; petiole, 1 to 2½ inches long, pubescent. About the first to show leaf development but *Hydrangea macrophylla* is a close second and often overlaps.

Buds: Imbricate, 4- to 6-scaled, divergent, brownish, tomentose; terminal much larger than laterals.

Stem: Young stems intensely brownish tomentose, stout, older stems (three years and more) with prominent lenticels, bark exfoliating to expose tawnyto cinnamon-brown inner bark, quite attractive but often overlooked. Large leaf scars, prominent, crescent- to halfmoon-shaped, vascular bundle scars 3 to 11; pith, light brown.

Flowers: Panicle, 4 to 12 inches long, 3 to 4(6) inches wide, stalked, branches bearing lateral umbel-like cymes of fertile flowers, each branch terminated by the so-called ray flower composed of 4, broad-ovate to sub-orbicular white sepals, usually overlapping to form a solid surface, sepals persisting turning pink, rose to rose-purple; fertile flowers bisexual, with 5 white, triangular, $\frac{1}{25}$-inch-long sepals, 5 white petals alternating with the sepals, obovate and cupped, twice or more as long as sepals, fragrant; 8 to 10 stamens, longer than the petals, styles 2, each with a 2-lipped stigma.

Colored pencil drawing of *Hydrangea serrata* 'Tiara'.

CHAPTER TEN

Hydrangea serrata
(Thunberg) Seringe

For inexplicable reasons, I have been unable to open my garden heart and allow this species to captivate. The plants and flowers are more refined than the "knock 'em dead" *Hydrangea macrophylla* taxa. Many hydrangea aficionados wax lovingly about the nuances of this species. Numerous cultivars exist, primarily lacecaps, with some mophead forms. Compared to *H. macrophylla*, an inordinate number of double-flowered forms are in cultivation. These are seldom available in everyday commerce and must be sought from specialty growers.

'Blue Billow', a seedling of the Korean form of *Hydrangea serrata*, was introduced by Richard Lighty, formerly of the University of Delaware, Longwood Gardens, and the Mt. Cuba Center, as a more cold hardy form. I grew it for a number of years with moderate success, but the lacecap blue flowers were not large or particularly showy and on occasion, late spring freezes made cooked collards of the leaves. Several 4-foot-high, large masses, abundantly endowed with rich blue lacecaps, were magnificent at the Atlanta Botanical Garden on 18 May 2003. Leaves are larger than typical and flat dark green. According to Yamamoto (2000), this Korean genotype should be classified as *H. serrata* subsp. *acuminata*. In terms of midwinter cold hardiness, i.e., tolerance when fully acclimated, this and other *H. serrata* taxa may supersede *H. macrophylla*. Unfortunately, all bets are off in fall and early spring when the foliage is more frost sensitive.

At the UGA Hydrangea Shade Garden, 16 taxa were outplanted on 18 and 19 June 2001 with 14 alive when evaluated on 29 April 2003: 'Amagi-amacha', 'Benigaku', 'Blue Deckle', 'Golden Sunlight', 'Iyō-Shibori',

Hydrangea serrata

'Kiyosumisawa' ('Pulchra'), 'Midoriboshi Temari', 'Miranda', 'Miyama-yae-Murasaki' ('Purple Tiers'), 'Shichidanka' ('Pretty Maiden'), 'Shirotae', 'Tiara', 'Woodlander', and 'Yae Amacha'. All had flat (no gloss) light to medium (a few with dark) green leaves, generally long and narrow. None acquired great size in the two growing seasons, with 'Benigaku' 21 by 20 inches, 'Kiyosumisawa' 17 by 20 inches, and 'Tiara' 20 by 29 inches; the rest were considerably smaller. 'Amagi-amacha', 'Benigaku', 'Miyama-yae-Murasaki', 'Tiara', and 'Woodlander' had high flower bud counts. On the taxa with high flower bud counts, both the terminal and axillary shoots produced inflorescences. All are so much more delicate in leaf and flower compared to *Hydrangea macrophylla* taxa that they can be identified by texture. Professional horticulturists and nurserymen should educate the buying public relative to the aesthetic nuances of *H. serrata*.

On 8 and 18 May 2003, I studied the *Hydrangea serrata* taxa at the JC Raulston Arboretum and Atlanta Botanical Garden, respectively, with largely the same consensus relative to greater hardiness, more flower buds from old wood, smaller duller leaves, and smaller stature compared to the many *H. macrophylla* taxa. Based on flower bud development stages and fully expressed flowers, *H. serrata* will be slightly earlier than the *H. macrophylla*, although overlap occurs depending on the cultivar and weather.

Hydrangea serrata 'Blue Billow'

The species is distributed in Japan and Korea. A specimen in the UGA botany herbarium was collected between 5,000 and 6,000 feet elevation on Mt. Iwaguro, Shikoku, Japan. Yamamoto (2000) describes the natural habitat in damp forest regions away from the coast; photos show *Hydrangea serrata* growing from moist cliffs and in the middle of a mountain stream, inundated by water. Corinne Mallet, who has traveled to Japan and observed the variation, lists subsp. *acuminata*, subsp. *yezoensis*, and subsp. *angustata*. This interpretation is based on Takeomi Yamamoto's distribution map. McClintock treats *H. macrophylla* subsp. *serrata* as all-encompassing, while Haworth-Booth lists *H. japonica*, *H. acuminata*, and *H. thunbergii* as distinct species. I present Mallet's treatment, as described in the Shamrock Newsletter No. 9, January 2003, pages 8 and 9. Admittedly, I am hard pressed to differentiate the various subspecies encountered in gardens; see "Cultivars and Varieties."

'Woodlander'

In garden terms, *Hydrangea serrata* is less robust than *H. macrophylla*, growing 3 to 5 feet high and wide. Leaves, 2 to 6 inches long, 1 to 2½ inches wide, are smaller, slender-pointed

(acuminate), cuneate, lanceolate to ovate-elliptic, sometimes ovate, finely or coarsely serrate, flat matt to dull green, glabrous above except on veins, pubescent below, often developing respectable fall color. Leaves often develop red tints in summer which become more prominent by fall; a good index for rapid separation from *H. macrophylla* is this early and often prominent coloration. Stems are thin, quite pubescent when young, finally glabrous, and may be colored and speckled. The lacecap inflorescences average 2½ to 5 inches diameter with clusters of showy sepals in (3s)4s(5s), ⅝ to 1 inch across. Sepals are either entire or prominently serrated. Sepal colors range from white, pink, rose, burgundy, to blue. Sepals may be blue in acid (aluminum) soils. Numerous single, double, lacecap, mophead, variegated and colored leaf forms have been selected through the centuries in Japan. Most will never arrive on American shores, but one look at Yamamoto's *Color Guide* (2000) makes for hopeful thinking. 'Grayswood', from which I have grown hundreds of seedlings, opens white, becoming rose with maturity. However, seedling populations, with remarkable similarity of foliage, have yielded white-, rose-, burgundy-, and blue-sepaled lacecap inflorescences, sepals entire to strongly dentate, singles and doubles. No mophead inflorescences occurred.

When fertile flowers are pollinated and as fruits develop, sepals then turn down to show backsides. With few exceptions, the sepals turn green or are tinged rose, burgundy, red. They lose their impact compared to the aging sepals of *Hydrangea macrophylla* taxa. This is something to consider, if the gardener wants to extend the color spectrum into late summer and fall. In fact, as I studied the *H. serrata* taxa at the JC Raulston Arboretum on 25 June 2003, their lack of oomph was painfully evident while *H. macrophylla* taxa were in spectral plumage. In a consumer's mind and budget, there would be no doubt about which hydrangea to purchase.

Culturally, at least in the South, the *Hydrangea serrata* complex does not have the staying power (oomph) of *H. macrophylla*. Across *H. serrata*, mildew resistance is slightly better than that of the *H. macrophylla* types. Light to moderate shade, even moisture, organic-laden soils, and wind protection provide the ideal. In 2002, I planted a group of 'Grayswood' seedlings under these conditions. The intense summer drought exacerbated the situation, with the leaves flagging like wilted lettuce. Twice-a-week watering kept them alive. My point: if *H. serrata* taxa are indeed more resilient, they do not typically demonstrate the tenacity often advertised. On 22 March 2003, these seedlings had produced leaves about ⅓ to ½ full size. Flower buds were fully evident in the broccoli stage by 9 April 2003; flowers were fully expressed by 18 May 2003. I noticed the same degrees of development for the many *H. macrophylla* cultivars. If *H. serrata* remained dormant later into spring, this would reduce the potential for injury due to late spring frosts.

Hardiness is considered greater in *Hydrangea serrata* than in *H. macrophylla*, perhaps a true Zone 6 (-10°F) without stem dieback. Subspecies *yezoensis* grows in the mountains of northern Honshu and southern Hokkaido, Japan, and should possess reasonable cold adaptability. According to Corinne Mallet, subsp. *yezoensis* is a remontant taxon and will flower on new growth. In our Georgia collections, several cultivars developed late season flowers. If there is any doubt about flowering response, wait until after spring to early summer flowering before pruning. Otherwise follow the procedures outlined in chapter 12.

The delicate nature of the species permits discreet meshing with perennials and in shrub borders. My take for any type of show is grouping and massing the plants. The greatest spectacles result from large numbers of single colors and even multiple cultivars.

Hydrangea serrata taxa are subject to mildew infestation, and seedlings of 'Grayswood', 'Tiara', 'Miranda', 'Tokyo Delight', and 'Golden Sunlight' contracted mildew comparable to *H. macrophylla* seedlings in our breeding program.

Propagation, production, care, and cultural considerations parallel those described for *Hydrangea macrophylla* in chapter 12.

Cultivars and Varieties

The following *Hydrangea serrata* subspecies descriptions reflect Corinne Mallet's and Takeomi Yamamoto's concepts of their occurrences in Japan and Korea. Obviously, not everyone agrees with this taxonomy.

Subspecies *acuminata* **Siebold** grows to 4 feet, usually less, leaves are medium green, thin, serrulate, narrow-oval, appearing crowded at ends of shoots, turn crimson in fall; lacecap inflorescences, terminal and axillary, with fertile and sterile flowers always colored, mid-June to mid-July with a possible second flush in late summer. Seedlings of subsp. *acuminata* developed numerous inflorescences from side shoots in their second growing season, flower buds visible in mid-April 2003. Full flower on 16 May 2003, with colors of white, pink, mauve, and blue. All seedlings had vertically streaked, speckled stems. Fall color was excellent reddish purple on several seedlings in November 2002. Shikoku, Kyushu, southern Honshu; widely distributed in Korea.

Subspecies *angustata* **Koidzumi** forms a small, 3-foot-high, dome-shaped shrub, with thin, many-branched stems producing terminal and axillary inflorescences; long narrow leaves, mid-vein lighter than the light green blade; the sepals and fertile flowers (i.e., all parts of the inflorescence) are white, becoming spotted carmine with maturity; flowering is prolific for about 3 weeks; many side branches along the length of the shoot produce flowers; eastern central region of Honshu at 2,000 feet elevation and above.

Hydrangea serrata
subsp. acuminata

Subspecies *yezoensis* **Koidzumi** is upright or rounded to 5 feet high. Stems are speckled. Leaves are oval, wrinkled, and pubescent on upper surface, margin sharply dentate, fall color yellow; lacecap inflorescences usually terminal, 4 to 6 inches wide, sterile florets well developed, 3 to 4(5) sepals, pink, blue, forming a crown around the fertile inner flowers; northern Honshu and southern Hokkaido, also Korea (questionable here, but if so would possibly explain 'Blue Billow' characteristics), growing in very acid soils. Subspecies *yezoensis* and *acuminata* grow together on the east coast of Honshu. This subspecies supposedly houses 'Rosea' and 'Otaksa', the progenitor taxa for many of the mopheads bred by the Europeans. These two cultivars are listed as *Hydrangea macrophylla* taxa in most literature.

Hydrangea serrata subsp. *angustata*

Hydrangea serrata Cultivar Chart

The following list of *Hydrangea serrata* cultivars was synthesized from American nursery catalogs, Internet sites, and personal observations. *The Japanese Hydrangeas Color Guide Book* (2000) by Takeomi Yamamoto features 300 photos of different hydrangeas, over half *H. serrata*, most of which I never knew existed, and brings this hydrangea aficionado to his knees. The variation, from singles, double, lacecaps, mopheads, colored and contorted stems, to variegated leaves, incites the trembles. *Hydrangea serrata* is every degree as diverse as its big sister, *H. macrophylla*.

Those marked with an asterisk (*) are best in tests based on data taken 17 May 2003 at the University of Georgia. Superior garden rating afforded those cultivars with respectable flower, foliage, habit, and vigor.

CULTIVAR	FLOWER TYPE	COLOR (-AL)	(+AL)	FLOWER NOTES	FOLIAGE & HABIT NOTES
'Acuminata'* (subsp. *acuminata*, 'Intermedia')	lacecap	white aging pink	blue sterile, blue fertile	sepals heavily serrate, pointed, 3s(4s); facing downward and showing green reverse after pollination; early to mid-summer	flat medium green crinkled leaves come to a narrow point; stems are red speckled; good autumn color on seedlings; 3 to 3½' by 3 to 3½'
'Akishino Temari' ('Akishino-temari')	mophead	soft pink		full heads	4' tall
'Amagi-amacha'* ('Amagi Amacha')	lacecap	white		diminutive heads, oval, entire sepals in 3s and 4s	extremely narrow light green foliage, yellow-white veins; delicate appearance; 3' tall; high flower buds
'Beni'	lacecap	red	red	holds color 10 July 2003 at Hawksridge Nursery	dull flat green leaves with red tints, from Dan Hinkley
'Benigaku'*	lacecap	white sepals aging pink becoming tinged with rose-red; lavender fertile		sepals in 3s and 4s; serrated; ages through pink to deep red; brilliant red coloration on 1 July 2003 at Hawksridge Nursery, Hickory, NC; mid-season picotee effect	remarkable deep green foliage, larger leaf; 3' tall; graceful stems; superior autumn leaf and stem color; high flower buds
'Blue Billow'	lacecap	pink	intense, dark iridescent blue	flower bud hardy to 5 to 10°F; early season; in heavy shade sepals age white	strong stems; coarse dark green leaves; fantastic fall color; one of the hardiest; 3 to 4' tall; most robust and floriferous *H. serrata* at Atlanta Botanical Garden
'Blue Bird'* ('Aïgaku', 'Bluebird')	lacecap	pink sterile; mid-blue fertile	pale blue to lavender-blue sterile; violet-blue fertile	flowers June to October; flowers turn upside-down as autumn approaches showing pink undersides; rounded sepals (4s) form a cross shape	robust grower; large flat dark green leaves; brilliant copper-red fall colors; 3 to 5' tall; stems without prominent spots; 'Aïgaku' was Japanese name; renamed by Haworth-Booth
'Blue Deckle'*	lacecap	pale pink	pale blue	serrated, frilly, small to medium size sepals; 4s; May to September; true remontant type	flat medium green leaves; dramatic fall leaf color; spotted stems; 3 to 4' tall; Haworth-Booth introduction
f. *chinensis* (questionable taxon similar to , 'Koreana', listed as 'Chinensis Koreana' by the Mallets)	lacecap	pure pink	light blue	my lone plant has delicate oval sepals	small, dwarf shrub, mounded habit; 2' at Atlanta Botanical Garden; rich green, hairless leaves; yellowish fall color

'Blue Deckle'

Hydrangea serrata
f. *chinensis*

CULTIVAR	FLOWER TYPE	COLOR (−AL)	(+AL)	FLOWER NOTES	FOLIAGE & HABIT NOTES
'Chiri-san Sue'	lacecap	pink sterile; pink fertile		double sterile florets	named for Sue Wynn-Jones of Wales; cuttings of a specimen observed in wilds of Korea in 1997 on Chiri-san, a mountain in the southern part of the peninsula; 4' tall; foliage light green; stems largely green
'Chishima'	lacecap	pink sterile; deep pink fertile		flat heads; large sterile sepals; large fertile flowers	
'Coerulea Lace'* ('Coerulea', 'Caerulea', also included in *H. macrophylla* list)	lacecap	pink	blue	repeat-flowering	flat medium green leaves; larger leaf than typical for a *H. serrata* type; received as *H. japonica* 'Coerulea Lace'; very cold hardy
'Diadem' ('Hashikuzu', 'Hoshkuzu')	lacecap	pink	pale blue	long flowering season; reliable flower bud hardiness	pale green leaves and plum fall color; vigorous, but compact shrub; ideal for small gardens and containers; 2 to 3' tall
var. *fertilis*	lacecap	white-pink	shades of light blue	listed as having purely fertile flowers, certainly not true on the plants I observed	a variety occurring on Cheiju Island; seedling variation should be expected; good fall color; light green leaves and stems
'Geisha Girl'*	lacecap	white aging to pink, rose		abundant small sepals and inflorescences	much like 'Tokyo Delight'; good grower with cold hardiness
'Golden Sunlight'	lacecap	white to light pink		larger serrated sepals and inflorescence than most *H. serrata*, sepals age to rose-burgundy	compact habit, yellow new leaves that turn green with age; actually green by late May in Athens; stems green; sport of 'Intermedia' discovered in 1989 in Boskoop, Netherlands
'Grayswood'	lacecap	white sterile; pink fertile	white sterile; blue fertile.	larger sepals than most *H.serrata*; age to deep rose-burgundy; flowers June to frost	pale green and darker green leaves with tips that turn reddish brown in early summer to late fall; 4 to 6' tall; old Japanese cultivar; renamed in England
'Intermedia' (see also 'Acuminata')	lacecap	white	blue	abundant inflorescences	much like 'Acuminata' except the largest *H. serrata* I ever witnessed at 6' tall

'Golden Sunlight'

'Intermedia'

CULTIVAR	FLOWER TYPE	COLOR (−AL)	(+AL)	FLOWER NOTES	FOLIAGE & HABIT NOTES
'Iyō-Shibori'	lacecap	pink marbled with deeper shades as well as white sterile; pink fertile	blue and marbled	small inflorescences; rounded overlapping sepals; 3s and 4s; beautiful coloring	narrow, intermediate size, flat light green foliage with a long acuminate tip; stems without prominent spots; not particularly vigorous
'Kiyosumisawa'* ('Kiyosumi', 'Pulchra')	lacecap	ruby-red buds opening to pink sepals picoteed in red; pink fertile		mid-summer; later sepals fade to white while keeping picotee effect; picotee effect evident as flower opens	new growth rich burgundy; remaining effective and colorful through summer in cool climates; 3 to 4' tall; leaves when stressed or nitrogen deficient turn red-purple in summer; stems prominently spotted
'Komachi'	mophead		blue	one of few Japanese mopheads with double florets; very full, irregularly shaped heads	compact stems to less than 4'
'Koreana' (dubious nomenclature, var. *koreana*, see f. *chinensis*)	lacecap	pink	blue	sepals in 4s, delicate and abundant	3' by 5', graceful plant
'Kurohime'	lacecap	pink	rich blue, purple	early flowering; deep pigmentation to sterile florets	3 to 4' tall; purple-black stems
'Maiko-ajisai' ('Maiko', 'Belladona')	mophead	pink and limey green	pink	small mophead inflorescence; abundant flowers	3' tall; very elegant dwarf shrub
'Midoriboshi Temari' ('Green Star')	lacecap (almost mophead)	pink sterile; pink fertile	blue to lavender sterile; pink fertile	elegant, long, bright pink pedicels; double sterile florets; long-flowering; irregularly shaped inflorescences	more upright habit; 5' tall; flat light green leaves; weak and not many flowers
'Miranda'*	lacecap	pink sterile; pink fertile	light blue sterile variegated with streaks and stripes of white and lighter colors; blue fertile	sepals in 4s	3½' tall; large flat light green leaves; stems without prominent spots; similar to 'Blue Bird' as I evaluated the two; good grower.
'Miyama-yae-Murasaki'* ('Purple Tiers')	lacecap	pink sterile; pink fertile	blue-purple sterile; blue-purple fertile	double sterile and fertile florets; large fertile florets; rounded sterile sepals; early flowering	extremely elegant; deeply toothed, long-pointed flat medium green foliage; red petioles; 4 to 5' tall; spotted stem

'Iyō-Shibori'

'Kiyosumisawa'

'Miranda'

'Miyama-yae-Murasaki'

CULTIVAR	FLOWER TYPE	COLOR (-AL)	(+AL)	FLOWER NOTES	FOLIAGE & HABIT NOTES
'Pink Beauty' see 'Preziosa'					
'Preziosa'* ('Preciosa', 'Pink Beauty')	mophead (and lacecap)	white, pink rose, red	violet-purple	flowers deepening to or spotted with ruby-red in autumn	dark purplish stems; 4 to 5' tall; considered a hybrid of *H. serrata* x *H. macrophylla*; full flower 3 June 2003 at JC Raulston Arboretum; terrifically susceptible to mildew
'Ramis Pictis'	lacecap	white	rose (like 'Rosalba')		
'Rosalba'	lacecap	white sterile; pink fertile	aging pink	sepals serrated; broad-rounded	3' tall; old cultivar, 1865; red petioles, speckled stems; looks much like 'Tokyo Delight' and 'Geisha Girl'
'Shichidanka' ('Pretty Maiden', 'Chiffon')	lacecap	pink	deep lavender to blue	lovely, demure, double flower; star-upon-star; pointed sepals	narrow, jagged-edged, flat dark green leaves; foliage takes on orange tints in autumn; 3½' tall; high flower buds; stems essentially unspotted
'Shirofuji' ('White-capped Mt. Fuji')	lacecap	white sterile; white or pink fertile	white sterile; white or blue fertile	star-like fully double or sterile florets	3½' tall; considered a good grower
'Shiro Maiko' ('Shiro-maiko')	mophead	striking creamy white opening lime green and fading to interesting green tint		all sterile florets; diminutive but full heads, to 4"; copious flowers	narrow, bright green leaves; often cultivated in containers in Japan; 3' tall
'Shironome'	lacecap	white to pink	blue	double sterile flowers; small flower heads; sepals age to pink	small, flat, light to medium green foliage; red autumn tints; largely green stems; 4' tall
'Shirotae'	lacecap to semi-mophead	white sterile and fertile		double sterile florets; starburst effect	flat medium green, narrow leaves; with white veins; 3 to 4' by 3 to 4'; green stems, weak grower
'Shishiva'	lacecap	pink	lavender-blue to blue	delicate, full lacecap	3' tall by 5' wide; abundant flowers 25 May 2003 at JC Raulston Arboretum, flat green leaves; red nodes and petioles

'Rosalba'

'Shichidanka'

'Shishiva'

'Tiara', fall color

CULTIVAR	FLOWER TYPE	COLOR (-AL)	(+AL)	FLOWER NOTES	FOLIAGE & HABIT NOTES
'Spreading Beauty' ('Hallasan 1')	lacecap	lilac pink sterile; pink fertile	lilac pink sterile; lilac blue fertile	flowers from July to late fall; flat semi-spherical heads	low, broad-spreading, 2' tall by 3' wide; reddish fall color; listed as hardy to Zone 4; from Robert and Jelena de Belder, Kalmthout Arboretum, Belgium
'Tiara'*	lacecap to almost mophead status	mauve-pink to crimson	blue	loaded with flowers; sepals in 4s; broad oval sepals	better than 'Diadem', which it resembles; 3 to 4' tall; flat medium green large leaves with purple tips turn red in fall; high flower buds; spotted stems
'Tokyo Delight'	lacecap	white deepening to pink as they age		early to late season; small corymb that makes up for it by quantity and layering; serrated sepals	graceful, upright habit; large flat dark green leaves with hints of red and purple in autumn; 4 to 5'; stems spotted; akin to 'Geisha Girl'
'Wilson 7820'	lacecap	pink with white/ green centers upon emergence	pink over time	3" heads; stays pink based on my observations	24 to 30" tall; compact broad-mounded; light green leaves; loaded with flower buds; one of the earliest to flower; very pretty and literally smothered with flowers at JC Raulston Arboretum on 25 May 2003
'Winterthur'	lacecap	white	rose	small sepals become spotted with maturity	not an impressive form, flowers are second class even for *H. serrata* types
'Woodlander'*	lacecap	white, shell pink	blue sterile; blue to purple fertile	rounded sepals in 3s/4s	dense growth, rounded habit, small, 3½' by 5'; large, flat medium green leaves take on purplish cast in fall; small leaves; high flower buds; green stems
'Yae Amacha'* ('Yae-no-Amacha')	lacecap	white	fading to pinkish white; violet-blue in our trials	few fertile florets surrounded by double sterile florets; smaller sepals in the center of each floret	3' tall; large, flat light green leaves; heavily wrinkled; stems spotted

'Yama Azisai' see 'Kurohime'

'Tokyo Delight'

'Wilson 7820'

'Woodlander', fall color

CHAPTER ELEVEN

Hydrangeas Worthy of Cursory Introduction

Several of these less well known, taxonomically unsettled species belong to the "black hole" of *Hydrangea* taxonomy and, although not validated by Mc-Clintock's 1957 revision of the genus, do surface on nursery Internet sites and catalogs. I have observed and/or grown plants of most included in this chapter, except *Hydrangea hirta* and *H. integrifolia*. These "stray" species are pinpointed to the degree possible and meshed (matched) with McClintock's interpretation of the genus.

***Hydrangea angustipetala* Hayata**, although listed as a separate species, is correctly lumped under *H. scandens* subsp. *chinensis*. Potential to 5 feet, usually less. Leaves are lustrous dark green, narrow, about $2^3/4$ inches long, $^3/4$ to 1 inch wide, deeply dentate, pubescent. My lone plant fits the leaf description perfectly. The lacecap inflorescences are comprised of cream-yellow fertile flowers and 4, white, spatulate sepals, the margins broadly dentate, rarely entire. Sepals age to yellow. Crûg Farm lists 17 forms collected from different sites throughout the native range. Considerable variation was evident in the Crûg Farm wild collections from deciduous to evergreen, with ray florets up to 2 inches diameter in f. *macrosepala*, and leaves narrow to broadly oblong. Depending on location of collection, hardiness would be variable. Zones 7 to 9? Partial shade and moist soil are recommended. In Haworth-Booth it is listed as *H. scandens* subsp. *chinensis* f. *angustisepala* Hayata; in Mallet, as *H. scandens* subsp. *angustipetala*. 'Tis safe to conclude,

Hydrangea angustipetala, foliage

for all the taxonomic hullabaloo, it will never become a garden icon. Variable over its range: Japan, China, Taiwan.

***Hydrangea hirta* (Thunberg) Siebold**. McClintock describes nativity as mixed forests and woods on Honshu and Okinawa at 660 to 3,300 feet elevation. Grows to 3 to 5 feet high. The dark green leaves, 1 to 4 inches long, 1 to 3 inches wide, are elliptic to obovate, abruptly acuminate, cuneate, sharply dentate, and pubescent on both surfaces. Known as the nettle-leaved hydrangea as the leaf resembles the nettle in general appearance. The coarse teeth are cut ⅛ to ⅓ inch into the margin of the leaf. The 1- to 4-inch-wide inflorescences are composed strictly of fertile flowers, typically blue, but also cream-white to pinkish white and delicately scented. Described as having delicate blue-tinged flowers by Crûg Farm. The stems, tinged red or mauve, are spindly. Mallet reported hybrids between this species and *H. luteovenosa*. *Hydrangea hirta*, *H. serrata*, and *H. luteovenosa* grow together in the wild. Possibly Zone 7, although Sandra Reed lists Zone 5.

***Hydrangea indochinensis* Merrill**. The validity of this species is taxonomically tenuous, but the foliage, with purple undersides, is unique among hydrangeas. The purple underside of the leaf is apparently not constant. The leaves are thick-textured, serrate, lustrous dark green above with prominent impressed veins. Lacecap inflorescences are composed of lavender-lilac to blue fertile flowers and ray flowers composed of 4 to 5 sepals, each rounded, overlapping, white, blue to pale lilac in color. My initial introduction was a single potted plant on the patio of Maurice Foster, Kent, England. This unique plant was 'Arthur Billard', and the sepals were pink with deeper purple-pink fertile flowers. The species is also listed by Crûg Farm Plants. Frost tender and hardy only to Zone 9(10). Again, probably best adapted to the West Coast. Merged by McClintock into *H. macrophylla* subsp. *stylosa*. Native to Vietnam and China.

Hydrangea integrifolia **Hayata**. An evergreen vine or scandent shrub, the dark green leaves, 2 to 7 inches long, 1 to 3½ inches wide, are thick textured and entire or slightly denticulate. The inflorescences, about 8 inches wide, consist of white, fertile flowers with sterile flowers, 2 to 3 sepals, scattered among. Fertile flowers have 4 to 5 sepals and petals, 8 or 10 stamens. Tardy to flower with a report of 15 years before doing so. Branches covered with reddish hairs with aerial roots developing along the stems providing sure footing as it climbs. Native to Taiwan and Philippines. Zones 8 and 9(10) on the West Coast.

Hydrangea lobbii **Maximowicz**. An evergreen species from the Philippines that is most legitimately included under *H. scandens* subsp. *chinensis*. Habit is upright to 5 feet. The leaves, lustrous dark green, narrow-ovate, serrate, glabrous, highlight the white lacecap flowers. The foliage remained free of mildew under greenhouse conditions. Each inflorescence has 4 to 5 white ray flowers composed of 4 lightly serrated sepals, typically approximately 1 inch

Hydrangea indochinensis 'Arthur Billard'

Hydrangea lobbii

across but up to 2 inches across. The plant has flowered in the UGA greenhouses, where it was an instant object of affection. After 10°F, residing in a container in the lath area, it perished. Described as growing in mossy forests of the high mountains at 3,300 to 8,000 feet from Luzon to Mindanao, also Taiwan. Reed lists adaptability as Zone 8; definitely less hardy, probably best suited to Zone 9(10) of West Coast.

***Hydrangea longipes* Franchet**. A medium-sized, spreading, deciduous shrub of loose habit. Leaves, 3 to 7 inches long, 1 to 3½ inches wide, sharply toothed, are bristly beneath. The red petioles, 2 to 8 inches long, receive accolades for their remarkable length. Flowers are white lacecaps, 4 to 6 inches wide, with ray florets to 1½ inches wide. Sepals age to rose-burgundy. Grows 6 to 7½ feet high. The lone specimen that I was able to study grew at Knightshayes, Tiverton, England; with 4 sepals, it had an amazing resemblance to *H. heteromalla*, although Crûg Farm mentioned its affinity to *H. aspera*, where they collected seed of *H. longipes* north of Boaxing, China. McClintock placed it with *H. aspera* subsp. *robusta*. Western China. Zone 7.

***Hydrangea luteovenosa* Koidzumi** (by some authorities same as *H. scandens* subsp. *liukiuensis*) resides in this pumpkin patch based on flower characteristics. Leaves (on herbarium specimen) were ½ to 1 inch long, petiole ⅛ inch long, hairy above, on veins below, gray interveinal areas. Stems are thin, with appressed hairs. Young stems are purplish black while those of *H. scandens* are gray. White entire sepals as described for *H. scandens*. My understanding is that the veins are yellowish, however, this characteristic was not evident on the herbarium specimen or photos of leaves. Twelve selections including mophead, double, pink- and yellow-flowered types are shown in *The Japanese Hydrangeas Color Guide Book*. A variegated ('Aureovariegata', 'Variegata', 'Nishiki') leaf form is offered in U.S. commerce. The leaf is splashed and streaked with yellow and cream. May be offered as *H. luteovenosa* or *H. scandens*.

Hydrangea scandens (Linnaeus f.) Seringe is a small, 3 to 6 feet high, deciduous shrub with flailing, splaying stems, dark blue-green leaves, 2 inches by 1 inch, weakly dentate, and lacecap inflorescences, the sepals white. It was the first hydrangea to flower at the Hillier Arboretum; my notes reflect late April to early May 1999. The lone plant in the UGA Hy-

Hydrangea scandens

drangea Shade Garden showed fully colored white sepals in mid-April 2003. The sepals are white, in groups of 3, developing in small (approximately 3-inch) inflorescences from the nodes. Usually 1 large sepal and 2 smaller, all entire, reminiscent of a Mickey Mouse hat. The cream-white fertile flowers are fragrant. Would appear useful in hybridization work because of the freedom and earliness of flower. Quite variable as the UGA botany herbarium's wild-collected specimen had narrow, to 2-inch-long, serrate, thinnish, acuminate, narrow cuneate, $\frac{1}{4}$-inch-petioled leaves with hooked trichomes on the upper and lower leaf surface and on the thinnish stems. Japan, Taiwan. Zone 7. Reed lists variable hardiness.

Also included under *Hydrangea scandens* is subsp. *liukiuensis* (Nakai) E. M. McClintock, and the wild-collected herbarium specimen had obovate, $1\frac{1}{2}$- to $2\frac{1}{2}$-inch-long leaves, petiole $\frac{1}{4}$ inch, leaf entire in the lower third, then deeply toothed to apex with relatively few crooked hairs randomly distributed on both surfaces. Petioles covered with hairs. Thin brown stems with hairs, crooked in shape, crawling along the surface. Inflorescence light blue, small, loose, with no showy sepals present. This last characteristic separates subsp. *liukiuensis* from *H. luteovenosa*. Native to Honshu, Kyushu, Shikoku, and Ryukyu according to McClintock.

***Hydrangea seemannii* Riley** is an evergreen vine, clinging like ivy via root-like holdfasts, the stems clothed with rusty brown stellate pubescence. The dark green leaves, 2 to 8 inches long by $^3/_4$ to $2^1/_2$ inches wide, are lanceolate to elliptic-lanceolate, entire to slightly serrated, leathery, conspicuously veined, and hairy below. Petioles are $^1/_2$ to 2 inches long. The inflorescences are slightly dome-shaped, fertile flowers irregularly presented, with ray flowers consisting of 4 entire, round sepals, the cluster 1½ inches across. Flower buds are enclosed by a conspicuous bract. Flowers open in July and August. Appeared somewhat confused in English gardens. I suspect what was sometimes labeled as *H. seemannii* was *H. serratifolia*. 'Rosemoor' is listed with no description. I surmise it is a selection from Lady Ann Palmer's garden, Rosemoor, in Great Torrington, England. Zone 8. Mexico, Sierra Madre mountains at 6,000 to 8,500 feet.

Hydrangea seemannii

***Hydrangea serratifolia* (Hooker and Arnott) Philippi f.** is a magnificent evergreen vine with thick, leathery, glossy dark green, oval, glabrous, entire, to remotely serrate leaves. Variable size from 2 to 6 inches long, 1 to 3 inches wide, elliptic, acuminate, tapered to the base and often cordate. Petiole ¼ to 1¾ inches long. The dome-shaped inflorescences to 6 inches high, 3 to 4 inches wide, with primarily white fertile flowers, the petals free and falling individually, open in July and August. Native to Chile and Argentina, where it grows 100 feet high in favorable locations. Occasionally listed as *H. integerrima* (Hooker and Arnott) Engler. Zone 9. Reed noted Zone 7.

Hydrangea serratifolia

***Hydrangea sikokiana* Maximowicz**. Possibly the rarest of all hydrangeas vaguely resembling the American *H. quercifolia* in leaf. Leaves, 6 to 8 inches by 3½ to 5½ inches, 2- to 3-lobed pairs, petioles 1 to 5 inches long and hairy, are not as deeply lobed throughout as *H. quercifolia*, more so in the upper half, sinuses toothed unlike *H. quercifolia*. Forest green in color and quite elegant. Leaves have crooked hairs principally on veins above, more prominent on veins below; the lower surface gray-green. This deciduous shrub grows about 5 feet high and wide, and is somewhat sparse at the base. Flowers, white, mature in mid to late June (Raleigh, North Carolina) in 6- to 8-inch-wide, lacecap inflorescences, the periphery punctuated with a few small, white ray florets, roughly 1 inch across, in groups of 4s, each sepal rounded, entire, overlapping. Lavender-blue sepal coloration occurred on lone plant in full sun at the JC Raulston Arboretum 25 June 2003. I became enamored with the species at Hillier and was able to collect seed in 2000. The resultant seedlings limped along for two years and most succumbed to the heat and humidity of Zone 7. However, a lone rooted cutting in a 3-by-3-by-3½-inch

Hydrangea sikokiana

propagation cell survived 10°F in the winter of 2002-03. Woods and mixed forests on Honshu and Kyushu. It is the only Asian species with lobed leaves. Plants I grew did not uniformly show the lobed character. In fact, a plant I gave to the JC Raulston Arboretum, which I photographed in flower on 12 June 2003, had only broad-ovate leaves without lobes. For long-term survival, suited only for Pacific Northwest into California. Listed as Zone 5 by Reed.

***Hydrangea umbellata* Rehder** (merged with *H. scandens* subsp. *chinensis* by McClintock). As I digest the literature and doggedly pursue the legitimacy of *Hydrangea* taxa, this appears the biggest morass of all. Haworth-Booth listed 12 formae under *H. scandens* subsp. *chinensis*. *Hydrangea umbellata*, a deciduous Chinese species, was given to me by David Parks, Camellia Forest Nursery, Chapel Hill, North Carolina. The narrow, ovate leaves are markedly larger than *H. scandens*, 2 to 4 inches long, fully serrated, and dark green. They are bullate (i.e., puckered above) with deeply impressed veins. Underside of the leaf is pubescent with conspicuous tufts of hairs in the axils of the veins. The white lacecap flowers, a mixture of white sepals and fertile flowers, are quite showy. Open in early May in Zone 7. Grows 4 to 5 feet high with stout, chocolate-brown, glabrous stems with vertical fissures evident. Pith is white, solid, and greater than one-half diameter of a one-year-old stem. Parks reported it one of the most cold-hardy hydrangeas. Also, no wilting at JC Raulston Arboretum on 8 May 2003, 89°F (13 degrees above normal), sited in full sun. *Hydrangea macrophylla* in same area were flagging. Also, no apparent cold damage, while *H. macrophylla* taxa showed variable degrees of stem dieback.

Hydrangea umbellata

This group, at least in American literature and gardens, is inadequately presented and represented, respectively. Hinkley (Heronswood) and Jones (Crûg Farm Plants) have introduced many variations of *Hydrangea scandens* subsp. *angustipetala*, which fall under subsp. *chinensis*. Crûg Farm describes *H. chinensis* f. *formosana* with narrow willowy leaves, white fading to yellow sterile flowers and *H. chinensis* from Sichuan with evergreen, broad-ovate,

Hydrangea umbellata, foliage

thick-textured, to 6-inch-long leaves. Flowers as above. Again, all are included by McClintock within subsp. *chinensis*. Check their Web pages (see Resources and Nursery Sources) for additional information.

CHAPTER TWELVE

Garden Care and Culture

Soils

Hydrangea macrophylla and *H. serrata* demand moist, actually consistently moist, well-drained, preferably acid soils, abundantly enriched with organic matter (leaves, mushroom compost, well-aged manures, etc.). Plants should also be mulched at a depth of 2 inches. I rototill the soil, layer compost, incorporate, repeat, and plant in groupings or masses. The raised beds are well drained and provide ideal root zone conditions. If soils are pH (6.0)6.5 to 7.5, flowers are typically pink, rose, to red. Also, at the higher pH levels, iron chlorosis and other nutrient maladies are more prevalent. At pH 5.5 and below, in mineral soils, flowers will be blue.

Moisture

Hydrangea macrophylla, more so than any other species, will signal when drought-stressed, with leaves drooping like a scolded dog. I estimate that an inch of water, once, perhaps twice, per week is sufficient if plants are cultured as described. In the South, leaves will flag even if ample moisture is present in the root zone when temperatures reach the high eighties and into the nineties. Leaves regain turgidity when temperatures abate.

Bailey (1989b) induced leaf malformation of *Hydrangea macrophylla* via thermal control at 92°F day/79°F night, but these temperatures had to be maintained to sustain development of distorted foliage. The cultivars were greenhouse types, a few of which are offered as garden plants.

On 8 May 2003, an unseasonably sunny, hot (89°F) day at the JC Raulston Arboretum, Raleigh, North Carolina, I evaluated the four major landscape hydrangea groups as well as a few outliers for heat stress responses. The evaluations were taken in mid-afternoon on plants sited in sunny, open locations and in the lath (shade) house. Ample soil moisture was available to all plants. *Hydrangea macrophylla* taxa were flagging (drooping) in the full sun locations, while *H. serrata* and *H. umbellata* (*H. scandens* subsp. *chinensis*) were turgid. Quite eye-opening was a planting of *H. paniculata* next to several *H. macrophylla* taxa in full sun. No stress (even young tender shoots) apparent on the former, while the latter had the appeal of cooked cabbage. In fact, *H. paniculata*, 'Brussels Lace', 'Greenspire', Pink Diamond, 'Tardiva', 'Unique', and 'White Moth' exhibited no heat stress. *Hydrangea quercifolia*, located in semi-shaded locations, was unaffected by the heat.

In the lath (shade) house, *Hydrangea macrophylla*, *H. serrata*, *H. quercifolia*, and the offbeat types—*H. aspera* subsp. *aspera*, subsp. *sargentiana*, a Villosa Group type, and 'Rocklon'—were not stressed. The latter four were less than 6 feet high and had been growing under the lath for as long as I have visited the arboretum (20 years). Only subsp. *sargentiana* had visible flower buds, and these were developing from mature (old, previous season's) wood. Just eyeballing the fuzzy foliage of the *H. aspera* taxa told me that if sited in full sun, they probably would not be alive.

The most ecological and economical strategy for watering hydrangeas is the utilization of drip irrigation. This involves drip tubing, extender lines, and emitters. Like Legos, the pieces are fitted to the main line to accommodate the spacing of plants and flow rates (volume, gallons per hour). If emitters are installed directly in the line they can be covered with mulch and are not obtrusive. I use the emitter system and also the spray stake method. The latter involves tubing attached to the main line connected to a stake that holds the sprinkler head. The diameter of the spray pattern and volume are controlled by the specific sprinkler head.

The entire system is attached to a garden hose (timer may be utilized) and run for an hour. This directed or targeted watering is more effective than the turf-type sprinklers. Check with a local irrigation company for specifics. One does not have to be an engineer to succeed.

Planting

In nursery commerce, hydrangeas are grown in containers, typically 1- and 3-gallon. The shoots (leaves and stems) should be healthy green and the plant habit full and dense. Ideally, flower buds and/or flowers will be present. Assess the quality of the root system by gently removing the media from the container and checking for white roots. Plant level with the top of the container medium or slightly higher and carefully loosen the root systems. Place the native soil around the root-ball, never compacting the backfill. Thoroughly water, which serves to fill any voids that may exist.

Much is made of digging a hole three times as wide as the root-ball. 'Tis okay if you have a personal gardener, however, I have dug all the holes for the thousands of plants—past and present—in the garden. Not a *single hole* was ever three times the diameter of the root-ball. Good soil preparation ahead of planting makes the process a piece of cake, and the hydrangeas perform like champs.

Sun/Shade

In the middle to deep South, site *Hydrangea macrophylla* and *H. serrata* in some degree of shade. Pine trees, the north and east sides of buildings, and woodland edges provide the requisite shade. Broadleaf trees like oaks, maples, beeches, and hickories are fierce competitors unless supplemental irrigation is provided. In our Zone 7b garden, hydrangeas of many ilk are positioned in varying degrees of shade. Most nurseries grow the hydrangeas under pine trees or in shade houses. The 50 percent saran shade covering is our mainstay. With this said, I see large, long-persistent plants of *H. macrophylla* in full sun in Zone 7. Although tired and weather-beaten by late summer and fall, they are sufficiently resilient.

Certainly, along the Atlantic and Pacific Coasts, plants grow successfully in full sun. Cape Cod, Nantucket, and Martha's Vineyard provide ideal conditions for successful culture. *Hydrangea macrophylla* is remarkably tolerant of maritime conditions and therefore is a good doer where aerial salts present cultural challenges. Bonnie and I traveled to Overbecks Garden (a National Trust property) in Devon, England, which sits on a bluff above the ocean. In "full" sun exposure, buffeted by maritime breezes (salt spray), grew *H. macrophylla* of shade-tree status (10 feet). I actually walked under the arching branches of the large clumps.

The reader should adjust the siting of hydrangeas (in general) to their particular region of the country, topography, soils, and microclimates that exist *in situ*. Common sense makes more sense than directions on paper, which at best should be viewed as a guide.

Fertilizer

Hydrangea macrophylla requires moderate to high nutrient levels and should be fertilized in late winter to early spring before leaf emergence. I use approximately 4 ounces of 10-10-10, scattered around the base of the plant and outward. This equals 0.25 ounces of actual nitrogen per plant. Slow-release fertilizers like Osmocote, Nutricote, and Polyon are excellent, and most nurseries are utilizing them in container production of the plants. Liquid fertilizers are also effective and provide more rapid greening. If chlorosis develops, use a product like Green Light iron and soil acidifier (see www.greenlightco.com), which contains sulfur, chelated (readily available to plants) iron, copper, and zinc. Two ounces per gallon of water is sufficient when applied to the root zone. Other iron chelate products are effective and readily available from local garden centers.

I do not want to mislead the reader about the importance of sensible fertilizer practices. My approach has always been cautionary; I use smaller quantities and apply them in split applications, for example, a late winter/early spring application, followed by an application after flowering. Too much nitrogen produces long, extended shoots that may not set the normal quantity of flower buds or simply do not harden sufficiently before an early fall freeze. Nothing is fertilized after 1 August in the Dirr garden. Good soil structure, organic matter, and tilth, combined with moderate fertilizer practices, are the best prescriptions. If you are confused by the myriad recommendations from experts, simply read the fertilizer rates recommended on the package and divide by two. The fertilizer company wants you to utilize its product successfully and not injure or kill the plants. Be safe!

Flower Color

Blue or pink colors are predicated on the amount of aluminum in the soil solution which can be absorbed by the roots. Although pH is often listed as the agent of color change, it is actually an instigator of (a precursor to) the process. If soils are acid, aluminum is available; if more alkaline, then aluminum is tied up in insoluble forms and not readily available for uptake. So the true story is that high acidity, i.e., low pH, solubilizes (or makes available) aluminum; the reverse occurs at low acidity (high alkalinity), i.e., high pH. Excess phosphorous in the soil will also tie up the aluminum in insoluble precipitates, even in acid soils. *Hydrangea macrophylla* grown in pine bark medium, pH 5 to 6, are typically pink. Why? The acidity is high, but almost no aluminum is present in the substrate (bark). Soil is composed of minerals, typically aluminum, silicon, iron, etc., and therein resides the difference. So how do growers produce blue hydrangeas in pine bark? Aluminum sulfate is added to the surface of the container at a prescribed rate, usually 0.75 to 1.5 ounces evenly distributed on the surface of the 3-gallon container medium. Greenhouse growers also apply it as a drench at the rate of 2.4 ounces per gallon solution with 8 ounces applied as a drench per 6-inch container. Greenhouse treatments start at budbreak and continue every 2 weeks for three additional applications. Growers have variable timetables for application but in our work as soon as flower buds are visible, a single application at the 1.5 ounce rate per 3-gallon is made. Water thoroughly after application to ensure solubilization of the aluminum and movement into the root zone. Too much is worse than too little: I have dwarfed and killed plants with excessive applications. *Hydrangea macro-phylla* displays a high tolerance to aluminum. Research (Ma et al. 1997, Ma 2000) showed that aluminum complexes with citric acid in the cell sap and may be detoxified in this manner.

Occasionally, elemental sulfur (flowers of sulfur) is recommended for acidifying the soil and thus mobilizing (solubilizing) aluminum. This is a borderline crazy approach and slow to effect the desired change. If the soil pH is high, live with pink, rose, and red hydrangeas—they are beautiful—or create raised beds, laden with acid organic matter, and apply aluminum sulfate that over time will lower pH and supply aluminum for ready blue-ing. *Hydrangea macrophylla* or *H. serrata*, in any shade of pink to red, is satisfying. Consider nature's gift to the garden, accept and enjoy. On the other hand, if soils are acid as lemons, lime may be added to raise the pH if pink, rose, and red flowers are desired.

Commercial production of *Hydrangea macrophylla* in the United States yields millions of plants annually

The crux of the color change is that aluminum ions complex with the pigment delphinidin-3-monoglucoside in the sepals to produce the blue coloration. A positive correlation between intensity of blue and aluminum foliar concentration has been demonstrated. Growers try to develop antique shades, somewhere between the rich blues and pinks by combining lime in the medium and aluminum applications. These in-between colors of hydrangeas are given the cutesy name "blurples." From my experiences, any pink-sepaled form, even the fickle 'Preziosa', can be blued and vice versa. Although various cultivars are often listed as pink or blue, I don't totally believe it. Lacecaps and mopheads respond in a similar fashion. The white cultivars typically are not affected and maintain their color; however, 'Mme Emile Mouillère' has a pink or blue eye depending on aluminum availability. This is true for some of the other white mopheads and lacecaps.

Bailey (1989a) listed several mitigating influences on sepal color. Aluminum uptake is antagonized by phosphorus, reduced by ammonium nitrogen (NH_4-N), and favored by nitrate (NO_3-N). For pink sepals, maintain high levels of nitrogen and low levels of potassium (K) and aluminum (<15 ppm); at pH 6.0 to 6.5, aluminum is only marginally available. For blue sepals, maintain a pH of 5.0 to 5.5, low levels of phosphorus, moderate levels of nitrogen, and high levels of potassium, and provide an ample supply of aluminum (>100 ppm): drench plants during September with aluminum sulfate (2.4 ounces/gallon), twice, 14 days apart. Anyone serious about commercial greenhouse production of hydrangea should acquire a copy of Bailey's book; it was geared to greenhouse potplant hydrangea production, but the principles apply to garden and nursery culture.

Pruning

Pruning is forever debated! Gardeners are told to remove the oldest stems, prune everything after flowering, and/or don't do anything. The truth is touched by all these admonitions. To understand the best pruning technique, examine the flower buds. Typically, *Hydrangea macrophylla* flower buds develop on old (mature) wood of the previous year and open in late spring and summer of the following year. Flower buds are formed at the terminals of the stems and, if not killed by cold, provide the show. However, additional flower buds are also present, often along the entire length of the stem. These lower buds also have fully developed floral primordia, but they simply do not open if the terminal flowers develop (they are regulated by a hormonal process called apical dominance). This means the terminal shoot, i.e., the bud before it breaks, controls the release (growth) of the buds below. If the top portion of the plant is killed, then these lower flower buds are released from this apical control. I know a Minnesotan gardener (Roger Sefelt, 1215 28th Ave. NE, Minneapolis, MN 55418-2927) who wraps the stems, covers with mulch, and flowers the common cultivars. The flowers are derived from the protected buds lower on the stems. Growers take advantage of the flower bud development along the length of the stem by pruning the upper 50 percent of the stems. The lower buds then develop shoots with flowers at their terminus resulting in a more compact plant for the customer (and easier shipping). This pruning takes place in January and February. Gardeners should learn to check for flower buds by examining the nodes along the stem. The large, $3/8$- to $5/8$-inch-long, plumpish, shiny green, red to brown structures often portend a great flower display. Also, a large bud will be evident at the end of the stem. If the vagaries of cold weather do not intercede, then the flowers will be spectacular. To maintain plant habit and structure, the larger stems may be removed on a three-year rotation, leaving the younger stems that carry the abundance of flower buds. This involves utilizing a pruning tool like long-handled loppers and making the cuts as close to the soil line as possible. I noticed this pruning approach was prevalent in England. In the United States, stems are often killed to the ground or at least partially injured and the large stems may not develop.

Gardeners often query about removing (pruning) old flowers (inflorescences) when they are raggedy and off-color (brown). My approach is to remove them as they become unpresentable. Simply make the pruning cut below the inflorescence. Often a pair of leaves subtends the inflorescence of *Hydrangea macrophylla*, *H. serrata*, and others. Typically, there are no viable vegetative buds at this node. This means, even if left, no new shoots will develop, only further down on the stem. Be careful with hard pruning in August and beyond, for new growth may occur. These tender shoots may not cold harden sufficiently by frost and could be seriously injured.

A recent study (Conwell et al. 2002) determined the "best" time for pruning container-grown *Hydrangea macrophylla* to ensure flower buds and fully developed inflorescences for the following spring and summer sales period. The results offer quantifiable evidence for when to prune. To my knowledge, this is the first published account with actual counts and not the usual anecdotal evidence, i.e., the plant flowered, looked good, was floriferous, very pretty, and other innocuous commentary. The procedure and results follow:

- Container-grown, 3-gallon, 20-inch-high 'Nikko Blue', 'Blue Wave', and 'Hobella' were pruned to one-half their length, 2 to 3 inches from the surface of the medium, or unpruned, monthly from May to September. Number of flowers and consumer quality index were assessed in early May of the following year.

- Plants pruned to one-half and 2 to 3 inches produced more flowers on average than the unpruned controls, i.e., 18, 15, 14 flowers per plant, respectively.

- August and September pruning treatments resulted in similar plant quality ratings among the three cultivars when evaluated in early May.

- Plants pruned May through August produced the most flowers the following year. September pruning resulted in an average of 8 flowers per plant for each of the three cultivars.

Conclusions? Flower buds are formed the summer and fall prior to flowering, and pruning, even down to the crown, at 2 to 3 inches, does not eliminate all the flower buds. In our work at the UGA Hydrangea Shade Garden, we counted as many as 40 flower buds nestled in the lower 6 inches of the stems of a potential introduction called 'Mini Penny'. The take-home lesson: as long as the flower buds are not totally eliminated by cold, flowers will be expressed even when plants are severely pruned. The unpruned treatment resulted in fewer flowers per plant than either pruning treatment; this tells me that although flower buds were present lower on the stem, the phenomenon of apical dominance did not allow them to be released from dormancy (control). Except for terminal flower-bud-only cultivars like 'Ayesha', it might make sense to tip prune the hydrangeas as the leaves emerge in spring. Many times the tips are dead and a general tidying-type pruning would serve two purposes: a more aesthetic plant and increased flowers.

CHAPTER THIRTEEN

Propagation:
Seeds, Cuttings, and Layering

Infructescences (fruit clusters), both lacecap and mophead, contain ripened, mature fruits. Those of lacecaps contain many, and when turned upside down, will shed seeds like salt from a shaker; the tiny seeds float in the wind and are lost forever. It is important to remember that fertile flowers and thus fruit also develop under the sepalous camouflage of the mopheads. I have yet to examine a mophead of *Hydrangea macrophylla* or *H. arborescens* that does not bear at least a few fruits. The precious seeds obtained from these mophead inflorescences were the precursors of the early French hybrid hortensias and to the present day offer unbelievable potential for improved cultivars, particularly through controlled breeding.

Seeds

Seeds should be collected in fall when the $1/4$- to $5/16$-inch-high, conical to urn-shaped (top-shaped) capsules turn brown and a small opening is visible at the top. The seeds, brown and dustlike in size, are not completely dispersed by the elements. I have collected infructescences in January and February that contained thousands of seeds. A 1-gallon clear plastic bag is placed over the infructescence, which is then removed from the parent plant, the bag inverted, and shaken. The tiny seeds are evident at the bottom. Seeds can be stored in glass jars or vials in the refrigerator. Do not allow the delicate seeds to dry for an extended period.

If the fruits are collected too early, for example September and October (Athens), drying will be necessary. The process is the same as above *except* the infructescences are placed on newspaper and dried at room temperature (65 to 75°F) for 5 to 7 days. Seeds will be visible on the paper as the capsules dehisce during the drying process. Occasionally capsules do not open, in which case a rolling pin or suitable pressure can be employed to crack the capsules. To afford an idea of the latitude for seed collection from *Hydrangea arborescens* 'Annabelle', our records indicated seeds were collected, cleaned, and planted November through February. Particularly with the mopheads, sepals, stalks, and chaff must be separated from the seed. We utilize a soil screen (variable size) that allows the small seeds to pass through. This has made seed cleaning a snap, compared to hand winnowing and "tweezer" use.

As to sowing and seedling culture, *Hydrangea* seeds require no special stratification treatments to germinate, i.e., have no seed coat and/or embryo dormancy. Seeds should be placed in a saltshaker (with filler) and lightly sprinkled on the surface of a suitable seedling mix. Fafard is a standard. *Never, never, never* cover the seeds. Place under mist (our approach) or keep evenly moist. The soil temperature is maintained at around 70°F. Seedlings are visible in 2 to 4 weeks, removed from mist when about $1/8$ to $1/4$ inch high, placed under 55 percent saran shade, and fertilized with 50 to 100 ppm N, once per week until about 1 inch tall. Seedlings are then carefully separated, placed one per 3-by-3-by-$3^1/_2$-inch plastic cell in Fafard 3B (Canadian sphagnum peat moss, aged pine bark, vermiculite, and perlite). The young seedlings are placed under mist for 7 to 10 days until established, returned to the greenhouse bench, fertilized with 100 ppm N and slow-release fertilizer (Nutricote 13-13-13 or 17-7-8 with minors; one-time application). When seedlings reach 4 to 6 inches high and danger of frost has passed they are transplanted to 3-gallon containers filled with 6.25 parts milled pine bark:1 part sand amended with 1.5 lb gypsum per cubic yard, 4 lb lime per cubic yard, slow-release fertilizer (Osmocote 24N-7P-7K) at a rate of 10 lb per cubic yard and micronutrients (Micromax) at 2 lb per cubic yard. For the Athens, Georgia, area, April to June transplanting allows sufficient time for plants to flower the first or second year.

In 2001-2002, 3,080 seedlings of *Hydrangea arborescens* 'Eco Pink Puff' and 'Wesser Falls' were grown as described above with *all* flowering by August 2002. Of these, 212 with the richest pink buds/flowers were selected and saved for continued evaluation. I have also grown several seedlings populations of 'Annabelle' using this protocol, and anywhere from 50 to 100 percent produced mophead inflorescences in the first growing season.

The procedure just described was used for *Hydrangea heteromalla, H. macrophylla, H. quercifolia, H. paniculata, H. serrata,* and *H. sikokiana* with similar results. Generally these species require a full season of growth, a winter, with flowering occurring in the second spring and summer, 16 to 18 months after seed sowing.

Cuttings and Selected Vegetative Propagation Approaches

In the woody world, the hydrangeas, particularly *Hydrangea arborescens, H. heteromalla, H. macrophylla, H. paniculata, H. quercifolia,* and *H. serrata,* are among the easiest to root from cuttings. Exceptions include *H. aspera* types and *H. involucrata,* although they are widely available from commercial growers. The major landscape *Hydrangea* species and cultivars root readily from softwood cuttings from April through July. The early rooted cuttings grow off more enthusiastically and by summer's end are robust plants, ready for transplanting to larger containers or overwintering as dormant rooted cuttings. These rooted cuttings often develop flower buds and will produce flowers the following spring and summer.

Single-node and multiple-node cuttings are suitable. Roots develop from internodal and nodal areas. The advantage of single-node (butterfly) cuttings is more plants per length of shoot. Split-node cuttings are sometimes used when cutting stock is in short supply. This involves splitting the stem in half, a good bud on both pieces, and then proceeding normally. I read *too many* recipes of *Hydrangea,* and particularly *H. macrophylla,* that prescribe at least two nodes, i.e., two or more sets of leaves for successful cutting propagation. This is simply not necessary because more space is taken, there is more leaf area to moisten, and, compared to single-node cuttings, one half or less the number of cuttings are realized. *Hydrangea macrophylla* supposedly has preformed root initials in the stem, like *Salix*, willow. Removal of the cutting from the parent plant is the stimulus for the root initials to develop, assuming the cutting is placed in a suitable environment. I observed greenwood (August, September) cuttings direct stuck outside in loose soil, covered with a wire frame, white plastic, syringed when necessary, that rooted in prolific numbers. The moral is that *any gardener* can increase the hydrangeas in the garden without needing the arsenal of the professional propagator. More care must be exercised when handling *H. arborescens* cuttings than others because the leaves are thin and easily damaged. Leaves are usually cut in half to reduce surface area because leaves of one cutting overlap those of another, preventing mist from fully covering all leaf surfaces. Commercial rooting cells are often small, $2\frac{1}{2}$ by $2\frac{1}{2}$ by $3\frac{1}{2}$ inches, and a full-leaf cutting overwhelms the space.

Cuts are made above each node (where the leaves are attached) and kept moist in bags or ice chests (without ice) until prepared for sticking. Take cuttings in the morning, if possible, when the plants are fully turgid. *Hydrangea* leaves wilt faster than many other woody species, so speed and attention to detail are important. Stem ends are dipped $\frac{1}{2}$ to 1 inch in a 1,000 ppm KIBA solution (any commercial rooting hormone will work) for 5 seconds and placed in the rooting medium to a depth of $\frac{1}{2}$ to 1 inch. Never place cuttings too deep in the medium for with depth and moisture, oxygen concentrations decrease. Oxygen is necessary for respiration and the metabolic functions that provide energy for cells to divide and form functional roots. For gardeners, products like Dip 'N Grow, Rootone, Hormodin, and Hormo-Root are available; check your local garden center or nursery for availability. These products are EPA registered and are safe when used according to label directions.

The cuttings are placed under intermittent mist with the cycles adjusted for time of year, day length, and hardness of cutting wood. Soft cuttings require the most attention but also root the fastest, usually within 2 to 4 weeks. Firmer cuttings take longer, up to 6 weeks. In our Georgia work, cuttings were rooted as early as April, as late as October.

Cuttings can be rooted at home using pots, plastic bags, shade protection, and syringing. Cover cuttings and the container with the plastic bag, place in indirect light, and syringe when the leaves start to wilt. However, the results do not generally parallel those achieved with mist.

Propagation of the "fuzzy" leaf taxa is often cited as touchy. In 2003, we tested this "theory" on 9 taxa utilizing 2 July 2003 softwood cuttings, 1,000 ppm KIBA, 3 perlite:1 peat medium, and mist. Rooting responses were *Hydrangea aspera*, 100 percent; *H. aspera* Kawakamii Group, 50 percent; *H. aspera* subsp. *robusta*, 100 percent; *H. aspera* 'Sam MacDonald', 100 percent; *H. aspera* subsp. *strigosa*, 75 percent; *H. aspera* x *H. involucrata*, 75 percent; *H. heteromalla*, 100 percent; *H. involucrata*, 100 percent; and *H. involucrata* 'Hortensis', 100 percent. Obviously, this group is easily rooted. Our propagation system is geared to careful water management, i.e., not too much or too little, and may enhance the success over what is often reported.

Hardwood cuttings, 6 to 8 inches long, collected in December and January (February) placed in well-drained soil or media like bark, with 1 to 2 inches of the top showing, will produce roots the following spring. I have used this technique with *Hydrangea macrophylla* cultivars with approximately 50 percent success. Great success was achieved with January cuttings, placed in bark in 3-gallon containers and left outside during the winter. Containers were left uncovered, and by early May 80 percent rooting occurred on three remontant taxa: 'David Ramsey', Endless Summer™, and 'Penny Mac'.

Along these same lines, dormant buds can be severed from the stem and placed on the rooting medium. The base of the bud should be lightly pressed into the medium. A large commercial nursery mentioned that if cutting wood is short, the single-bud technique is used.

In the dormant season it is possible to divide *Hydrangea arborescens*, *H. macrophylla*, *H. quercifolia*, and *H. serrata* with a sharp spade or knife. The stem and attached root pieces can be replanted around the garden or transplanted to a container. Cut the severed stems back to about half their length to induce new shoots. The resulting plants develop into more dense specimens.

Layering

Layering is an ancient technique whereby stems, still attached to the parent plant, are placed in a small hole or trench, covered with loose soil, and held in place with rocks, bricks, wood, or pins. Roots form on the covered parts and can be severed from the parent plant the following year. Layering is typically accomplished in late summer and fall into winter with new plants ready for removal one year later. Fall-layered 'Grayswood' seedlings in the Dirr garden had sufficient roots for transplanting by April the following year.

I have also observed dormant stems of *Hydrangea macrophylla*—removed from the parent plant in late fall and winter, placed in a shallow trench, and covered with soil/organic matter—produce shoots, with roots, often with flower buds, from the buried nodes. The effect reminds of a row of beans or corn in the garden, except the vegetable is now a hydrangea. *Hydrangea macrophylla* 'Dooley' showed great propensity for this type of vegetative propagation. I suspect most *H. macrophylla* types would also fall in line.

Resources

Dip 'N Grow, Inc.
P.O. Box 1888
Clackamas, OR 97015-1888
tel: 866.347.6476
e-mail: sales@dipngrow.com
www.dipngrow.com

Coor Farm Supply Service, Inc.
3 Malta St.
P.O. Box 525
Smithfield, NC 27577
tel: 800.999.4573
fax: 919.934.1216
e-mail: coor@dockpoint.net

Park Seed Wholesale, Inc.
2 Parkton Ave.
Greenwood, SC 29647-0002
tel: 800.845.3366

Florikan
1523 Edger Place
Sarasota, FL 34240
tel: 941.377.8666

Scotts-Sierra Hort. Prod. Co.
14111 Scottslawn Rd.
Marysville, OH 43041
tel: 888.270.3714
www.scotts.com

CHAPTER FOURTEEN

Pests and Diseases

Hydrangeas are remarkably disease- and insect-free, except for the universality of powdery mildew. Other maladies rise and fall with varying environmental conditions. In our greenhouses, mildew, spider mites, and aphids are constant problems. Mite-feeding on *Hydrangea paniculata* was so intense that the foliage turned bleached brown and the plants were unsalvageable. Aphids prefer soft, succulent shoots, and when plants are forced in the greenhouse, it is like displaying an "Eat at Joe's (for free)" sign.

Diseases of *Hydrangea macrophylla* and other species are listed on the American Phytopathological Society Web site (www.apsnet.org), and Auburn University's excellent Web site (www.aces.edu/pubs/docs/A/ANR-1212/) provides in-depth information on diseases that affect hydrangeas and their controls; it is tough to navigate and can be backdoored (www.aces.edu)—then go to 1) publications, 2) agriculture, 3) plant pathology, 4) ornamentals, and, finally, 5) diseases of hydrangeas.

Bacterial Diseases

Bacterial blight. *Pseudomonas solanacearum* E. F. Sm.
Bacterial leaf spot. *Pseudomonas cichorii* (Swingle) Stapp.

Fungal Diseases

Anthracnose. *Colletrichum gloeosporioides* attacks flowers and leaves, creating circular to irregular brown spots. Hot, wet weather favors the development of the disease. Plants that are heavily fertilized are more susceptible. Prevalent on *Hydrangea macrophylla*.

Botrytis blight. *Botrytis cinerea* Pers.: Fr. Affects leaves, buds, and flowers, appearing as a ghostly gray mold-type growth, almost like bread mold. Leaves, when touched, literally disintegrate and fall apart. Fungicides are available for control. Most common on greenhouse-grown hydrangea; however, it occurs in overwintering houses when consecutive days of cloudy, rainy, humid weather occur. All *Hydrangea* species (major) are susceptible. Optimal temperature for the development of this disease is around 65°F.

Fungal leaf spots. *Cercospora hydrangeae* Ellis and Everh. in Atk. Cercospora leaf spot disfigures the leaves when it develops in late summer and fall. Symptoms are tan to gray lesions with dark purple halos. The lesions are roughly circular and sunken. Affects *Hydrangea arborescens*, *H. macrophylla*, *H. paniculata*, and *H. quercifolia*. Seldom kills plants but disfigures. Initiates in mid-summer, most noticeable by fall. Disease is most prevalent on plants in poor health. Frequent rains in late summer increase severity of infection.

    Corynespora cassiicola (Berk. and M. A. Curtis) C. T. Wei. A recent paper (Leite and Barreto 2000) describes multiple purple spots on flowers and leaf necrosis on *Hydrangea macrophylla* in highland localities of Brazil.

    Phyllosticta hydrangeae Ellis and Everh.

    Septoria hydrangeae Bizz.

Mushroom root rot. *Armillaria mellea*, *A. tabescens*. Also called armillaria root rot, this disease occurs in landscape plantings of hydrangea, particularly *Hydrangea quercifolia*. The causal fungi are common in the soil. I have observed this on *H. quercifolia*, especially on drought-stressed or weakened plants. A branch appears wilted and when watered, the leaves remain flaccid and limp. The fungus attacks the shoot under the bark often at the root collar. In short, proper cultural conditions are the best protection against the disease. Keep the plant healthy and vigorous.

Phytophthora root rot. *Phytophthora nicotiana* (formerly *P. parasitica*). Common on *Hydrangea quercifolia* in container culture. It also occurs on other hydrangeas. Sudden wilting of the foliage, yellowing, leaf drop, and stunting are symptomatic. The young feeder roots are brown rather than whitish. Typically, excessive watering (and underwatering) contributes to the development of the disease. Maintain excellent drainage and even moisture.

Powdery mildew. *Erysiphe polygoni* DC. Mildew is troublesome outdoors in spring and fall, when day temperatures are warm, nights are cool, and humidity is high. In September and October (Athens), plants that were clean suddenly become gray. Note that yellow or purple blotches may also appear from mildew infestation. The greenhouse environment is also perfect for mildew development, seemingly year-round. In our tests for mildew resistance, rooted cuttings are placed on greenhouse benches. Without any fungicidal treatment, mildew appears in spades. If a seedling or cultivar does not develop mildew, then resistance is significant.

Hydrangea serrata, *H. paniculata*, and *H. arborescens* are mildew susceptible. Certainly, *H. macrophylla* is the worst, followed in descending order by the above. Taxa such as 'Lilacina', 'Veitchii', 'Ayesha', and 'Lady in Red' are resistant (not immune), while 'Nikko Blue', 'Preziosa', 'Holstein', 'Générale Vicomtesse de Vibraye', and many old French and German cultivars are susceptible. Based on our Georgia work, immunity to mildew does not exist within *H. macrophylla*, and the best hope is for high resistance.

The following evaluation data (18 September 2001, UGA Hydrangea Shade Garden, Athens, Georgia) affords a quantifiable index of mildew susceptibility. All plants were growing under 50 percent saran shade, cheek to jowl. Obviously, mildew inoculum was abundant. Worthwhile emphasizing that of the *Hydrangea macrophylla* taxa, only 'Veitchii' had *no* mildew. The scale: 1 = no visible mildew; 2 = 1 to 25 percent of leaf surface affected; 3 = 26 to 50 percent of leaf surface affected; 4 = 51 to 75 percent of leaf surface affected; 5 = 76 to 100 percent of leaf surface affected.

Hydrangea arborescens
'Eco Pink Puff'—1
'Wesser Falls'—1

Hydrangea macrophylla
'All Summer Beauty'—4
'Alpenglühen'—2 (1-gallon)
'Ami Pasquier'—2 (1-gallon)
'Ayesha'—2 (on 1- and 3-
    gallon)
'Blushing Pink'—2 (1-gallon)
'Dooley'—4 (1-gallon)
'Firelight'—3
'Forever Pink'—3 (on 3-gallon),
    2 (on 1-gallon)
'Freudenstein'—3
'Frillibet'—2
'Geisha Girl'—2 (1-gallon)
'Général Vicomtesse de
    Vibraye'—4 (on 3-gallon), 3
    (on 1-gallon)
'Goliath'—3 (on 3-gallon), 2
    (on 1-gallon)
'Hillier Blue'—4
'Holstein'—4
'Lilacina'—2 (on 1- and 3-
    gallon)
'Mme Emile Mouillère'—3 (on
    1- and 3-gallon)
'Mariesii Variegata'—2 (on 3-
    gallon), 3 (on 1-gallon)

'Mousmée'—3 (1-gallon)
'Nigra'—3 (on 1- and 3-gallon)
'Nikko Blue'—4 (on 3-gallon),
    5 (on 1-gallon)
'Pia' ('Winning Edge')—2
'Soeur Thérèse' ('Sister
    Theresa')—2 (1-gallon)
'Souvenir du Pdt. Paul
    Doumer'—2 (1-gallon)
'Veitchii'—1
'Westfalen'—4 (on 3-gallon), 2
    (on 1-gallon)
'White Wave'—2 (on 3-gallon),
    1 (on 1-gallon)

Hydrangea paniculata 'Chantilly
    Lace'—1

Hydrangea scandens—1

Hydrangea serrata
'Kiyosumisawa' ('Pulchra')—1
'Miranda'—2
'Miyama-yae-Murasaki'
    ('Purple Tiers')—2
'Preziosa'—4
'Shichidanka' ('Pretty
    Maiden')—1
'Tiara'—2
'Tokyo Delight'—2 (1-gallon)
'Woodlander'—2

Root rot. *Pythium* spp.

Rust. *Pucciniastrum hydrangeae* (Magn.) Arth.

Southern blight. *Sclerotium rolfsii* Sacc. [teleomorph: *Athelia rolfsii* (Curzi) Tu and Kimbrough]

Viral Diseases

Viral diseases are among the reasons hydrangeas cannot be directly imported into the United States and must be held in quarantine.

Phyllody. Hydrangea ringspot virus; has been eliminated from *Hydrangea serrata* via tissue culture.

Ringspots. Other ringspots that affect hydrangeas include tobacco ringspot virus, tomato spotted wilt virus, and tomato ringspot virus.

Virescence. Mallet reports this condition, in which the sepals are green and show irregular development. She noted two collections of hydrangeas were devastated in Japan. Leaves may also be distorted and show unusual greenish color combinations. I have not read about this problem in the American literature, but on occasion, I have observed a condition that appeared to coincide with this description on an isolated rooted cutting in the greenhouse. Agent responsible is apparently a phytoplasma.

Principal Insect Pests

Aphids savor the new growth, cause stunting and distortion, and coat the leaves with sticky honeydew. Check the young shoots if growth is less than expected. Simply wash off or use Safer Soap. Do not overreact.

The four-lined plant bug causes round, brown, sunken spots on the leaves. I have yet to observe damage via the insect.

Japanese beetles will occasionally browse on the foliage of *Hydrangea aspera* and *H. paniculata*. I have not observed significant damage to hydrangeas in general from this pest.

A leaf tier webs the leaves over the tip of the branches. This small larval insect has caused problems on seedlings and forced plants in the greenhouse. Leaves are rolled, distorted, with cottony mass when unrolled. Pick off and destroy damaged leaves. *Hydrangea arborescens* appears the most susceptible.

Rose chafers are light tan beetles with red, spindly legs, though they can be darker. I have not seen them in action.

Oystershell scale infests the upper stems of hydrangeas but is seldom a significant problem.

Mites feed on the underside of the leaves, causing spotting and yellowing and defoliation. They are more problematic in warm greenhouses or polyhouses. If mite activity is suspected, remove a leaf and shake above a white piece of paper. If specks (really tiny) are moving, mites are present. Through thousands of seedlings of many hydrangea species, minimal mite problems have developed. Tough to control for homeowner. Keep plants healthy and vigorous.

Japanese beetle damage on *Hydrangea aspera* subsp. *sargentiana*

Other Pests

Slugs, those rather nasty slimy creatures, apparently are pests where excessive moisture is present. Haworth-Booth (1984) gives more press to these creatures than any insect pest of hydrangea. Baits and beer ("only the good stuff") will slow them down.

Unfortunately, deer relish *Hydrangea macrophylla* and other hydrangeas and must be kept at bay. In fact, one of my gardening buddies, to whom I offer the stray breeding seedlings, seeks cover to avoid saying no. The deer made him hydrangea- and Dirr-shy.

CHAPTER FIFTEEN

Hydrangea Potpourri

Toxicity

Several references surfaced relative to dermatitis from contact with *Hydrangea macrophylla*. Flower buds and leaves are the toxic parts of the plant. I do not know anyone who has experienced problems, but this cautionary note may prove helpful. *Hydrangea macrophylla* contains cyanogenic derivatives (hydrogine), which could induce nausea, vomiting, headaches, and breathing difficulties if ingested.

In France, nurserymen and florists in repeated contact with the plants developed dry, cracked skin inflammation; only one case was described in an amateur (from Shamrock Newsletter No. 9, January 2003, page 5, excerpted from an article by Jean-Claude Rzeznick, in *Les Nouvelles Dermatologiques*, September 2002). Occurrence is rare and then only in the case of those who repeatedly touch plants.

Herbal Uses

A body of information exists on the use of *Hydrangea arborescens* roots for health purposes. The Internet is rich with the history, lore, and curative properties as well as sources. In brief, the dried root, rhizome, and leaves are used medicinally. Cherokee Indians used a root decoction or tea as a diuretic, cathartic, and emetic. A poultice, made from the bark, was used for burns, wounds, aching muscles, and sprains. Bark was chewed for stomach problems and heart trouble.

It is most often cited for its solvent properties, which assist with the breakdown and further dissolution of stones and deposits in the urinary system. Has been utilized for hundreds of years in folk medicine to contribute to the elimination of deposits in the bladder and kidney. Soothes irritated mucous membranes and relieves backache caused by kidney problems. Also, recognized in the treatment of inflamed or enlarged prostate glands.

Other adaptations for medicine are described but possibly exceed the limits of imagination as far as preventative and curative properties. Both capsules and a tincture are available.

Cutting Hydrangeas

Here follow guidelines for cutting hydrangeas for use as fresh cut flowers, as presented by Donna Mills of Floral & Hardy Farm, 1824 Old Barnwell Rd., Lexington, SC 29073; e-mail: floralandhardyfarm@hotmail.com; tel: 803.957.4594:

1. Water plants thoroughly the day before cutting them.
2. Take a bucket filled with tepid water into the garden; plunging stems into water immediately will make a difference in their vase life.
3. Make sure buckets are clean. Use a little bleach to kill bacteria.
4. Cut flowers when 90 percent of florets are open. Some varieties are subject to wilting if cut too early.
5. Remove lower leaves that will be under water.
6. Maintain water at about 100°F for best hydration.
7. If wilting occurs, use a hydrating solution such as Quick Dip, available at most floral suppliers.
8. Place in a floral preservative, either purchased from a florist or floral supplier or homemade. Two favorites: 1 tablespoon sugar + $\frac{1}{2}$ teaspoon bleach + 2 tablespoons lemon juice per 24 ounces water; 1

part 7-Up or Sprite (with sugar, not diet) to 1 part water + ½ teaspoon bleach per 24 ounces water.

9. Store in a cool place out of drafts and out of direct sunlight.

10. Spray with Floralife FloralMist for maximum life.

Drying and Dyeing Hydrangeas

As presented by Judith King of www.hydrangeashydrangeas.com

The secret to beautifully dried hydrangeas is choosing the right time of year
to harvest. This is far more important than the method one uses. While it is
tempting to cut the flowers at the height of their color, fresh, recently
opened flowers rarely dry well in the open air. Hydrangeas do best when allowed to dry a bit on the plant before picking. Experiment with harvesting
from August through October.

'Penny Mac', flowers
drying on the plant

As to actual methods of drying, easist of all is to leave flowers on the plant; some hydrangeas dry beautifully in shades of lavender, purple, green, pink, and burgundy while on the shrub. Another simple method: cut the flowers just as they begin to lose their "fresh" color, arrange them in a vase, with or without water, and leave them to dry. To retain extremely natural hydrangea color, use silica gel to dry fresh blooms. Do not use a microwave!

The method of drying hydrangeas with silica gel will result in vivid colors and an amazingly natural appearance. While this process is very simple, it must be pursued over a number of weeks to obtain enough dried flower heads to make an arrangement.

DRYING HYDRANGEAS WITH SILICA GEL

1. Use plastic Tupperware-type containers that are large enough to hold flowers without crushing them.
2. Cut fresh, recently opened hydrangeas from the shrub on the morning of the day they are to be put into the silica.
3. Cut stems very short so they will fit in containers.
4. Place hydrangea head in the container on a thin layer of silica gel. (Experiment with stem being up or down.) Gradually sift silica around the head, working it into the center and under all petals.
5. When the first flower is covered, continue to layer whole or parts of flower heads with silica gel to within a ½ inch of container lid. Do not force them to fit in the container, or they will be unnaturally shaped.
6. Secure lid on container and label with date.
7. Four days later, pour contents very slowly onto newspaper and pluck out hydrangeas.
8. Gently tap them clean and place in plastic bags for storage until ready for use.

Do not leave hydrangeas in silica for more than four days, or they will be too brittle (unless silica is more than two to three years old). To lengthen a stem that has been cut short, tape a dry stem to hydrangea with florist tape. This is not necessary for a wreath (duh!).

Dyeing dry hydrangeas is a messy process; protect the kitchen floor, your clothes, and other items from dripping dye. Before dyeing, consider spot-spraying the dry flowers with white spray paint. Concentrate spray on the centers of each floret. Spray all darkened areas of the flower. This method is especially useful for prolonging the beauty of older flowers.

Mix Rit Dye according to directions and bring to boil. Rit Dye can produce either deep or light colors. The deepest colors can be achieved by making sure the Rit Dye mixture is boiling before dipping the dry hydrangea heads into it; for lighter effects, leave head in dye less time or use lighter color dye.

Stunning Christmas tree ornaments, wreaths, and arrangements can be made with dry hydrangeas. Leave flower heads natural, or spray them gold, silver, or (believe it or not) red. In arrangements, combine hydrangeas with fresh ivy, nandina berries, or holly. On the tree, use a gold bow with each hydrangea head.

Hydrangea macrophylla trained as a standard, Longwood Gardens

Designing with Hydrangeas

Initially, like a cantankerous mule, I resisted the thought of a section on design. In fact, the entire book was written, proofed, and proofed again before the following thoughts were penned.

Much is made of design, in my estimation an exercise in pencil farming that impresses concepts to paper. This footprint is followed to various degrees to produce a landscape painting. My first (and only) legitimately focused design centered on the development of a red border, emulating Lawrence Johnston's great creation at Hidcote. Over the years, I visited Hidcote on 15 occasions; my fascination with the genius of the design *and* execution grew ever more intense. Yet, try as I might, the area designated as the Dirr red border is still higgledy-piggledy. The moral: garden (and design) to your abilities, taste, and budget. To copy is foolish. There is only one red border, and it is forever sacrosanct.

Now for hydrangeas. I'd rather be up against a firing squad than try to re-count the numerous combinations and permutations that have pleased me. At Trelissick, a National Trust garden in Cornwall, 360-some cultivars were enmeshed, like a wildflower meadow, simply with greater wallop. A mass planting is spectacular and can stop a getaway car of bank robbers. The gi-ant masses are the domain of larger properties, where sweeps of blue, pink, red, and/or white truly mesmerize the eyes. In 1979, while visiting Cape Cod, Bonnie and I spied a walk lined with blue *Hydrangea macrophylla*. Whenever we discuss the impact of color, specifically from hydrangea, the phrase "Do you remember . . ." surfaces.

The negative side of these massive monoculture plantings is that cold can occasionally eliminate the flowers. The 70-plant mass, bordering a tree line at the Heritage Plantation, Sandwich, Cape Cod, Massachusetts, had three flowers when I observed it in 1991. A spring freeze had eliminated the flower buds. 'Nikko Blue' was the cultivar, and the foliage alone cannot carry the design.

Hydrangea macrophylla spilling into the walk

RHS Garden Wisley effectively integrates hydrangeas (several species), rhododendrons, small trees, and perennials in the Battleston Hill section. The hydrangeas peak in July and August, but there is always something of interest. However, at the same garden, in the Pinetum area, a large collection of *Hydrangea macrophylla* cultivars were sited in a low area where frost settled. In April 1999, a devastating frost laid waste to most of the plants and a decision was made to give (share) the collection with Abbotsbury Subtropical Garden, on the coast of Dorset.

Siting is important, especially for the frost sensitive taxa. Avoid low areas. Avoid wind-swept, full-sun areas, since foliage emerges early on most hydrangeas and can suffer desiccation and tattering; utilize fences, evergreens, and the north and east sides of the house, to provide protection. In the Dirr garden, every *Hydrangea macrophylla*, *H. serrata*, *H. quercifolia*, *H. scandens*, and *H. anomala* subsp. *petiolaris* enjoys various degrees of shade. *Hydrangea paniculata* 'Webb's' is the only taxon in full sun.

The greatest design attribute in addition to the wow color/size factor is the timing of floral presentation. Reflect on the species and cultivars discussed in this book. In Athens, the broadleaf canopy of trees is fully expanded by late April. The spring floral extravaganza (azalea, dogwood, redbuds) is kaput. Yet, hydrangeas spring into color-motion from mid-May to October. What better group of plants to provide summer floral color that lingers into fall? The colorful red-burgundy leaves of *Hydrangea quercifolia* even loiter into December, with new foliage evident in March.

For maximizing the length of the flowering experience, consider the flowering times of the various species. For the major landscape species, *Hydrangea quercifolia* is first, 15 to 31 May peak window in Athens, then *H. serrata* and *H. macrophylla*, which overlap, although in our evaluations the *H. serrata* taxa are generally in full flower before the *H. macrophylla*. Within *H. macrophylla*, Endless Summer™ was in full flower on 17 May 2003, 'Générale Vicomtesse de Vibraye' almost at peak, 'Lilacina' with sepals just emerging, and 'White Wave' with buds just expanding, still green, without visible sepals. This expansive variation is great for the knowledgeable designer, who can provide their clients with significant color for several months.

Hydrangea arborescens and cultivars parallel and/or follow the above group with flower buds expanding but still green. 'Annabelle', for example, would have dark green flower buds (inflorescences) expanded about ¼ to ½ their full size. Typically, mid-June is the peak show period for 'Annabelle' in the Dirr garden. Last in the sequence is *H. paniculata*; flower buds were not visible on 17 May 2003; July and August are the principal flowering times. Truly exciting, the color that can be brought to bear on the garden via wise hydrangea selection.

Gardeners are forever bemoaning the lack of flowering shrubs for shade. *Hydrangea arborescens*, *H. macrophylla*, *H. quercifolia*, and *H. serrata* are beyond reproach for low light conditions. If *H. quercifolia* never flowered, it would still be a great asset to the shady border. The fact that it flowers profusely under such conditions, at least in Zones 7 to 9 of the Southeast, is like 20 percent interest. The Atlanta Botanical Garden's excellent hydrangea collection is sited under hickories, oaks, and tuliptrees. As I experienced it on 18 May 2003, the profuseness of flower production was spectacular; the garden's key is good soil preparation and timely irrigation.

In English garden literature and gardens, shrub borders are discussed and presented, respectively. The idea of meshing shrubs into a presentable whole appears foreign to American gardens. Certainly, herbaceous perennial borders are fashionable and seemingly on the menu of every garden symposium. When was the last time the reader listened to a *knowledgeable* speaker address the principles and practices of the shrub border? For over 20 years, Bonnie and I have fitted and retrofitted such a border with abelia, viburnum, tea-

Hydrangea macrophylla (left) and *H. serrata*

Hydrangea arborescens 'Annabelle' and cohorts

Hydrangea aspera subsp. *sargentiana*, the dead-stick appearance of early spring

olive, camellia, and oakleaf hydrangea. There is texture, color, fragrance, seasonality, and minimal maintenance. Hydrangeas do not have to be the star of every show. One here, another over there, meshed with shrubby cohorts, results in a pleasing composition.

Hydrangea macrophylla and *H. serrata* make good container plants as long as the drainage is even and the moisture constant. 'Générale Vicomtesse de Vibraye', in a large terra-cotta container, was effective for two months. A vacation for 10 days proved costly. We should have remained home and cared for the Générale.

Hydrangeas do not make great foundation plants, with their dry, dead-stick appearance, potential for dieback, and deciduous nature. In the South, *Hydrangea macrophylla* was often planted in front of older homes—magnificent in May and June, less so in the heat of summer. The dried brown inflorescences (and dead stems) are seldom removed and stick out like sore thumbs in late summer and fall, particularly if rainfall was sparse. At Arlington Court, in Devon, however, the Manor House was skirted with *H. macrophylla*. Perhaps they do make good foundation plantings.

If rules exist for the use of hydrangeas in contemporary garden making, I suggest the reader disobey. If ever a group of plants, when in full plumage, overshadowed their subordinates, the hydrangeas do, eloquently and forcefully. May your garden be graced by at least one of the hydrangeas discussed in the book.

Hydrangeas at Trelissick

A border of *Hydrangea macrophylla*

CHAPTER SIXTEEN

The Future:
Breeding and Improvement

Hydrangea breeding, largely via open-pollinated seedlings, was initiated in the early 1900s by Lemoine of Nancy and Mouillère of Vendôme, France. Their introductions of *Hydrangea macrophylla* are still among the most popular, but by no means are the French the only contributors to *H. macrophylla* improvement. Anyone interested in the numerous breeders, particularly with *H. macrophylla*, should consult Haworth-Booth and the Mallets (a brief history is presented in the *H. macrophylla* chapter herein). Open-pollinated breeding means the mother or seed-producing plant was randomly pollinated by any number of males or pollen-bearing plants. Typically, bees are the principal vectors for pollen transfer, although I have observed all manner of insects moving to and fro from the opening flowers, no doubt serendipitously spreading pollen. Amazingly, Pilatowski (1982) identified 52 species of insects from inflorescences of *Hydrangea*, mainly in the area of Highlands, North Carolina. The insects represented seven orders and 27 families.

In our work at the UGA Hydrangea Shade Garden, open-pollinated seedling populations of *Hydrangea arborescens* and subsp. *discolor*, *H. heteromalla*, *H. macrophylla*, *H. paniculata*, *H. quercifolia*, *H. serrata*, and *H. sikokiana* were grown to flowering. The learning curve was steep, and over time production protocol was developed that facilitated flowering in one to two growing seasons; please refer to chapter 13 for specifics. For breeding activities with the various species, refer to their specific treatments, later in this chapter.

Our protocol for controlled- and open-pollinations is as follows:

CONTROLLED CROSSES

1. Plants moved to warm greenhouse in early January from outdoor growing area. Day temperature ±75°F, night ±65°F.

2. Flowers are fully expressed and ready to shed pollen in 10 to 12 weeks. Three to five inflorescences are pollinated per plant, the others removed. The majority of the crosses are completed by the end of March.

3. Pollen is collected in plastic vials and stored at approximately 40°F or collected fresh and utilized immediately.

4. Pollinations are accomplished in the morning between 6:30 a.m. and 10:00 a.m.

5. Flowers of the maternal parent are carefully emasculated (stamens removed) with tweezers. This may not be necessary based on Reed and others' reports of self-sterility, but we do not take chances.

6. Pollen is transferred to the stigma with a fine camel-hair paintbrush, and the flower is labeled with maternal parent, pollen parent, date, and the individual making the crosses. All utensils, brushes, etc., are sterilized in isopropyl alcohol.

7. Pollinated flowers are not bagged since there are no insects or breezes and the bags might injure the succulent flower parts.

8. Plants are moved outside in May and carefully monitored for insects and diseases.

9. When the infructescences (fruit clusters) are mature and turn brown, they are harvested, dried, and cleaned to remove seed (see chapter 13).

10. Seed is sown immediately as described in chapter 7, *Hydrangea macrophylla*. Seed can also be placed in glass vials, properly labeled, and stored in the refrigerator until the normal spring planting sequence. If sown early (i.e., fall), seedlings must be carefully tended because of lower light levels in winter. Overwatering is the largest problem. Also, mildew can wreak havoc on the young seedlings. We utilize 60 watt bulbs to simulate long days and keep the seedlings in active growth.

OPEN POLLINATIONS (ALL OUTSIDE)

1. Plants for breeding (♀) by insects are placed in rows of three, alternating with the pollen (♂) parent(s).
2. Plants are grown in a 55 percent saran shade house and monitored for nutrition, insects, and diseases.
3. Normal flowering times for *Hydrangea serrata* and *H. macrophylla* are mid-May to mid-June in Athens, and fruit maturation occurs in October and November.
4. Collection, cleaning, and sowing are as for controlled crosses.

The most obvious truism, learned via growing over 15,000 hydrangea seedlings, is that the maternal parent exerts an unbelievably profound influence on the offspring. On occasion, I wondered whether the male was involved in the fertilization process. The seedlings inherit the foliar and growth characteristics as well as the disease (mildew) susceptibility of the mother plant. The flower characteristics are the most variable (a wonderful happenstance), with mopheads and lacecaps often occurring in the same population; sepals—round, entire, toothed, large, small, and in every imaginable color. At times, the resultant flower characteristics are unexplainable.

From 1999 to 2002, immense seedling populations (4,072) representing 27 *Hydrangea macrophylla* and *H. serrata* taxa (see list that follows) flowered at the Center for Applied Nursery Research, Dearing, Georgia, and Dudley Nurseries, Thomson, Georgia. All 'Forever Pink' and 'All Summer Beauty' produced mophead flowers; all 'Grayswood' produced lacecap inflorescences. Taxa like 'White Wave', 'Nigra', and 'Nikko Blue' produced both lacecap and mopheads. Seeds were collected from all the taxa, growing cheek by jowl in the shade houses at our UGA production location. Sandra Reed, United States Department of Agriculture, United States National Arboretum, McMinnville, Tennessee, showed that *H. macrophylla* was essentially self-infertile, meaning pollen from the same flower (plant) cannot affect fruit development and/or viable seed formation. I suspect that this varies with the species and cultivars. For example, selfed 'Dooley' (*H. macrophylla*) produced mopheads, as did selfed 'Annabelle' (*H. arborescens*). In 2001, open-pollinated 'Veitchii' (white lacecap) possibly outcrossed with 'Dooley' and/or 'Nikko Blue' in a garden setting yielded, out of approximately 800 seedlings, a 3:1 ratio of lacecap to mophead.

The *Hydrangea macrophylla* and *H. serrata* taxa utilized in the 1999-2002 breeding program were as follows:

Hydrangea macrophylla (mopheads)	*Hydrangea macrophylla* (lacecaps) unknown taxon
'All Summer Beauty'	'Lady in Red'
'Ayesha'	'Lanarth White'
'Dooley'	'Libelle'
Endless Summer™ ('Bailmer')	'Lilacina'
'Forever Pink'	'White Wave'
'Freudenstein'	'Veitchii'
'Générale Vicomtesse de Vibraye'	
'Goliath'	*Hydrangea serrata*
'Holstein'	'Golden Sunlight' (lacecap)
'Mme Emile Mouillère'	'Grayswood' (lacecap)
'Nigra'	'Miranda' (lacecap)
'Nikko Blue'	'Preziosa' (mophead)
'Otaksa'	'Tokyo Delight' (lacecap)
'Penny Mac'	
'Westfalen'	

Again, if the maternal parent is mildew prone, then the offspring, for the most part, inherit the problem. All the 'Forever Pink' and 'All Summer Beauty' seedlings were rampant with mildew in late summer and fall of 2002 and were scrapped. 'Ayesha', 'Lilacina', 'Veitchii', and 'White Wave' show good resistance, not immunity, and provide the best chance for success. However, two selections, Ayesha-07-02 and Ayesha-08-02, yielded polar opposite data, with the former highly mildew resistant; the latter covered with the disease. Both were growing side-by-side in the evaluations.

I do not believe there are guarantees for greatness from any maternal parent, only a more realistic "chance." In our work, controlled crosses in the greenhouse have become de rigueur. The parental types (taxa) that give the maximum opportunity to attain the stated goals are crossed. The use of the best foliage, flower, and mildew resistant types crossed with the remontant (reblooming) taxa provides the springboard for a quantum leap into the next generation of everblooming garden hydrangeas. I reflect on the *Hydrangea macrophylla* breeding time frame, noting that almost 100 years have dissipated since the great French breeders worked their magic for the growers and gardeners of the world. I believe that with patience and persistence, our program at the University of Georgia will incorporate compactness, superior foliage, fall color, disease resistance, strong stems, stem color, and remontant flowering into a single genotype.

Other breeders and scientists are also striving to improve hydrangeas via unique and/or more difficult approaches. Breeders are dreamers, conceptualizing and visualizing the future, then tenaciously and tediously trying to seize that elusive dream with a plant that equates with the goal(s). For example, if the genes of *Hydrangea arborescens* and *H. paniculata*, which are cold hardy and, more importantly, flower on new growth, could be incorporated into *H. macrophylla* and *H. quercifolia*, which flower on old (previous season's growth), then the resultant hybrids could successfully grow and flower from Nome, Alaska, to Tallahassee, Florida. With the advances in biotechnology, there is little doubt that these Star Wars plants will eventually become reality.

For the present, allow me to elaborate on the work of Nobuhiro Kudo and Yosiji Niimi (1999b), in which the development of a plant was dependent on the use of cotyledonary segments of embryos derived from crosses of *Hydrangea macrophylla* 'Blaumeise' ('Blue Sky') x *H. arborescens* 'Annabelle'. No viable plants resulted from conventional hybridization: the progenies exhibited hybrid lethality at the young seedling stage. Of 15 callus lines (cultures), only one regenerated plantlets, which were transplanted to soil. Hybridity was confirmed by leaf, chromosome, and DNA (RAPD) markers. Kudo and Niimi found that viable seeds were recovered from the crosses only when *H. macrophylla* served as the maternal parent.

Reed (2000a) reported similar results when *Hydrangea macrophylla* served as the female parent in crosses of *H. arborescens*, *H. paniculata*, and *H. quercifolia*. In the same paper, she reported that selfed flowers of *H. arborescens* and 'Annabelle' produced no viable seed. Our work with selfed 'Annabelle' resulted in many seedlings. Selfed *H. macrophylla* taxa, except for 'Alpenglühen' (8 seeds germinated), and *H. serrata* produced no viable seed. Of seven selfed *H. quercifolia* taxa, only 'Pee Wee' yielded seeds that germinated (5 in number). With selfed *H. paniculata*, 'Brussels Lace', 'Burgundy Lace', and 'Unique', only 'Unique' produced seedlings (18 in number).

Pilatowski crossed *Hydrangea arborescens* × subsp. *discolor* with no fruit set; subsp. *discolor* × subsp. *radiata* = 10 percent fruit set; *arborescens* × subsp. *radiata* = 0 percent fruit set; subsp. *discolor* × *arborescens* = 0 percent fruit set; subsp. *radiata* × *arborescens* = 0 percent fruit set; and subsp. *radiata* × subsp. *discolor* = 10 percent fruit set. His sample size was small (10 flowers), but it points to barriers between and among the various taxa. His contention for taking subsp. *discolor* and subsp. *radiata* to species *H. cinerea* and *H. radiata*, respectively, is that although they overlap in nature, they do not interbreed and produce hybrid swarms. In short, they maintain their genetic purity and thus their unique phenotypic characteristics.

Sandra Reed's work indicates that most of the common landscape species and cultivars of hydrangea are self-incompatible. This would mean that breeders do not need to emasculate (remove stamens) from the plant to be pollinated; however, I have reservations. Our work to date with selfed 'Annabelle' and 'Dooley' produced viable seed and flowering seedlings with largely mophead inflorescences.

Kudo and Niimi (1999a) present more valuable information for readers interested in interspecific *Hydrangea* breeding:

- Pollen of *Hydrangea macrophylla* and *H. arborescens* stored at -4°F retained germination capacity for a long time; at 23°F, viability was retained for up to 5 months.

- Fresh and stored pollen of both species germinated well on the stigma in self, intraspecific, and interspecific pollinations.

- In self and intraspecific crosses, the two species set fruits (capsules) and produced mature seeds.

- Seeds germinated, but showed arrested growth after development of the cotyledons, and then died.

■ A plant was produced from cotyledonary callus, not via normal seed germination.

What comes to light via the work of researchers Kudo, Niimi, and Reed is that wide, interspecific crosses yield minimal to no viable seed. The seeds that do germinate die off quickly or develop into weak, spindly plants. Embryo rescue via tissue culture is potentially the only way to salvage plants. Reed's work trying to incorporate the cold hardiness and reflowering traits of *Hydrangea paniculata* into *H. macrophylla*, after thousands of crosses, resulted in only five *H. macrophylla* 'Kardinal' x *H. paniculata* 'Brussels Lace' hybrid seedlings that survived. Characteristics were similar to *H. paniculata*. Only one was sufficiently vigorous and provided potential for backcrossing. These five hybrids were verified by DNA (Reed et al. 2001).

When breeders dare to travel where most never dream, guarantees are never in absolute terms. Reed's papers (see References) should be required reading for anyone daring enough to take the quantum leap into the world of *Hydrangea* improvement.

It is worth noting that Haworth-Booth reported Monsieur L. Foucard, Orléans, France, produced a remarkable hybrid between *Hydrangea macrophylla* var. *rosea* ('Rosea') and *H. paniculata* in 1910. The hybrid produced pink flowers and clearly showed its parentage in the intermediate character. The plant was lost during World War I. Another unusual hybrid was orchestrated by Monsieur Henri Cayeux, Le Havre, France, when he crossed *H. macrophylla* var. *rosea* ('Rosea') and *H. petiolaris* (*H. anomala* subsp. *petiolaris*) and produced a curious plant that he named x*H. hortentiolaris*. This was destroyed in World War II. Truly quite amazing that until the 1990s no one attempted to duplicate the successes of these unusual crosses or at least publish the results! History provides a foundation for future activities. I believe the possibilities for *Hydrangea* improvement are monumental, and the current rumblings portend the volcanic eruptions that will occur.

Certainly most of the improvement has been targeted toward *Hydrangea macrophylla* and logically so, since this is the major commercial species in the world. Most selections of *H. quercifolia* are seedling variations that were capitalized on by opportunistic plantspeople, collectors, and nursery personnel.

Eddie Aldridge's great 'Snowflake', discovered in 1969, patented in 1971, is still the acknowledged premier cultivar. Don Shadow, Shadow Nursery, Inc., Winchester, Tennessee, has grown thousands of seedlings of Snow Queen® ('Flemygea') and others without introducing a single clone. Likewise, I have grown numerous 'Alice' and 'Amethyst' seedlings and have yet to target any that are better than the maternal parents. The wonderful array of *H. quercifolia* cultivars already offers compactness ('Pee Wee', 'Sikes Dwarf'); large habit, flowers, and ease of culture ('Alice'); and largely sterile and/or double flowers ('Harmony', 'Roanoke', 'Snowflake'). Any selection should be scrutinized against the current cast of stars. No doubt, superior forms exist in the wild; it is just a matter of stumbling upon them.

Reed is crossing *Hydrangea quercifolia* 'Pee Wee', 'Sikes Dwarf', and Snow Queen®, trying to develop compact cultivars with good flowering characteristics and autumn foliage. Open-pollinated 'Pee Wee' and 'Sikes Dwarf' yielded no dwarf seedlings, indicating that compact habit is a recessive trait. She has a plant that has shorter internodes and thicker stems than 'Pee Wee'. To repeat, oakleaf hydrangea is a tough act to follow (or improve upon).

Hydrangea paniculata and its dominant cultivar, 'Grandiflora' (introduced circa 1867 from Japan) have populated every country in the world where culture is possible. Largely, the impetus for new cultivars arrived with the 1968 introduction (de Belder's) of 'Unique', large-flowered and -sepaled, a seedling of 'Floribunda'. The de Belders, of Kalmthout Arboretum, Belgium, grew many seedling populations of 'Unique' and by my count introduced five, along with five others from different parents. I have grown large seedling populations of 'Brussels Lace' and Pink Diamond and, in their early years, was simply not enamored with the results. Then in 2001-2002 energetic and focused evaluations of the 491 seedlings pinpointed 24 selections. Several have superior dark green foliage, strong stems that hold the flowers upright, and large sepals that cover the fertile flowers. They resist the blistering heat of Zone 7b and are presentable in October. One clone, Brussels Lace-17-01, turns brilliant rose-burgundy in late summer. Brussels Lace-04-01 and Brussels Lace-22-02 are 22 by 33 inches and 14 by 20 inches, respectively, after three years. Both are compact mounds of dark green foliage with small panicles of showy sepals and fertile flowers.

Final Thoughts

According to Haworth-Booth (1984), most *Hydrangea macrophylla* cultivars, including 'Joseph Banks', 'Otaksa', 'Rosea', 'Mariesii', 'Veitchii', and *H. japonica*, are hybrids of mixed parentage. He further stated that these clonal cultivars of *H. macrophylla*, used as foundations, already contained the "blood" (genes) of the three woodland species. See H. serrata (chapter 10) for a discussion of the three subspecies that equate with Haworth-Booth's woodland species.

This theory is also espoused by the Mallets in *Hydrangea International Index of Cultivar Names* (2002), in which they address the presentation of names thusly:

> For certain cultivars resulting from extensive cross-breeding, the species name can only be given for information as a plant may contain genetic material from several species or subspecies. Thus many cultivars previously classified under *macrophylla* are now written without a species name, e.g., *H.* 'Arburg'. Only "pure" *H. macrophylla* such as *H. macrophylla* 'Izu-no-Hana' are written with the species name.

Hydrangea macrophylla 'Izu-no-Hana'

The authorities just cited have evaluated more hydrangeas than this author could hope to see in five lifetimes. However, the thought always surfaces relative to the purity of the seedling populations of *Hydrangea macrophylla* taxa. In our work, most are similar in leaf, stem, and habit characteristics to the ideal for *H. macrophylla*; likewise for *H. serrata* seedlings. In breeding, if the parentage was mulligan stew (mixed), then subsequent generations removed from the original hybrid cultivar should show segregates representative of the original contributors. For example, *Abelia*, *Buddleia*, *Gardenia*, *Lagerstroemia*, *Nandina*, and *Viburnum* open-pollinated maternal parents produced unbelievable variation in the seedling populations.

Wilson (1923) noted that he was unable to assign hybrid status to any of the 40 French hybrid *Hydrangea macrophylla* he received from Messrs Dreer & Co., Riverton, New Jersey. In *none* could he find any signs of *H. serrata* and its forms.

Mark Fillan, Fillan's Plants, England, mentioned that he is evaluating exciting hybrids between *Hydrangea macrophylla* and *H. serrata*. Also, in the Shamrock Newsletter No. 10, April 2003, Tetsu Hirasawa reported natural hybrids of the two species on the Izu Peninsula. I have often reflected on why breeders have not incorporated the genes of *H. serrata* into *H. macrophylla*, although speculation centers on the hybrid nature of many of the mopheads. If natural hybrids occur, then the potential for controlled crosses is realistic.

Potential for mutation breeding is genuine, and mutagenic agents like colchicine and ethyl methanesulfonate may induce polyploidy or gene mutations, respectively. This approach is common among daylily and magnolia breeders who strive for large flowers. Can the reader imagine 'Otaksa Monstrosa' (immense mophead) or 'Beauté Vendômoise' (immense sepals) with even larger flowers? Certainly the opportunity exists for creating thicker, darker green leaves and stronger stems via chemical mutagens. The entire process: spray young seedlings while in active growth with aerosols of the mutagenic agent and hope the apical meristem is altered. Usually the seedlings impacted are phenotypically larger. Various indices such as leaf length:width ratios are utilized to assess change. Ideally, chromosome counts will verify polyploidy. *Hydrangea macrophylla*, *H. anomala* subsp. *petiolaris*, *H. arborescens*, *H. aspera*, *H. scandens*, *H. paniculata*, *H. heteromalla*, and *H. quercifolia* have $n = 18$ chromosomes. *Hydrangea paniculata* 'Floribunda' and 'Praecox' are tetraploids with 72 chromosomes. From a collection in Angers, France, of 121 *H. macrophylla* tested, 21 were triploids ($3n = 54$). All other cultivars were $2n = 36$ ($n = 18$). Some variation in *H. aspera*, $2n = 30$, $2n = 34$, $2n = 36$, was reported in *Theoretical and Applied Genetics* 103:45-51 (2001).

Another chemical agent, ethyl methanesulfonate, also has potential for mutation breeding. The chemical modifies cytosine, one of the nitrogen bases that constitute DNA. I know of one situation where it has been utilized for *Lagerstroemia* (crapemyrtle) improvement. Apparently the chemical affects gene expression, and the effects are totally random. The seeds are soaked for a period of time, and the effective concentration needs to be determined for each plant type. Seeds are sown and the resultant progeny evaluated for unique characteristics. Chromosome numbers (ploidy) are not affected as with colchicine. Simply, genes are altered, repressed, and/or expressed, leading to genetic and potentially phenotypic changes.

Lastly, another source of new and/or potentially useful cultivars is the chimera, or branch sport. A chimera represents a change in tissue composition that typically occurs in the meristem. These anomalies are manifested in different ways, with leaf variegation one of the most common (and easily observed). *Hydrangea serrata* 'Golden Sunlight' is a branch sport derived from 'Intermedia'. *Hydrangea macrophylla* 'Merritt's Supreme' produced several commercial sports, including 'Oregon Pride' and the 1996 patented potplant variety 'Ravel'.

In England, I was shown a white mophead branch sport of the classic white lacecap, 'Veitchii'. At Trelessick Garden, a sport of 'White Wave', called 'Penguin', with compact habit and abundant flowers caught my eye. 'Ayesha', with cupped, heavily textured sepals, is a branch sport. I have observed reversion shoots from 'Ayesha' to the typical thin sepal form at RHS Garden Wisley, England.

'Ayesha'

Most of the variegated leaf forms like 'Quadricolor', 'Lemon Wave', and 'Wave Hill' are branch sports. Typically, they are not stable and revert to albino and all-green shoots. Amazingly, 'Mariesii Variegata', which unfortunately is not stable, is one of the larger sellers in U.S. commerce.

In our program, many variegated seedlings occurred in the breeding process. Not a *single* one has been stable.

My advice to those who grow hydrangeas is to be on the lookout for the

strange anomalies called chimeras or sports . . . Occasionally, something beautiful and garden-worthy materializes.

The *Hydrangea* improvement story will continue to unfold as amateurs and professionals take up the mantle. The beehive-like activities in *Magnolia* and *Rhododendron* breeding and improvement foreshadow the potential opportunities for *Hydrangea*. The American Hydrangea Society (see Resources and Nursery Sources, under "Associations") will bring together those who love hydrangeas and foster the sharing of plants and ideas. Visitors from across the United States, France, England, New Zealand, and Japan have traveled to Athens, Georgia, seeking and sharing. The *Hydrangea* world will grow smaller.

RESOURCES AND NURSERY SOURCES

Associations

American Hydrangea Society
P.O. Box 11645
Atlanta, GA 30355-1645
http://dir.gardenweb.com/directory/ahs2/
Write the Society for a membership
and to receive the newsletters of the
American Hydrangea Society—
timely, new, and valuable information
from the experts.

**Friends of the Shamrock Hydrangea
Collection**
Collection d'Hydrangea Shamrock
Route de l'Eglise
76119 Varengeville-sur-Mer
France
http://ourworld.compuserve.com/ho
mepages/Jacoll/Shamrock.html

Hydrangeum vzw
Attn: Luc Balemans
Veldekensstraat 40
9070 Destelbergen
Belgium
tel/fax: 011.32.9.355.71.83
e-mail: hydrangeum@hotmail.com

Institut National d'Horticulture
Attn: Hélène Bertrand, National
Collection of Hydrangeas
2 rue Le Nôtre
49045 Angers cedex
France
tel: 011.33.2.41.22.54.54
(direct from the States)
fax: 011.33.2.41.73.15.57
(direct from the States)
e-mail: INH@angers.inra.fr

Information Web Sites

All About Hydrangeas
www.hydrangeashydrangeas.com

Pete's Hydrangeas
www.conweb.com/hydrangea

Noble Plants
www.nobleplants.com

Gardens to Visit

Check the American Association of
Botanical Gardens and Arboreta Web
site for other gardens around the
United States: www.aabga.org

Aldridge Gardens
3530 Lorna Rd.
Hoover, AL 35216
tel: 205.682.8019
www.aldridgegardens.com

The Arnold Arboretum
125 Arborway
Jamaica Plain, MA 02130
tel: 617.524.1718
www.arboretum.harvard.edu

Atlanta Botanical Garden
1345 Piedmont Ave. NE
Atlanta, GA 30309
tel: 404.876.5859
fax: 404.876.7472
www.atlantabotanicalgarden.org

Birmingham Botanical Gardens
2612 Lane Park Rd.
Birmingham, AL 35223
tel: 205.414.3900
www.bbgardens.org

Brooklyn Botanic Garden
1000 Washington Ave.
Brooklyn, NY 11225
tel: 718.622.4433
www.bbg.org

Brookside Gardens
1800 Glenallan Ave.
Wheaton, MD 20902
tel: 301.949.8230 or 301.962.1400
www.mc-mncppc.org/parks/brookside

JC Raulston Arboretum at NCSU
Dept. of Horticultural Science,
Box 7522
Raleigh, NC 27695-7522
Arboretum location: 4415 Beryl Rd.,
Raleigh
tel: 919.515.3132
www.ncsu.edu/jcraulstonarboretum

Lyle Littlefield Ornamental Garden
University of Maine
5722 Deering Hall
Orono, ME 04469-5722
tel: 207.581.2918
www.ume.maine.edu/~nfa/lhc/little.htm

Minnesota Landscape Arboretum
3675 Arboretum Blvd.
Chaska, MN 55318-9613
tel: 952.443.1400
www.arboretum.umn.edu

The Morton Arboretum
Route 53
Lisle, IL 60532
tel: 708.328.8025
www.mortonarb.org

Norfolk Botanical Garden
Kaufman Hydrangea Collection
6700 Azalea Garden Rd.
Norfolk, VA 25318-5337

tel: 757.441.5830
fax: 757.853.8294
www.norfolkbotanicalgarden.org

The Scott Arboretum
Swarthmore College
500 College Ave.
Swarthmore, PA 19081
tel: 215.328.8025
www.scottarboretum.org

Stephen F. Austin Mast Arboretum
P.O. Box 13000 SFA Station
Stephen F. Austin State University
Nacogdoches, TX 75962-3000
tel: 936.468.4343
www.sfasu.edu/ag/arboretum

UGA Hydrangea Shade Garden
University of Georgia
Dept. of Horticulture
Athens, GA 30602
tel: 706.542.2471
www.uga.edu/~hort

United States National Arboretum
3501 New York Ave. NE
Washington, DC 20002
tel: 202.245.2726
www.usna.usda.gov

Van Dusen Botanical Garden
5251 Oak St.
Vancouver, BC V6M 4H1
Canada
tel: 604.878.9274
www.city.vancouver.bc.ca/parks/parks
&gardens/vandusen

Washington Park Arboretum
University of Washington
Seattle, WA 98195
tel: 206.543.8800
http://depts.washington.edu/wpa/

Nursery Sources

Aesthetic Gardens (mail-order retail)
On-line catalog only.
www.agardens.com

Apalachee Nursery (wholesale)
1333 Kimsey Dairy Rd.
Turtletown, TN 37319
tel: 423.496.7246

Arrowhead Alpines (mail-order retail)
1310 N. Gregory Rd.
P.O. Box 857
Fowlerville, MI 48836
tel: 517.223.3581
fax: 517.223.8750
www.arrowheadalpines.com

Bailey Nurseries, Inc. (wholesale)
1325 Bailey Rd.
St. Paul, MN 55119
tel: 800.829.8898
fax: 800.829.8894
www.baileynursery.com

Bell Family Nursery (wholesale)
6543 S. Zimmerman Rd.
Aurora, OR 97002
tel: 503.651.2848
www.bellfamilynursery.com

Carolina Nurseries, Inc. (wholesale)
739 Gaillard Rd.
Moncks Corner, SC 29461
tel: 800.845.2065

Carroll Gardens, Inc.
(mail-order retail)
444 East Main St.
Westminster, MD 21157-5540
tel: 800.638.6334
www.carrollgardens.com

Country Gardens (mail-order retail)
36735 SE David Powell Rd.
Fall City, WA 98024
tel: 206.222.5616
fax: 206.325.6907
www.nwlink.com/~dafox

Creek Hill Nursery (wholesale)
17 West Main St.
Leola, PA 17540
tel: 888.565.0050 or 717.556.0000
fax: 717.556.0001

The Crownsville Nursery
(mail-order retail)
P.O. Box 797
Crownsville, MD 21032
tel: 410.849.3143
fax: 410.849.3427
www.crownsvillenursery.com

Crûg Farm Plants
(retail, no mail-order)
Griffith's Crossing
Caernarfon
Gwynedd, LL55 1TU, Wales
011.44.1248.670232 (direct from
the States)
www.crug-farm.co.uk

Digging Dog Nursery
(mail-order retail)
P.O. Box 471
Albion, CA 95410
tel: 707.937.1130
fax: 707.937.2480
www.diggingdog.com

Dudley Nurseries, Inc. (wholesale)
P.O. Box 429
Thomson, GA 30824
tel: 800.542.4484
fax: 706.595.8166
www.radudley.com

Fairweather Gardens
(mail-order retail)
P.O. Box 330
Greenwich, NJ 08323
tel: 856.451.6261
fax: 856.451.0303
www.fairweathergardens.com

Flowerwood Nursery (wholesale)
15315 Kelly Rd.
P.O. Box 665
Loxley, AL 36551
tel: 251.964.5122

Forestfarm (mail-order retail)
990 Tetherow Rd.
Williams, OR 97544-9599
tel: 541.846.7269
fax: 541.846.6963
www.forestfarm.com

Gossler Farms Nursery
(mail-order retail)
1200 Weaver Rd.
Springfield, OR 97478-9691
tel: 541.746.3922
www.gosslerfarms.com

Greenleaf Nursery (wholesale)
28406 Hwy. 82
Park Hill, OK 74451
tel: 918.457.5172
fax: 918.457.5550
www.glnsy.com

Greer Gardens (mail-order retail)
1280 Goodpasture Island Rd.
Eugene, OR 97401
tel: 800.548.0111 or 541.686.8266
fax: 541.686.0910
www.greergardens.com

Griffith Propagation Nursery
(wholesale)
2580 Antioch Church Rd.
Watkinsville, GA 30677
tel: 888.830.3236 or 706.310.0027
fax: 706.769.4618

Hawksridge Farms, Inc. (wholesale)
P.O. Box 3349
4243 Highway 127 South
Hickory, NC 28603
tel: 800.874.4216
www.hawksridgefarms.com

Heronswood Nursery, Ltd.
(mail-order retail)
7530 NE 288th St.
Kingston, WA 98346
tel: 360.297.4172
fax: 360.297.8321
www.heronswood.com

Hines Nurseries (wholesale)
12621 Jeffrey Rd.
Irvine, CA 92620-2199
tel: 800.444.4499 or 949.559.4444
fax: 949.651.8978
www.hineshort.com

Hydrangeas Plus (mail-order retail)
P.O. Box 389
Aurora, OR 97002
tel: 866.433.7896 or 503.651.2887
fax: 503.651.2648
www.hydrangeasplus.com

Joy Creek Nursery (mail-order retail)
20300 NW Watson Rd.
Scappoose, OR 97056
tel: 503.543.7474
fax: 503.543.6933
www.joycreek.com

Klehm's Song Sparrow
(mail-order retail)
13101 E. Rye Rd.
Avalon, WI 53505
tel: 800.553.3715
fax: 608.883.2257
www.songsparrow.com

Louisiana Nursery (mail-order retail)
5853 Highway 182
Opelousas, LA 70570
tel: 337.948.3696
fax: 318.942.6404

McCorkle Nurseries (wholesale)
4904 Luckey's Bridge Rd. SE
Dearing, GA 30808
tel: 800.533.3050

Microplant Nurseries, Inc.
(wholesale)
13357 Portland Rd. NE
Gervais, OR 97026
tel: 503.792.3696

Monrovia Nursery Company
(wholesale)
18331 East Foothill Blvd.
Azusa, CA 91702
tel: 800.999.9321
fax: 626.334.3126
www.monrovia.com

Nurseries Caroliniana (wholesale)
22 Stephens Estate
North Augusta, SC 29860
tel: 803.279.2707
www.nurcar.com

Oregon Hydrangea Company
(wholesale)
15696 Hwy. 101 South
Brookings, OR 97415
tel: 800.469.3136 or 541.469.3136
fax: 541.469.0563

Piroche Plants Inc. (wholesale)
20542 McNeil Rd.
Pitt Meadows, BC V3Y 1Z1
Canada
tel: 604.465.7101
fax: 604.465.7103

Pride of Place Plants, Inc. (wholesale)
674 Cromarty Ave.
Sidney, BC V8L 5G6
Canada
tel: 250.656.7963
fax: 250.655.0306
www.prideofplaceplants.com

Roslyn Nursery (mail-order retail)
211 Burrs Lane
Dix Hills, NY 11746
tel: 631.643.9347
fax: 631.427.0894
www.roslynnursery.com

Shadow Nursery, Inc. (wholesale)
254 Shadow Nursery Rd.
Winchester, TN 37398
tel: 931.967.6059

Spring Meadow Nursery, Inc.
(wholesale)
12601 120th Ave.
Grand Haven, MI 49417-9621
tel: 800.633.8859
www.springmeadownursery.com

Superior Trees, Inc. (wholesale)
P.O. Box 9325
Lee, FL 32059
tel: 850.971.5159
fax: 850.971.5416

Wavecrest Nursery (mail-order retail)
2509 Lakeshore Dr.
Fennville, MI 49408
tel: 888.869.4159 or 616.543.4175
fax: 616.543.4100
www.wavecrestnursery.com

Wilkerson Mill Gardens
(mail-order retail)
9595 Wilkerson Mill Rd.
Palmetto, GA 30268
tel: 770.463.2400
fax: 770.463.9717
www.hydrangea.com

Willowbend Nurseries, Inc.
(wholesale)
4654 Davis Rd.
Perry, OH 44081
tel: 440.259.3121

Woodlanders, Inc. (mail-order retail)
1128 Colleton Ave.
Aiken, SC 29801
tel and fax: 803.648.7522
www.woodlanders.net

REFERENCES

Adkins, J. A., M. A. Dirr, and O. M. Lindstrom. 2002. Cold hardiness potential of ten *Hydrangea* taxa. *J. Environ. Hort.* 20:171-174

Bailey, D. A. 1989a. *Hydrangea Production*. Timber Press, Portland, Ore..

———. 1989b. Stimulation of "hydrangea distortion" through environmental
manipulations. *J. Amer. Soc. Hort. Sci.* 114:411-416.

———. 1992. Hydrangea pp. 365-383 In: R. Larson (ed.). *Introduction to
Floriculture*. 2nd ed. Academic Press, San Diego, Calif.

Bell, A., and T. Bell. 1997. Special names for special plants. *American
Nurseryman* 186(12):86-91.

Bertrand, H. 1992. Identification of *Hydrangea macrophylla* Ser. cultivars. *Acta
Horticulturae* 320:209-212.

———. 2000. Management and knowledge of the *Hydrangea* collection of
Angers. Morphological characters and data analysis. *Acta Horticulturae.*
508:173-177.

Bir, R. E. 2000a. Landscape survival of *Hydrangea macrophylla* and *serrata* cultivars. *Proc. Southern Nurs. Assoc. Res. Conf.* 45:456-457.

———. 2000b. Flowering of *Hydrangea macrophylla* and *serrata* cultivars in
USDA Zone 7 landscapes. *Proc. Southern Nurs. Assoc. Res. Conf.* 45:458-459.

———. 2002. Rebloom or doom. *Nursery Management and Production*
18(11):43-45.

Bir, R. E., and J. L. Conner. 2002. Reblooming bigleaf hydrangeas. *Proc.
Southern Nurs. Assoc. Res. Conf.* 47:125-127.

Blom, T. J., and B. D. Piott. 1992. Florists hydrangea blueing with aluminum
sulfate applications during forcing. *HortScience* 27:1084-1087.

Bowman, D. P. 1999. *Hydrangeas*. Friedman/Fairfax, New York.

Buma, D. R. 2002. The Kaufman hydrangea collection: beauty, education, and
marketing. *The Public Garden* 17(2):40-41.

Cerbah, M., E. Mortreau, S. Brown, S. Siljak-Yakovlev, H. Bertrand, and C.
Lambert. 2001. Genome size variation and species relationships in the
genus *Hydrangea. Theor. and Applied Genetics* 103:45-51.

Church, G. 1999. *Hydrangeas*. Cassell, London.

Condon, M. 2003. Love those paniculatas. *The American Hydrangea Society
Newsletter* 9(1):1, 3-6.

Conwell, T. B., K. Tilt, D. Findley, H. Ponder, and K. Bowman. 2002. Pruning decisions for containerized hydrangeas. *Proc. Southern Nurs. Assoc. Res. Conf.* 47:495-498.

Copeland, L. L., and A. M. Armitage. 2001. *Legends in the Garden*. Green Leaves Press, Atlanta, Ga. Distributed by Timber Press, Portland, Ore.

Demilly, D., C. Lambert, and H. Bertrand. 2000. Diversity of nuclear DNA contents of *Hydrangea*. *Acta Horticulturae* 508:281-284.

Dirr, M. A. 1983. *Hydrangea arborescens* 'Annabelle'. Cover illustration and text. *American Nurseryman* 157(2):31.

———. 1987. *Hydrangea quercifolia*. *American Nurseryman* 166(5):174.

———. 1992a. *Hydrangea macrophylla*: a vision in blue and pink. *Nursery Manager* 8(1):30-32.

———. 1992b. *Hydrangea*: magnificent treasures for southern gardens. *Perennial Notes* Vol. 4(4).

———. 1993. *Hydrangea arborescens*. *Nursery Manager* 9(2):24-25.

———. 1996. *Hydrangea paniculata* merits a second look. *Nursery Management and Production* 12(1):16-17, 98-100.

———. 1998. *Manual of Woody Landscape Plants*. Stipes Publishing. Champaign, Ill.

———. 1999. Opportunity exists for gardener-friendly *Hydrangea*. *Nursery Management and Production* 15(1):16-17, 96-97.

———. 2000. *Hydrangea quercifolia* virtues are many, the liabilities few. *Nursery Management and Production* 16(6):14-15, 97-101.

———. 2001a. A reliably wonderful oakleaf hydrangea. *The Atlanta Journal-Constitution Home and Garden Section*, Thursday, 7 June.

———. 2001b. *Hydrangea paniculata* 'Chantilly Lace'. *The American Hydrangea Society Newsletter* 7(2):7.

———. 2001c. Pursuing continuously flowering hydrangeas. *The American Hydrangea Society Newsletter* 7(2):1-2.

———. 2002a. In search of a perfect *Hydrangea*. *Nursery Management and Production* 18(6):16-17, 95-96.

———. 2002b. Woody plant improvement at the University of Georgia: advances in *Hydrangea* breeding and selection. *Landscape Plant News* 13(2):5-9.

———. 2003. Evaluation program yields dynamite hydrangeas, nandinas. *Nursery Management and Production* 19(4):14-15, 71-72.

Dirr, M. A., and C. W. Heuser. 1987. *The Reference Manual of Woody Plant Propagation*. Varsity Press, Inc., Athens, Ga.

Handreck, K. A. 1997. Production of blue hydrangea flowers without aluminum drenches. *Comm. Soil Sci. Plant Anal.* 28:1191-1198.

Haworth-Booth, M. 1984. *The Hydrangeas*. Constable, London.

Hillier, J., and A. Coombes, eds. 2002. *The Hillier Manual of Trees and Shrubs*. David & Charles, Newton Abbot, United Kingdom.

Hinkley, D. J. 1998. Mopheads. *Horticulture.* 95:37-40.

Lambert, C., H. Bertrand, J. Lallemand, and M. Bourgoin. 2000. Characterization of a collection of *Hydrangea macrophylla* using isozyme analysis. *Acta Horticulturae* 508:295-296.

Lawson-Hall, T. 2001. Laced with charm. *The Garden* 126:592-595.

Lawson-Hall, T., and B. Rothera. 1995. *Hydrangeas: A Gardener's Guide*. Timber Press, Portland, Ore.

Leite, R. S., and R. W. Barreto. 2000. Petal spotting of hydrangea flowers caused by *Corynespora cassiicola*: old pathogen—new disease. *Mycologist* 14(2):80-83.

Lindstrom, J. T., M. C. Pelto, and M. A. Dirr. 2003. Molecular assessment of remontant (reblooming) *Hydrangea macrophylla* cultivars. *J. Environ. Hort.* 21:57-60.

Kudo, N., and Y. Niimi. 1999a. Production of interspecific hybrids between *Hydrangea macrophylla* f. *hortensia* (Lam.) Rehd. and *H. arborescens* L. *J. Japan Soc. Hort. Sci.* 68:428-439.

———. 1999b. Production of interspecific hybrid plants through cotyledonary segment culture of embryos derived from crosses between *Hydrangea macrophylla* (Lam.) Rehd. and *H. arborescens* L. *J. Japan Soc. Hort. Sci.* 68:803-809.

McClintock, E. 1956. The cultivated hydrangeas. *Baileya* 4:165-175.

———. 1957a. A monograph of the genus *Hydrangea*. *Proceedings California Academy of Sciences* 29(5):147-256.

———. 1957b. Hydrangeas. *Horticulture Magazine.* 36:270-279.

Ma, J. F. 2000. Role of organic acids in detoxification of aluminum in higher plants. *Plant and Cell Physiology*. 41:383-390.

Ma, J. F., S. Hiradate, K. Nomoto, T. Iwashita, and H. Matsumoto. 1997. Internal detoxification mechanism of Al in hydrangea: identification of Al form in the leaves. *Plant Physiology* 113:1033-1039.

Mallet, C. 1994. *Hydrangeas: Species and Cultivars*. Vol. 2. Centre d'Art Floral, Varengeville, France.

Mallet, C., and R. Mallet. 2002. *Hydrangea International Index of Cultivar Names*. Association Shamrock. Varengeville, France.

Mallet, C., R. Mallet, and H. van Trier. 1992. *Hydrangeas: Species and Cultivars*. Vol. 1. Centre d'Art Floral, Varengeville, France.

Pilatowski, R. E. 1982. A taxonomic study of the *Hydrangea arborescens* complex. *Castanea* 47:84-98.

Reed, S. M. 2000a. Compatibility studies in *Hydrangea*. *J. Environ. Hort.* 18:29-33.

———. 2000b. Development of an *In Ovolo* embryo culture procedure for *Hydrangea*. *J. Environ. Hort.* 18:34-39.

———. 2002a. Flowering performance of 21 *Hydrangea macrophylla* cultivars. *J. Environ. Hort.* 20:155-160.

———. 2002b. Breeding hydrangeas. *American Hydrangea Society Newsletter* 8(11):1, 3-7.

Reed, S. M., G. L. Reidel, and M. R. Pooler. 2001. Verification and establishment of *Hydrangea macrophylla* 'Kardinal' x *H. paniculata* 'Brussels Lace' interspecific hybrids. *J. Environ. Hort.* 19:85-88.

Rose, N., Selinger, D., and J. Whitman. 2001. *Growing Shrubs and Trees in Cold Climates*. Contemporary Books. Chicago, Ill.

Sebastian, T. K. and C. W. Heuser. 1987. *In vitro* propagation of *Hydrangea quercifolia* Bartr. *Scientia Horticulturae* 31:303-309.

Soltis, D. E., Q. Y. Xiang, and L. Hufford. 1995. Relationships and evolution of Hydrangeaceae based on rbcL sequence data. *Amer. J. Bot.* 82:504-514.

Stoltz, L. P. 1984. *In vitro* propagation and growth of hydrangea. *HortScience* 19:717-719.

Takeda, K., T. Yamashita, A. Takahashi, and C. F. Timberlake. 1990. Stable blue complexes of anthocyanin-aluminum-3-p-coumaroyl- or 3-caffeoyl-quinic acid involved in the blueing of Hydrangea flower. *Phytochemistry* 29:1089-1091.

Trehane, P., C. D. Brickell, B. R. Baum, W. L. A. Hetterscheid, A. C. Leslie, J. McNeill, S. A. Spongberg, and F. Vrugtman (editorial committee). 1995. *International Code of Nomenclature for Cultivated Plants*. Quarterjack Publ., Wimborne, United Kingdom.

Wilson, E. H. 1923. The hortensias *Hydrangea macrophylla* DC and *Hydrangea serrata* DC. *J. Arnold Arboretum* 4:233-246.

Yamamoto, T. 2000. *The Japanese Hydrangeas Color Guide Book*. English translation by Bryan Woy available from Association Shamrock, Route de l'Eglise, 76119 Varengeville-sur-Mer, France, fax 011 33 02 35 85 30 20, e-mail jacoll@compuserve.com

Yeh, D. M., and H. H. Chiang. 2001. Growth and flower initiation in hydrangea as affected by root restriction and defoliation. *Scientia Horticulturae* 91:123-132.

Zheng-yi, W., and P. H. Raven. 1994. *Flora of China*. Vol. 8. Missouri Botanical Garden. St. Louis, Mo.

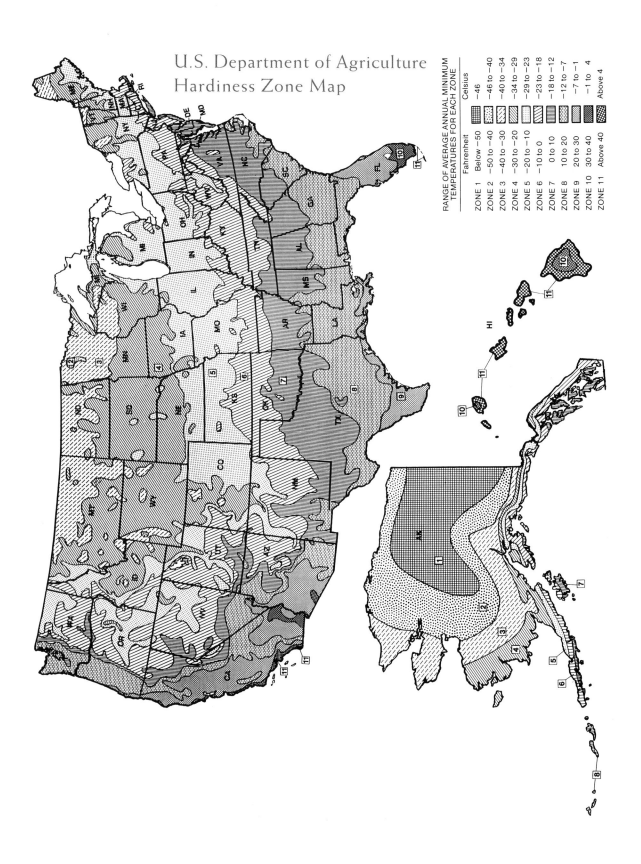

U.S. Department of Agriculture
Hardiness Zone Map

RANGE OF AVERAGE ANNUAL MINIMUM
TEMPERATURES FOR EACH ZONE

	Fahrenheit	Celsius	
ZONE 1	Below −50	−46	
ZONE 2	−50 to −40	−46 to −40	
ZONE 3	−40 to −30	−40 to −34	
ZONE 4	−30 to −20	−34 to −29	
ZONE 5	−20 to −10	−29 to −23	
ZONE 6	−10 to 0	−23 to −18	
ZONE 7	0 to 10	−18 to −12	
ZONE 8	10 to 20	−12 to −7	
ZONE 9	20 to 30	−7 to −1	
ZONE 10	30 to 40	−1 to 4	
ZONE 11	Above 40	Above 4	

INDEX